c 1967   The Californ
main

2 1765 0007 8857 3

D1233782

DATE DUE

The California Oath Controversy

DAVID P. GARDNER

The California Oath Controversy

UNIVERSITY OF CALIFORNIA PRESS

BERKELEY AND LOS ANGELES 1967

378,1012
G226c
1967

University of California Press
Berkeley and Los Angeles, California
Cambridge University Press
London, England
Copyright © 1967, by
The Regents of the University of California

Library of Congress Catalog Card Number: 67-16840
Printed in the United States of America

For Libby
and Karen, Shari, and Lisa

378.1012
G226c
1967

PREFACE

It is my purpose in this work to write an account of the loyalty oath controversy that for three years convulsed the largest university in the nation and one of the world's leading centers of letters and science. The trauma suffered by the University of California over an oath of loyalty required of the University's faculties and staff by the Board of Regents in 1949 anticipated nearly all the issues that were to arise and afflict America's universities and colleges during that troubled time: oaths of loyalty and Communist disclaimers required of teachers on pain of dismissal; penalties to be levied upon teachers for refusing to cooperate with legislative committees investigating subversion; sanctions to be imposed by intramural bodies against colleagues for lack of candor when queried about possible Communist ties; implications for academic freedom and constitutional liberties carried by rules disqualifying Communists and other alleged subversives from university employ; and challenges by boards of trustees and faculties to traditional forms of university governance.

The California conflict, along with the University of Washington cases in late 1948 and early 1949, inaugurated a nadir in the history of American academic freedom. While California's agony, in a sense, reflected the pathology of the country's seemingly inescapable preoccupation with communism and security, the University's turmoil over the oath contributed in part to the neurosis that in postwar America encouraged those forces ranged against freedom of inquiry and dissent. The dispute abetted more than it restrained hostility toward scholarship and intellectual freedom and strengthened, at least in California, public suspicion of scholars engaged in free inquiry and independent thought. While the University of California loyalty oath controversy is inextricably a part of the legal, political, and educational history of mid-twentieth century America, the issues which constituted the conflict remain essentially unresolved and promise, perhaps more firmly than before, to erupt again into public debate. I sincerely hope, therefore, as there has been much excited but largely uninformed comment about the controversy and the principles that gave it life and direction, that this book will serve to illuminate both the event itself and the critical questions for American higher education and intellectual freedom emerging from it.

The controversy, as a landmark in the academic history of the United States, has already been widely noticed and treated by scholars for nomothetic purposes. Some have used it as a polemic for academic freedom. Still others, in the heat of battle, published in order to influence the course of the dispute itself. To illuminate the event and the issues from the vantage ground that only time and evidence could gain, it seemed to me, would repair in part the incompleteness of earlier works caused by the inaccessibility of original documents, the bias of involvement, the press of deadline journalism, and the unwillingness of principals or their heirs to cooperate. Because the use of original documents, private journals, and official records was restricted or repressed, previous studies necessarily relied on hearsay, secondary sources, and the testimony of participants of a particular persuasion. Access to the minutes of the Regents' executive sessions, for example, was refused until December, 1951; use of the relevant administrative files was restricted; study of the transcription of oral interviews with certain of the key men was not possible; admission to the files of the faculty Committee of Seven was denied until 1958; and so forth. To compound the problem of secrecy, which is functional in such crises, the men who published were often ex parte to the controversy itself, for example, Professors George Stewart, John Caughey, Ernst Kantorowicz, Dixon Wecter, Joseph Tussman, Max Radin, Lawrence Harper, among others. The nearly inevitable consequence has been that the literature has fed upon itself and given rise to myth and legend. For whatever light this volume casts on the history of the incident, however, I am indebted in part to my predecessors, whose works, although incomplete and admittedly often biased from personal involvement, proved invaluable to me in my efforts to capture the spirit, passion, and drama of the encounter.

While pointing out the limitations of earlier works may I comment on my own. The Berkeley campus of the University of California has been very much a part of my life. I grew up a short distance from it, as a child knew well many of its professors and administrators — for they were neighbors and their children schoolmates — used its spacious grounds as a playfield, and as a student earned from its faculties two graduate degrees. As an adult, I serve both as a member of the faculty and as an administrator at the University's Santa Barbara campus. I admit freely to a special feeling for the University, and perhaps, consequently, I treat unfairly those whose regard for the University's welfare became essentially inconsequential in their struggle to gain personal advantage.

A brief word about the text. I have preferred a prosaic style to a more aphoristic or flamboyant one. One need not gild real drama. I have deliberately made sparse use of biographical data. To make ample use, I feared, would encourage the reader to impute to the individual the characteristics of his associations. Finally, in an effort to ensure impartiality, and because so much of the conflict turned on semantics, the story has been told through the words of the principals whenever possible.

This study would not have been possible without help
from the faculty, the administration, the Regents, and the
alumni of the University of California. In naming but a few
whose assistance was particularly critical, I in no way imply
less gratitude to the several others for whose help I shall
remain ever thankful.

I acknowledge the cooperative and courteous assistance of
University librarians at the Bancroft Library at Berkeley, the
Department of Special Collections at Los Angeles, and
the general library at Santa Barbara. Thanks go also to those
who staff the offices of the Secretary of the Regents, the
Academic Senates at Berkeley, Los Angeles, and Santa
Barbara, and the California Alumni Association for their
several courtesies.

I owe a great debt of gratitude to Dr. Robert Gordon
Sproul, President Emeritus of the University, and to his
secretary, Miss Agnes Robb, whose willingness to cooperate
in every regard in my research made it possible to gain access
to documents absolutely essential to the study. And, in like
manner, I acknowledge my thanks to Mrs. John Francis
Neylan and to her attorney Herman Phleger. Because of
their cooperation and interest in furthering the research,
and with the assistance of Dr. George Hammond, Director
Emeritus of the Bancroft Library, I was allowed access to
and use of the Neylan papers on the loyalty oath found in the
Bancroft Library.

For time and trouble in my behalf, my special thanks to
Dr. Clark Kerr, former President of the University of Cali-
fornia; Mr. James H. Corley, Vice-President Governmen-
tal Relations, Emeritus; Regent Mrs. Edward H. Heller;
Regent Emeritus Paul Hutchinson; Regent Emeritus Don-
ald H. McLaughlin; the late Admiral Chester Nimitz; and
Regent Edwin Pauley. For their courtesy, encouragement,
and assistance, I am grateful to Professors Walton Bean, John
Caughey, Milton Chernin, Malcolm Davisson, Paul Dodd,
R. A. Gordon, J. A. C. Grant, John Hicks, Joel Hildebrand,
Neil Jacoby, T. J. Kent, Frank Kidner, Frank Newman,

Stephen Pepper, Raymond Sontag, Wendell Stanley, and George Stewart; and particularly to Professors T. R. McConnell, Albert Lepawsky, and Frederic Lilge for their patient and constructive criticism and for their personal encouragement. Sidney Hook, of New York University, and Walter Metzger, of Columbia University, read an earlier version of the manuscript and provided many helpful criticisms.

My thanks also to Chancellor Vernon I. Cheadle of the University's Santa Barbara campus for his help in arranging a leave of absence for me at a critical stage in the study.

To my friends and colleagues at Berkeley and Santa Barbara and to members of my family is owed my enduring gratitude. Their encouragement helped me to maintain enthusiasm and drive when seemingly unsurmountable obstacles threatened the research. Particularly do I wish to say "thank you" to my wife, whose quiet patience and encouragement sustained me during the several years this work was in preparation. And to my three small daughters, for picnics missed, stories unread, and games unplayed, goes my promise to recover lost time.

DAVID P. GARDNER

CONTENTS

Chapter One

Introduction

I

To report the story of any great controversy is manifestly to engage myth and reality, opinion and fact, legend and truth. When a dispute is long and complex, such as that which engrossed the University of California during the period 1949 to 1952, fact and fiction become more difficult to separate. However, there is one grand myth of the loyalty oath conflict, tenaciously clung to by some out of ignorance and by others for ideological reasons, which might be exposed to light at the outset: that this was mostly a conflict over principles. It was not. In its main outlines and principal events it was a power struggle, a series of personal encounters between proud and influential men. Ideals and beliefs boldly enunciated early in the dispute were surrendered little by little as tribute to personal hostility, stubbornness, and bad manners. And in the end most of those who held uncompromisingly to their ideals — that small band of scholars unwilling to sign the oath — were victims of the battle, not its chief protagonists.

The *San Francisco Examiner* editorial of Tuesday morning, August 1, 1950, declaimed: "While American youth is being conscripted to die fighting Communistic barbarism in Korea and elsewhere it is proposed to accord to thirty-nine professors and assistant professors on the many campuses of the University of California the privilege of defying a simple regulation to protect the institution which is engaged in research vital to national defense."[1] The "simple regulation" — a Communist disclaimer — noted by the *Examiner* had already by that time embroiled the University of California in a major controversy that had lasted for sixteen months and was to continue for another two years.

The battle had made adversaries primarily of faculty and Regents, but it had also pitted faculty member against faculty member and Regent against Regent. By August of 1950, members of the faculty refusing to sign the disclaimer and their protagonists on the governing board had become intractable; in the major confrontation later that month they were found to be nearly alone, resented by many of their colleagues, and criticized for an intransigence that their associates regarded only as harmful to the general welfare of the University.

"The great majority of the faculty are weary of the discussion [controversy]," wrote the chairman of the Academic Senate's Committee on Academic Freedom to University President Robert Gordon Sproul on August 18, 1950, and "they are unwilling to continue it. . . . Apathy, fear, insecurity — all play a part. . . . I believe that anxiety concerning the possibility of disaster to you [Sproul] is the most general feeling which motivates faculty members at present. On the other hand," he continued, "there is no spontaneous movement to give you general support. This is also, I believe, attributed to weariness and confusion."[2] The non-signers of the Communist disclaimer and their antagonists among the Regents, though weary, were neither apathetic nor confused as they pressed with equal ardor for a last engagement. And as the adversaries labored, so also did those members of the faculty seeking to avert the collision. Strenuous efforts were made by members of the faculty to induce the non-signers to sign. The appeals not only proved unsuccessful but also provoked resentment from those being importuned. "I think you . . . would do better," answered one non-signer in refusing the entreaties of a colleague, "instead of continuing the pressure on non-signers to sign, which only humiliates the faculty and sacrifices the matter of principle, if you put all the pressure you can on the Regents to keep their word."[3] Interpreting dissension of this sort as clear evidence of a fatal disunity in the faculty, the non-signers' chief adversary, Regent John Francis Neylan, reported to a friend that the opposition was crumbling. Neither the Regent and his allies on the governing board nor the faculty non-signers crumbled, however, and on August 25, 1950, thirty-one members of the University of California faculty were dismissed by a two-vote majority of the Board of Regents for refusing to sign the disclaimer. The irony was that not one of those dismissed was accused by any Regent of being a Communist or in sympathy with any other organization allegedly subversive. Furthermore, each had been found by the Academic Senate Committee on Privilege and Tenure to be a competent scholar, an objective teacher, and untainted by disloyalty to the country. How the Regents of the University of California came to sever from the institution's service men and women against whom no charge of professional unfitness or personal disloyalty had been laid is an extraordinary study in futility.

II

The issues that gave life to the controversy, and the tactics and strategies that gave it direction were much associated with the principles of governance and the mechanisms of control on which the University's organizational and administrative structure rested. And as the dispute is traceable principally through the interaction of the several parts of the institution, some brief mention of the University's form is suggested.

In the spring of 1949, the University of California, a vast educational enterprise, was the country's largest university and ranked among the nation's best. There were general campuses at Berkeley and Los Angeles, college campuses at Davis and Santa Barbara, major research centers at Berkeley,

Lick Observatory, La Jolla, and Riverside, and professional schools at Berkeley, Davis, Los Angeles, and San Francisco. Nonacademic employees numbered 6,250. Members of the faculty and others engaged in the academic work of the institution totaled some 3,200.[4] The University was vested as a public trust in the corporate body known as The Regents of the University of California, which constitutionally enjoyed full powers of organization and governance except for legislative interest in the appropriation, security, and administration of its funds. The Board of Regents was composed of twenty-four members, sixteen of whom were appointed by the governor of the state for terms of sixteen years. The remaining eight were ex officio members and included the governor as president of the Board, the lieutenant governor, the speaker of the State Assembly, the president of the State Board of Agriculture, the president of San Francisco's Mechanic's Institute, the state superintendent of public instruction, the president of the University, and the president of the alumni association. The Regents were mostly prominent men of affairs; and in this respect members of the Board in 1949 were no different from those who had served previously.[5] Although nine had been Regents for a decade or more, fifteen had come on the Board since 1940.

The president of the University, as executive head of the institution, was appointed by the Regents and responsible to them. He served also as chairman of the Academic Senate. Robert Gordon Sproul, President of the University since 1930, enjoyed in 1949 the support and loyalty of the faculty, the staff, the alumni, and the Regents. An alumnus of the University, Berkeley class of 1913, Sproul entered its service in 1914 as a cashier and held successively the positions of assistant secretary, assistant comptroller, secretary and comptroller of the Board of Regents, and vice-president of the University until his election as president. A reliance on the faculty for advice on academic matters, an insistence on the prerogatives of the presidency in all other matters relating to the executive function, and a respectful regard for the Board and its responsibilities had gained for Sproul the confidence and cooperation of the faculty and the Regents.

The University's Academic Senate, functioning under the general authority of the Organic Act which founded the University in 1868 and in accord with broad delegations of regental authority, was an integral part of the administration and enjoyed advisory responsibility in the appointment, promotion, and dismissal of colleagues; in the determination of educational policy; in the formulation of the budget; and final authority in the internal organization and conduct of the Senate itself. The President relied heavily on the recommendations of the Senate, and the Regents in turn expected that the President's proposals to the Board on matters of interest to the Senate had previously enjoyed the considered opinion of the faculty. This system of shared responsibility had proven to be a reasonably productive one for a quarter of a century. By 1949, however, forces at work within the University were chipping away little by little at the adequacy of the organizational and administrative structure and at the effectiveness of the responsible officers. Some of the cause and much of the course of the controversy is traceable to the effect these forces had on the formal and informal lines of communication and the means of control and constraint within the institution.

In 1949 the administration of the University was still strained by the exigencies of World War II and by the pressures of enrollment and adjustment following the close of hostilities in 1945.[6] Although the appointment of Clarence Dykstra as Provost of the Los Angeles campus in 1945 had helped to distribute the administrative burden in the University, the retirement in 1947 of Professor Monroe E. Deutsch, Provost of the Berkeley campus and Vice-President of the University, and the failure of the Regents to appoint a successor, countered whatever gains had been made in the appointment of a Provost at Los Angeles. Thirty line officers, exclusive of staff, had reported to the President even during Deutsch's tenure. To this number were added twenty-two deans, directors, and other administrative officers when Deutsch's retirement left vacant the Provost's position at Berkeley. The organization and staffing of the President's office had not kept pace with the complexities and pressures facing it. This weakness contributed in part to the administrative difficulties experienced by the President's office early in the controversy and which throughout the dispute plagued Sproul in his relations with the Board of Regents.

The Academic Senate in a similar sense had failed, in its complex and somewhat cumbersome mechanism, to allow for ways and means of sampling opinion on matters affecting its members. There were advisory committees, one for the northern faculties and one for the southern, responsible to the Senate for informing the President on faculty views and attitudes and for advising him on matters of general University policy and welfare. The committee, however, met only infrequently, advised and informed irregularly, and were without formal means of ready access to general faculty opinion apart from the service of their members on other committees and personal friendship with colleagues.

The Senate was also in the process of transferring power from the old guard to the younger men of promise. The senior men had for years worked closely with the President and knew many of the Regents personally. On the other hand, they did not know well the newer men on the faculty, many of whom had been appointed since the close of World War II. At the same time, the younger men were less well known to many of their colleagues, were not experienced in working with the President, and were not widely acquainted with the Regents. In the crisis brought on by the oath, these factors combined to deny in the Senate a commanding voice in which full confidence and reliance could be placed as the representative opinion and advice of the faculty. Consequently, in negotiations with the President and with the Regents, those serving the Senate were placed time and again in the position of representing opinion later found to be unrepresentative of the faculty majority. This was a critical weakness for which the Senate paid dearly.

Although the Regents had delegated broad powers and responsibilities in educational matters to the Academic Senate and had respected the President's executive role as the medium through which Senate recommendations and advice were represented to it, the Board, nevertheless, retained a substantial interest in the administration of the University. The Board's Committee on Finance and Business Management had for some time served, in effect, as an "executive committee" in the sense that the President brought to it not only matters of finance and business management, but other matters relating to the general welfare of the institution.

A member of long standing on this committee was Regent John Francis Neylan. A person of powerful physique and bearing, Neylan, as a young man, figured prominently in bringing Hiram Johnson and the Progressive Republican party to power in California and had served in Governor Johnson's administration as chairman of the California State Board of Control (1911–1917). Neylan's stature and influence in California's political and legal circles gained as he engaged in a successful practice of the law in San Francisco and grew intimate with the William Randolph Hearst family interests radiating from San Simeon. Neylan, at the time of the oath controversy, was serving the second of two sixteen-year terms as a Regent of the University, having been appointed initially by Governor C. C. Young in 1928 and again by Governor Earl Warren in 1944. Regent Neylan and President Sproul had been close personal friends for years and had worked together harmoniously. But for whatever reasons — the burden of business after World War II, the number of newer appointments to the Board, the overwhelming number of matters pending — Neylan and Sproul by 1949 were less cordial than before. Where the relationship between Neylan and Sproul had been a source of stability between the office of the President and the Board of Regents, it was by the time of the oath a potentially disruptive factor. During the controversy Neylan and Sproul held differing opinions and drew further apart. Paradoxically, in the course of the dispute, each reversed his position regarding the oath. This further aggravated the deteriorating relationship and contributed to an already confused, complex, and sensitive situation.

Although the organizational and administrative weaknesses detailed here very likely helped prolong the controversy and probably were in part responsible for it, the answers to how the conflict began and why it persisted lie elsewhere. One should bear in mind, however, the respective roles of the Regents, the office of the President, and the Academic Senate and the internal conditions of strain existing within and among them as the University moved toward the turmoil that overtook it in the early spring of 1949.

III

How the Regents of the University of California on March 25, 1949, came to amend an oath of allegiance already required of the faculty and staff by adding to it a disclaimer affidavit of nonmembership and nonbelief in any organization that advocated the overthrow of the government is a disingenuous adventure. The Board acted that day in response to two immediate but quite unrelated concerns: a State Senate constitutional amendment pending in the California legislature that proposed to take from the Regents and give to the legislature the power to ensure the loyalty of officers and employees of the University; and a disagreement within the administration and the Board over the interpretation of regental regulations governing the use of University facilities. The confluence of these two forces on the morning of March 25, 1949, and the inducement each offered to the President and the Regents to respond, can be rationally interpreted as cause for enactment of the oath only if independently understood.

IV

In early 1949, California's Un-American Activities Committee, established eight years earlier by joint action of both houses of the California legislature, introduced a thoroughgoing and comprehensive legislative program consisting of thirteen bills designed to "isolate, expose and remove from positions of power and influence persons who are a dangerous menace to our freedom and security."[7] Known popularly as the Tenney bills after the committee chairman, Senator Jack B. Tenney, Democrat of Los Angeles, the legislation sought to strengthen and supplement existing laws dealing with subversion.[8]

Tenney, a former piano player and song writer, entered public life in 1936 when he was elected to the California State Assembly on the Democratic ticket. Shortly thereafter, he was elected vice-president and then president of Local 47, American Federation of Musicians, in Los Angeles. For the next three years, both as legislator and as union official, Tenney was associated with liberal and "left-wing" causes.[9] Following defeat in his bid for reelection as president of Local 47 in December of 1939, Tenney turned against several of the same liberal causes he had supported only shortly before. In the next session of the California Legislature, he emerged as a leading proponent of a bill designed to deny the Communist party the right to a place on the ballot.[10] Tenney was appointed the following year as chairman of the Fact-Finding Committee on Un-American Activities and served continuously in that position until his resignation in mid-1949.

Senate Constitutional Amendment 13 (SCA 13), one of the thirteen bills introduced by Tenney and his associates, threatened intrusion of the legislature into prerogatives of the Regents that in 1879 and 1918 were specifically delegated by the state's highest law. It proposed to amend Section 9, Article IX, of the State Constitution, which gave full powers of governance and organization to the corporate body known as The Regents of the University of California, by assigning to the legislature power to determine the loyalty of University employees. SCA 13 was referred to the Senate Committee on Education. When hearings on the Tenney bills began in March, SCA 13 was *not* among those heard and neither were five of the other twelve bills introduced. The remaining seven constituted the serious legislative proposals of the Un-American Activities Committee.

As late as mid-May, the prospects for enactment of the *seven* bills appeared favorable. Each had passed the Senate with a heavy affirmative vote. But in the lower house only three of the seven bills were reported out of committee. On June 24, 1949, Assemblyman Yorty of Los Angeles moved that the remaining three bills be withdrawn from the file and re-referred to the Committee on Rules.[11] The motion carried. Five days later a motion to withdraw one of the bills from committee was defeated by a vote of 57 to 16. The Tenney bills had lost in toto.

Writers of the oath controversy have uniformly reported that the Tenney bills, particularly SCA 13 and/or threats of budgetary penalties, prompted the Regents to enact the oath.[12] The evidence suggests, however, that the bills were less cause than they were cover and, probably, in and of themselves would not have provoked the Regents or the president to require the oath. Rather, the "threat" posed to the University by the bills, and by SCA 13 in particular, proved convenient to recall later in the controversy when the administration was pressed hard to report why the oath was needed. But, as will be shown, they were not the significant factor in the decision of the Regents to adopt an oath. Rather, the bills in their entirety were important to the University in a different way; *for to whatever extent they turned the political temper of the times into articulated issues, then in that measure they indirectly influenced the mood of the Regents the day the oath was adopted.* And one need only recall briefly the mood of the nation in 1949 to grasp the meaning of the Tenney bills.

A "curtain" had fallen across the face of Eastern Europe and from behind it the Communist strategy for world dominion was allegedly planned. Communist takeovers in Rumania and Czechoslovakia, civil war in Greece, radical unrest in Western Europe, civil war in China, and the gradual dissolution of the British Empire were regarded as threats to the defense and security of the United States. The Communist party, U.S.A., was adjudged by many to be a fifth column within the body politic, and as a people in fear is no more discerning than a people in anger, the nation lashed out to secure domestically what seemingly eluded it internationally. The great quest for security that captured the nation's attention for much of the immediate postwar decade turned easily for some into a fetish as it served both their personal ambitions and the preoccupation of their followers. Abetted by the sensational spy trials in 1949 and 1950 of Alger Hiss, Whittaker Chambers, Judith Coplon, Klaus Fuchs, and others and encouraged by the federal government's move in March of 1949 to prosecute eleven of the nation's top Communists for violation of the Smith Act, Senator McCarthy at the national level and Tenney in California, Canwell in Washington, Ober in Maryland, and others of similar persuasion in state governments moved boldly to delimit the liberties of Communists, fellow travelers, and a host of other alleged subversives. The Feinberg Law in New York, the Ober Anti-Subversive Laws in Maryland, the Tenney bills in California, among others, and a rash of local ordinances all directed against "subversion" in the schools and/or the civil service reflected a nation's exaggerated response to a fear magnified by the very steps taken to allay it. America was disquieted and the uneasiness of the times could not help but penetrate the consciousness of the trustees of California's state university.

V

As the Tenney bills brought the question of loyalty home to California, the Regents of the University of Washington were demonstrating its relevance to higher education. Dean Edward H. Lauer of the College of Arts and Sciences at the University of Washington, on September 8, 1948, initiated complaints against six tenured members of the Washington faculty. Each, accused of present or past membership in the Communist party, earlier in the year had been called as a witness by the State of Washington's Legislative Committee on Un-American Activities, known popularly as the Canwell Committee, and on that occasion either had refused to testify as to his relationship with the party or had admitted past membership but denied present membership. Raymond B. Allen, President of the University, sought later to gain further information from each of the six about the charges made. Because of their unwillingness to cooperate with the president and because of their testimonies at the Canwell Committee hearings, the complaint was made and dismissal of the six sought.[13]

Against Professors Herbert J. Phillips and Joseph Butterworth all charges except current membership in the Communist party were dropped. Each had admitted his present membership in the party to the faculty's Committee on Tenure and Academic Freedom; and this admission had cleared the way for the University of Washington to determine whether or not it would deny employment to members of the Communist party *ipso facto*. The recommendation of the Committee on Tenure and Academic Freedom in the Phillips and Butterworth cases was not unanimous. Of the eleven members of the committee, five held that under the Administrative Code of the University, membership in the Communist party *ipso facto* was *not* ground for dismissal. Three others concurred with the five that the respondents *not* be dismissed but disagreed with them on matters of reasoning and factual considerations. Two other members of the committee felt that Professors Butterworth and Phillips, by reason of their active present membership in the Communist party, should be dismissed. A final member agreed with the two who would dismiss, but for different reasons.

The Board of Regents conducted its own hearings on January 22, 1949, and voted, subsequently, to dismiss Professors Phillips and Butterworth as of February 1, 1949. Another of the six was dismissed, not for current membership in the Communist party, but for lack of candor when queried about his relationship with the party. The remaining three, although not dismissed, were required to sign a Communist disclaimer and placed on two years probation.

The dismissals were the first major challenge to the stated position of the American Association of University Professors (AAUP) that membership in the Communist party did not *ipso facto* constitute ground for dismissal:

There is, then, nothing in the nature of the teaching profession which requires the automatic exclusion of Communists, and the attempt to exclude them would threaten our educational system. . . . In the light of present facts, it is the unanimous opinion of the Active members of Committee A that there is nothing now apparent in reference to the Communist Party in the United States, or to international conditions, that calls for a departure from the principles of freedom and tenure by which the Association has been guided throughout its history. On the basis of those principles, this Association regards any attempt to subject college teachers to civic limitations not imposed upon other citizens as a threat against the Academic profession, and against the society that profession serves.[14]

For the AAUP, professional unfitness could not be inferred from association nor determined by imputing to an individual the characteristics known generally to identify any category or organization. The AAUP commitment sharply contradicted the principles enunciated by the President and Regents of the University of Washington and was contrary as well to the position of the American Association of Universities, which held membership in the Communist party to be disqualifying.

The California legislature, on March 17, 1949, passed Assembly Concurrent Resolution 47 (ACR 47) which commended the Regents of the University of Washington for their dismissal of known Communists from the faculty. As the resolution had instructed, Chief Clerk of the Assembly, Arthur Ohnimus, on March 23, 1949, sent copies of this legislative action to members of the Board of Regents of the University of California and to its President and Provost.[15] The California legislature had taken cognizance of the Washington incident as a substantive issue and had expressed its opinion unequivocally to the governing board and administration of the University of California. While it does not appear that ACR 47 played a direct part in the Board's adoption of the oath two days later,[16] it is certain that the dismissal of Professor Herbert Phillips from the University of Washington because of his membership in the Communist party, and his appearance on the Los Angeles campus of the University of California shortly thereafter, was a principal cause.

VI

Dr. Clarence Dykstra, Provost of the Los Angeles campus of the University of California, signed permissions on February 15, 1949, granting authority to the Graduate Students' Association to sponsor a debate on campus between Professor Herbert Phillips, recently dismissed member of the University of Washington faculty, and Professor Merritt Benson, professor of journalism at the same university.[17] The subject of the debate was whether one who was a member of the Communist party could also be an objective teacher and impartial researcher for truth. (Owing largely to the influence of the Washington cases, the question had already evoked national interest and was to be widely discussed during the spring and summer of 1949.)[18] Provost Dykstra viewed the debate as a forum at which both sides were to be presented but attendance was to be restricted to graduate students.[19] The undergraduates' response was to circulate a petition urging that Professors Phillips and Benson be permitted to address the entire student body. On the evening before the debate petitions bearing 2,210 signatures were forwarded to the officers of the Associated Students for action. Although the officers took no formal notice of the petitions, they authorized the president of the student body to ask the Provost for an open meeting. In response, Dykstra indicated that no change in arrangements was possible at that late hour. Furthermore, on the morning following the debate Professor Benson was scheduled to leave the city.[20]

The refusal prompted the faculty and students at Los Angeles to voice a long-standing complaint that vital political and religious issues could not be discussed on campuses of the University of California. (University Regulation 17, first adopted by the Regents in 1934, governed the use of University facilities and denied them to those whose use of such facilities fell within certain prohibitions specified in the State Constitution, namely Article IX, Section 9, in which the University as a public trust was required to be free of all political or sectarian influences.) Dykstra believed that Regulation 17 did not prevent the discussion of controversial questions so long as both sides were presented, and so long as the meeting was under the sponsorship of a recognized University organization. "On the other hand," as Dykstra recognized, "no partisan or sectarian meeting is to be allowed." [21] Dykstra considered the Phillips–Benson debate to be clearly permissible within the rules of the University, and in reporting the situation to Sproul for the latter's use in answering criticisms being voiced by some members of the Board, he said:

It seems to me that when permission was asked to hold the above-mentioned meeting that if the subject was of sufficient interest for the newspapers, the magazines, commentators, and Town Hall of New York to discuss openly, mature students should be allowed to hear a debate between two people who were in the middle of the controversy, both of whom had already debated the question at Reed College in Portland, and probably are expected to debate it again. In my opinion, it is of high importance to raise the question of thought control on our campuses and strike early if it appears that such control is raising its ugly head.[22]

The Los Angeles papers reported the debate and the exclusion of undergraduates from it.[23]

Phillips' appearance was discussed at length by the Regents of the University of California in executive session on February 25, 1949. Chairman of the Board at this time was Edward A. Dickson of Los Angeles. Dickson, a Regent of the University since 1913, when he was appointed at the age of thirty-four by Governor Hiram Johnson, enjoyed considerable influence in southern California both within Los Angeles financial and civic circles, and among the area's several newspapers. Regent Dickson, as had Regent Neylan, crusaded for Progressive Republican candidate Hiram Johnson in the latter's successful bid for the governorship in 1910. He had edited and published the *Los Angeles Evening Express* from 1912 to 1931 and then had turned his interest and energies to the growing savings-and-loan movement in southern California. Dickson was principally responsible for persuading the Board of Regents to found a campus of the University at Los Angeles in 1919 and counted among his friends many members of the faculty and administrative staff there. He had also been a strong backer of Sproul's when the latter was elected to the presidency in 1930, and continued to regard him highly in 1949. Dickson had followed the Washington cases closely and was much concerned with the appearance of a known Communist (Phillips) on any campus of the University.[24] A report of the incident at the University of California at Los Angeles (UCLA) was made by the President from a letter written to him by Dykstra on February 23. Sproul called the Board's attention to the relevant constitutional prohibitions against political and sectarian influence in the University, to University Regulation 17, which implemented the constitutional prohibition, and to resolutions of the Board dealing with the employment of Communists by the University.[25] The Board was critical of Dykstra for having authorized the use of University facilities in seeming contravention of existing University policy (Regulation 17) and for a purpose that was regarded by some Regents as an affront to the University of Washington. Regent Paul Hutchinson, president of the UCLA Alumni Association, in defense of Dykstra, pointed out that President Allen of the University of Washington had recommended to the Provost one of the participants in the debate; and that in his (Hutchinson's) opinion the University regulation in question might not be as clear as the Board supposed.

In deference to Hutchinson's views, no action was taken by the Regents against Dykstra. Instead, the Provost was invited to represent his position personally at the Board's April meeting. A special committee, under the chairmanship of Regent Hutchinson, was appointed "to draft a resolution for adoption by the Board setting forth the Regents' views as expressed at today's meeting, and providing that all facilities of the University are to be barred to Communist party members." [26] Appointed to serve with Hutchinson (whose term as Regent was to expire June 30, 1949) were Regent Victor R. Hansen, Los Angeles attorney, and Regent John Francis Neylan.

"Involvement of University of California in the Washington University Communism Case" was item 5 on the agenda of the President's Administrative Advisory Committee meeting in Berkeley on February 28, 1949. The item was included on the agenda primarily because of the Phillips–Benson debate at UCLA. The key administrative officers of the University (including Sproul and Dykstra) and members of the northern Senate's Advisory Committee were in attendance. Sproul reported that the Regents saw no reason why "invited speakers should have the doubtful privilege of belonging to the Communist Party when members of our own staff are denied it." Also, said Sproul, the Board was concerned with the inappropriateness of debating the policies of a sister institution when the policies in debate coincided with those held by the University of California— particularly in view of possible "legislative restrictions on the University because of an alleged liberality toward Communists on the part of the administration."[27] The minutes of this meeting report:

> It was the consensus that while inviting a member of the Communist Party to speak on campus under controlled conditions is essentially different from hiring or retaining one to take individual charge of a course, and that a judicious use of Communists on the "Exhibit A" principle might actually be an effective antidote to radical tendencies among young and impressionable students; nevertheless, in view of the attitude of public leaders, and the recognition of that attitude by the Regents of the University any exceptions to the general policy implied by the Regents would be dangerously unwise. To avoid errors in judgment *the faculty should be more widely informed of the full scope of the policy under which the University is now operating* [emphasis added].[28]

Provost Dykstra faced, coincidentally with the Phillips–Benson debate, a related problem which had arisen in connection with an invitation by UCLA's Institute of Industrial Relations to Professor Harold J. Laski to deliver two lectures on the University's Los Angeles campus. Laski, controversial member of the British Labour party, a member of its Executive Committee, and a professor at the University of London, had been invited to the United States by the Sidney Hillman Foundation for a series of ten lectures. On December 10, 1948, Stewart Meacham, director of the Hillman Foundation, wrote to the UCLA Institute of Industrial Relations asking if the University wished to invite Laski. Laski was offered by Meacham to both Berkeley and Los Angeles.[29]

On January 26, 1949, the UCLA Institute of Industrial Relations and the Department of Political Science asked the Provost for authorization to ask Laski to lecture on campus. Professor Edgar Warren, director of the Institute, was asked by Dykstra if Laski was to appear at Berkeley as well. When assured in the affirmative, permission was given to invite Laski to UCLA.[30]

Toward the end of January, Professor Abbot Kaplan of UCLA's Institute of Industrial Relations was in New York and visited with Meacham of the Hillman Foundation. Kaplan learned that Laski would be able to speak either at Los Angeles or at Berkeley — not at both, as had been earlier thought possible. As permission had already been given by UCLA's Provost, Kaplan and Meacham agreed that Laski's University of California lectures would take place on the Los Angeles campus.[31] Five weeks passed, however, before Dykstra was advised that Laski was not scheduled at Berkeley. Once informed, the Provost asked Edgar Warren to get in touch with Professors Clark Kerr and Peter Odegard of Berkeley's Institute of Industrial Relations and Department of Political Science respectively, and ask them to inquire of the President if Laski could be heard on the Berkeley campus and also whether, available or not, Laski would be welcome there.[32] The President responded on March 10 by teletype to Warren with a copy to Dykstra. Sproul said that he was unfamiliar with the situation and in any event was reluctant to intervene as Dykstra had full power to act.[33] With the Phillips–Benson debate still freshly in mind, Dykstra remained anxious for further clarification. However, further effort to secure an elaboration of the President's attitude proved unrewarding.[34]

The University's Charter Day celebrations at Los Angeles on March 21 afforded Dykstra the opportunity to talk personally with Sproul about the invitation to Laski. Dykstra reports the President as saying that "the appearance of Laski on our campus would not be pleasing to the Board of Regents because some have charged Laski with being ultra-left and the Regents have a very firm policy as to Communists and *alleged Communists* [emphasis added]."[35] Taking this to mean that the President wished the invitation withdrawn, Dykstra advised Warren to call off the Laski lectures.[36]

The Provost had allowed no publicity about the Laski invitation, and only the principals knew that Laski was to speak at UCLA. When the University advised the Hillman Foundation that because Laski could not speak at Berkeley he would, therefore, be unable to speak at UCLA, the Foundation chose to challenge the decision. Jacob Potofsky, president of the Amalgamated Clothing Workers of America, on behalf of the Foundation, reported the University's decision to the press and suggested that Laski's political views and the appearance the previous month at UCLA of Professor Phillips were what really prompted the University to withdraw its invitation and not for the reason given by the University. Potofsky's rather aggravated response may in part have been prompted by similar refusals to Laski occurring elsewhere. The Harvard Law School Forum, for example, was to have sponsored an address by Laski at a public school auditorium in Cambridge. The school board denied use of the auditorium to Laski, however, and Sanders Theater on the Harvard campus was chosen as an alternate site. The report of Laski's acceptance of the Harvard invitation was carried nationally, and the UCLA incident was woven into the story.[37] To force the University's hand, Potofsky, on March 24, wired to Dykstra and Sproul and offered to have Laski speak at both Berkeley and Los Angeles.[38]

Upon receipt of this wire, Dykstra called Sproul at the Santa Barbara campus where the Regents were gathering for their March meeting. Dykstra asked that he be allowed to send one of two wires in reply to Potofsky. The first read: "We have your proposal to present Laski on both major campuses of the University. Have just had President Sproul on the phone with regard to Berkeley campus and he joins me in accepting early April dates." The second read: "Since you have now offered Laski to both campuses my reason for withdrawing my earlier consent no longer applies and I am glad to reinstate my approval of having Laski on this campus on the dates as given." President Sproul advised Dykstra to send neither wire until he had talked with the Regents about the problem.

VII

It was these two issues — the dismissal of two tenured members of the faculty at the University of Washington for current membership in the Communist party, and the use of University facilities on the Los Angeles campus by a Communist (Phillips) and a leader of the British Labour Party (Laski) — that caused the administrative officers and the Board of Regents of the University of California to be concerned with the clarity and explicitness of University regulations governing both the employment of faculty and staff and the use of University facilities. *On the eve of the March 25, 1949, meeting of the Board of Regents, these matters were of immediate importance.* The evidence clearly suggests that the Tenney bills, particularly SCA 13, and legislative cognizance of the University of Washington cases (ACR 47) were not substantive concerns but, rather, acted as catalysts to bring about a quick "solution" of the two principal issues. They also served, very likely, to suggest the *means* of solving administratively the unrest and uncertainty generated within the University by the Washington cases and the UCLA incidents. Thus, given the political temper of the times, the Regents' unanimous response to the need to strengthen and delineate University policy prohibiting the employment of, and use of facilities by, Communists — enactment of the oath, in part — undoubtedly appeared to them not only rational but wise as well on the morning of March 25, 1949 — even to those Regents who later were

Chapter Two

Prelude to Controversy

I

The Board of Regents assembled in Ebbett's Hall on
the Santa Barbara campus on the morning of March 25,
1949, for its regular monthly meeting. The attendance of
only eleven members out of a Board of twenty-four suggested
a normal agenda. The Hutchinson committee, appointed the
previous month to study the use of University facilities,
was not to report its recommendations to the Board until
April. And Provost Dykstra was not to appear before the
Regents in explanation of the Phillips–Benson debate until
the following month. As was customary the Board had
scheduled its committee meetings for the morning and early
afternoon.[1] Regular session was to follow at 2:30 p.m. Minutes of the committee meetings that day report no discussion
of the oath, the use of University facilities, the Tenney bills,
or any other subject even remotely connected with the general issue of communism.[2]

The Phillips–Benson and Laski incidents were the subject
of brisk conversation, however, during the usual "rump sessions" that preceded and followed the regularly scheduled
committee meetings; and between sessions that morning occurred a series of informal conversations among the Regents
and administrative staff on the general subject of communism and the University's response to it. From these discussions emerged the decision to amend the already required
oath of allegiance.[3] The attorney for the Regents, Jno. U.
Calkins, Jr., was asked to draft the amendment for presenta-

tion to the Board in regular session that afternoon. Calkins and James H. Corley, University comptroller and its legislative advocate in the State Capitol, worked on a draft over the *lunch hour.* The amendment drawn up was based "on the oath prescribed by Congress for labor leaders under the then provisions of the Taft-Hartley Act." [4]

As were all regular sessions of the Board, the Regents' meeting that afternoon was open to the press and public. During the session no mention was made of communism or of the related matters which had so concerned members of the Board earlier in the day. Corley reported the legislative situation in Sacramento but made no mention of the Tenney bills either collectively or individually. Corley did acknowledge that the University was having trouble with its budget but indicated that this was not an attack against the University, but rather an attempt to balance the state budget and avoid additional taxation. [5] Following Corley's report, Regent Dickson called for an executive session. *Everyone except the Regents, the President, and the secretary of the Regents left the room.* A brief discussion ensued concerning the Laski incident at UCLA. Regent Dickson, sympathetic with the decision to cancel the invitation to Laski, spoke briefly and expressed his opinion that the Regents take action to prevent the use of University facilities by those who would employ them for propaganda purposes. Regent Hansen moved that the matter be referred to the President, but when reminded of the Hutchinson committee already studying the problem, withdrew his motion in favor of referral to that committee. [6] *And then the Board returned to regular session.*

The President was recognized and the amendment to the oath of allegiance was offered. The record deserves to be quoted in full:

PRESIDENT SPROUL: There is a matter on which I should like the hand of the President upheld and his authority clarified having to do with the subject. Before I introduce it, and if you wish to consider it, it will be necessary for unanimous [sic] consent [a necessary condition to admit to consideration any item not previously a part of the day's agenda]. By resolution adopted by the Regents on June 12, 1942, it is required that all appointees subscribe to the following oath:

"I do solemnly swear (or affirm) that I will support the Constitution of the United States and the Constitution of the State of California, and that I will faithfullly discharge the duties of my office according to the best of my ability."

I propose that the said resolution be amended to substitute the following for the oath now required:

"I do solemnly swear (or affirm) that I do not believe in, and I am not a member of, nor do I support any party or organization that believes in, advocates, or teaches the overthrow of the United States Government, by force or by any illegal or unconstitutional methods; that I will support the Constitution of the United States and the Constitution of the State of California, and that I will faithfully discharge the duties of my office according to the best of my ability."

The added material has to do with the oath that the man is not "a member of, nor do I support any party or organization that believes in, advocates, or teaches the overthrow of the United States Government, by force or by any illegal or unconstitutional methods."

REGENT AHLPORT: I suggest that you put the negative portion of that at the end, and make the affirmation to the Constitution first. I move unanimous consent.

REGENT HANSEN: I second.

(The Regents voted unanimously to consider the matter of a new oath of allegiance.)

PRESIDENT SPROUL: As to the change in the form of the motion — the Attorney drafted this for me.

ATTORNEY CALKINS: I put it both ways, and finally decided it would have more emphasis if it were at the start.

REGENT AHLPORT: I like the affirmation of allegiance first, and then put the negation last.

PRESIDENT SPROUL: I move it in the amended form.

(The Regents voted unanimously to adopt the oath in the following form:)

"I do solemnly swear (or affirm) that I will support the Constitution of the United States and the Constitution of the State of California, and that I will faithfully discharge the duties of my office according to the best of my ability; that I do not believe in, and I am not a member of, nor do I support any party or organization that believes in, advocates, or teaches the overthrow of the United States Government, by force or by any illegal or unconstitutional methods."

REGENT TEAGUE: I am wondering if you will have an opportunity to present that new oath to men who are already members of the faculty.

PRESIDENT SPROUL: It will be in the new contract.

REGENT DICKSON: This oath will apply to all persons connected with the University whether they are faculty members or administration. The Los Angeles City Council just recently adopted a similar rule and required all City employees to take that oath of office. We had three members who refused to take the oath and they were discharged immediately.[7]

With the rapid disposition of two additional matters of business, the Regents adjourned.

The importance of this sequence of events cannot be overemphasized. Executive session of the Board normally followed the regular session. The meeting of March 25 was an exception. Before going into an *interim* executive session that day, the great bulk of the Board's business had been accomplished. When the interim executive session was called, the press, the public, and the staff — everyone except the President, members of the Board, and the secretary — left the room. Those who left knew that the day's business was very nearly completed, and most likely assumed that final matters would be considered in executive session. Their belief in this was confirmed when the meeting broke up shortly afterwards.[8] The Regents, however, upon completing their discussion of the Laski matter, moved back into regular session *but in doing so neglected to inform those outside.* As the remaining business was quickly handled, the thought that there were those outside who should have been inside apparently never occurred to those who were concentrating on the business at hand. And so the oath was born and its birth known only to those who gave it life and to a secretary who recorded it. Every consideration that influenced the President and the Regents that day is not known. Much, however, is certain, and the President's position in all of it is of paramount importance, particularly in view of the criticism to which he was latter subjected by a fraction of the Board and by a part of the faculty. There is no question that President Sproul favored adoption of the oath on March 25, 1949.[9] It is also certain that the members of the Board voting that afternoon were as favorably disposed toward the oath as the President.[10] Although it is not clear who first suggested the idea of an oath, it does appear that the President and the Regents were receptive to the idea as a means of elaborating upon the University's policy prohibiting the employment of Communists.[11] Although the President did not meet or consult with his academic advisors about the adoption of an oath prior to its enactment, he had discussed with them the *policy* the oath was later meant to implement more precisely.[12] Moreover, in the absence of formal Academic Senate advice, an oath had been adopted once before in the University, with no resulting dissent by the faculty and staff.[13] Finally, it appears that Sproul intended no violence either to the integrity of faculty self-government or to the privileges and tenure of the members of the faculty.[14] What seems most probable is that that oath served the President's immediate purposes in several ways.

For the Regents, the use of University facilities by a Communist was related to the question of the employment of Communists on the faculty.[15] A special committee of the Board (Hutchinson committee) had been appointed the previous month to study the issues arising from the Phillips–Benson debate and was to report its recommendations to the Board in April. In March the situation had been further complicated by the Laski incident. The President, as executive officer of the University, apparently considered it to be his responsibility, not the Regents', to deal with the UCLA incidents, and by supporting what he considered to be an "innocuous" amendment to the oath of allegiance he would in one stroke obtain several objectives. (As has already been noted [n. 11], who in fact first proposed or initiated the oath is uncertain. Sproul clearly supported it, however, and technically "proposed" it to the Board the afternoon of March 25, 1949. The President, as executive officer, of course, "proposed" all of the Board's business to the Regents except that introduced by individual members.) For Sproul, the oath would implement more explicitly the Regents' policy on the non-employment of Communists; narrow the problems then under study by the Hutchinson committee to the single question of the use of University facilities and, thus, in part, return administrative initiative to the President; obtain a firmer expression of regental policy so as to strengthen his hand in dealing with Dykstra, who was administratively accountable to the President; and provide a more definitive response to those on the faculty who were reported by the chairman of the Senate's northern Advisory Committee to be in support of the position of the American Association of University Professors on Communist teachers and to those on the faculty and staff who were uncertain of the University's policy on the employment of Communists.[16] Because University regulations on the use of facilities by Communists were not definitive, the administration had found itself in an awkward position in the appearance at UCLA of Professor Phillips. The Laski lectures had further complicated matters. The oath of allegiance was not definitive either, as it no more explicitly proscribed Communists than did the regulations on the use of facilities. *Apparently, Sproul wished to "strengthen" the oath of allegiance in order to implement further the already existing University prohibition against employment of Communists, in the same way that the Hutch-*

inson committee wished to "strengthen" regulations govern-
ing the use of University facilities in order to deny them to
those who would use them as a "platform" for propaganda.
The question as to whether a loyalty oath was appropriate
seemed to Sproul "to have been answered seven years ago
and the answer accepted by all concerned," for since 1942
the faculty, without notable objection, had subscribed to an
oath of allegiance.[17] Sproul seemingly believed that to amend
the oath of allegiance by adding a disclaimer affidavit would
cause no more concern among the members of the faculty
than had the adoption of an oath in 1942. If the distinctions
between an oath of allegiance and a disclaimer were recognized, they were not, apparently, regarded as critical.

The oath seemed to recommend itself to Sproul the morning of March 25, 1949, as a key to the solution of several
problems then pending, such as use of University facilities,
University policy on employment of Communists, and administrative authority. That it would soon create even greater
difficulties was apparently not seriously considered by the
President or by any Regent present.

II

The Regents' secretary and treasurer, Robert M. Underhill, was out of the country when the oath was enacted and
did not return until early the following month. In mid-April
Underhill learned of the disclaimer when the 1949–50 appointment letters containing the new oath were delivered from
the printer.[18] He immediately contacted Sproul's assistant,
Dr. George A. Pettitt, who was responsible for the University's Office of Public Information, only to learn that Pettitt
knew nothing of the new oath.[19] Underhill and Pettitt agreed
that the faculty and staff should be advised of the requirement immediately. A regular monthly publication, the *Faculty Bulletin*, was scheduled to be printed and mailed within
the next four days, and it was decided to use that medium
for the notification, rather than to prepare and mail a sepa-

rate notice. It was May 9, however, two and a half weeks later, before the *Faculty Bulletin* was in the mails, with the delay due principally to "jam ups on the University Press." [20] The notice in the *Bulletin* read:

SECRETARY OF THE
REGENTS

The Regents of the University have directed me to include in acceptance letters when 1949–50 appointments are made an oath of allegiance in the form to be set forth therein, and that all faculty and employees must take the oath as part of the acceptance. This procedure is about to go into effect for new appointees for the remainder of this fiscal year, but persons taking the oath of allegiance now will not be required to do so again on next annual appointments. Salary checks cannot be released until acceptance letters have been returned to this office properly signed before a Notary Public.

ROBERT M. UNDERHILL
Secretary of the Regents [21]

The oath was referred to but not quoted, as it was thought by Pettitt to have been adopted in executive session. Furthermore, if it were published and members of the faculty objected to it, the objection, Pettitt feared, might serve to strengthen the Tenney bills.[22] Thus, it was early June before the full text became generally known and only then because of direct inquiries made by members of the faculty.

Two and a half months had passed from the day the Regents enacted the oath to the time it was reported to the faculty. The delay was crucial. The wording of the oath was made public at the close of the academic year, just in time for the final scheduled Academic Senate meeting of 1948–49 — a meeting normally routine in character and only sparsely attended. The timing caused some of the faculty to suspect administrative intent to minimize Senate opposition. Consequently, resentment, suspicion, and doubt arose in the faculty toward the administration and cost the

President and the Regents a rather generous measure of goodwill and cooperation.

III

Meanwhile, the Regents continued to grapple with University policy governing the use of facilities. The Hutchinson committee reported to the Board in April that it would not be ready with its recommendations until May. Provost Dykstra's request that Laski be reinvited was denied. The Board withdrew its request that Dykstra appear in defense of his actions with regard to the Phillips–Benson debate and referred the matter to the President.[23] The oath was not discussed by the Regents during their April meetings.

Regent Hutchinson, in the hope of having a statement to submit to the Board in late May, circulated a draft of a resolution to his fellow committeemen for review. The draft proposed in part that "no member of the Communist organization shall be employed or retained in the service of this University nor accorded the use of University facilities."[24] The statement was essentially an elaboration of the University's 1940 policy on the non-employment of Communists, to which was tied an explicit prohibition against the use of facilities by members of that party. By the time of the May meeting of the Board, however, the committee had yet to agree on a recommendation. Hutchinson promised to report in June and Sproul was asked to help the committee with its work.[25]

As May slipped into June, Regent Hutchinson seemed to sense impending danger and wrote to Neylan of his concern for the timeliness of the Board's action on his committee's report. "I do not think the University has a Communist problem," Hutchinson said, "and the action of the Board without a timely reason might give rise to the impression that we did have such a problem."[26] The thought that Board action might better be delayed, however, soon vanished when faculty resistance to the new oath was widely reported by the press.

IV

The last meeting of the year for the Academic Senate's northern section was scheduled for June 7, 1949. As it was expected that the oath would be debated on the floor of the Senate, key members of the faculty were encouraged by the administration to be present to prevent a "blowup."[27] The meeting, attended by some two hundred members of the Senate's northern section (representing the campuses at Berkeley, Davis, Lick Observatory, and San Francisco), was brief and on only one occasion dealt with the oath, namely, when upon adjournment a special meeting was called for June 14 to consider a resolution to be offered by Professor Edward Tolman of psychology concerning the new requirement.[28]

Headlines appearing in the nation's newspapers during the seven days June 7 to June 14, 1949, did not create an atmosphere "friendly to cold logic or clear processes of the intellect."[29] The *New York Times* reported on June 12, 1949, for example, that "spy stories played a large part in the news last week — and in the thinking of the nation. Analysis of the New York newspapers disclosed that 32 per cent of the first page space was devoted to the 'spy' theme or matters closely related to it. . . ."[30] The Hiss perjury trial had begun two weeks earlier, the trial of the eleven Communists indicted under the Smith Act was beginning its fourth month, the congressional investigation of the Atomic Energy Commission's security measures was in its second week of hearings, the House Committee on un-American Activities was holding hearings in Washington, D.C., on subversion allegedly occurring during World War II at the University's Radiation Laboratory at Berkeley, and the same committee had just announced its intention to survey college textbooks for dangerous or subversive ideas.

The University added some column inches of its own to this already impressive reporting of Communist influence and the nation's response to it by disclosing publicly the Regents' decision to require a Communist disclaimer of the University's faculty and staff. "We don't like the idea of oaths — nobody does," Pettitt was reported as saying, "but in the face of the cold-war hysteria we are now experiencing, something had to be done. The new oath," Pettitt continued, merely makes "more explicit the oath of allegiance to the state and nation." [31] Senator Tenney's response to the announcement was to give reluctant approval — he had hoped for something more — and to drop his own legislative proposal for a compulsory loyalty oath (Senate Bill 280, which would require a Communist disclaimer of all state employees — a piece of legislation then pending in the lower house). [32] President Sproul's unqualified retort to the Tenney remark was that the oath "originated within the Board of Regents" and "has absolutely no connection with Senator Tenney"; [33] and Sproul was joined publicly by Regent Edward Heller, who stated that Tenney had nothing whatsoever to do with the disclaimer required by the Board. [34]

In the midst of this tumult four hundred members of the northern section of the University's Academic Senate gathered in Berkeley to consider the oath. [35] President Sproul, as chairman of the Academic Senate, presided. Professor Tolman introduced the business of the day in the form of a resolution which affirmed the loyalty of the members of the Senate to the nation and to the state, objected to the speed with which the oath was being imposed, raised issues of academic freedom and tenure, and in conclusion, requested that the amendment to the oath of allegiance enacted March 25, 1949, be deleted. Tolman, one of Berkeley's senior and most distinguished scholars and one of the nation's most prominent psychologists, had served the University for thirty-one continuous years — since his appointment to the faculty in 1918; and he held membership in the American Academy of Arts and Sciences, the American Philo-

sophical Society, and the National Academy of Sciences —
three of the country's most eminent learned societies. The
Tolman resolution was debated at length. The most important plea in support of the resolution was made by Professor Ernst H. Kantorowicz, one of the University's prize
scholars and one of the world's renowned medievalists,
whose remarks that day, as an expression of the feeling and
intensity of some of the members, deserves to be fully
quoted:

Statement Read Before the
Academic Senate Northern Section
June 14, 1949

As a historian who has investigated and traced the histories
of quite a number of oaths, I feel competent to make a statement
indicating the grave dangers residing in the introduction of a new,
enforced oath, and to express, at the same time, from a professional and human point of view, my deepest concern about the
steps taken by the Regents of the University.

1. Both history and experience have taught us that every
oath or oath formula, once introduced or enforced, has the ten-
dency to develop its own autonomous life. At the time of its
introduction an oath formula may appear harmless, as the one
proposed by the Regents of this University. But nowhere has
there been a guaranty that an oath formula imposed on, or ex-
torted from, the subjects of an all-powerful state will, or must,
remain unchanged. The contrary is true. All oaths in history that
I know of, have undergone changes. A new word is added. A
short phrase, seemingly insignificant, will be smuggled in. The
next step may be an inconspicuous change in the tense, from present to past, or from past to future. The consequences of a new
oath are unpredictable. It will not be in the hands of those im-
posing the oath to control its effects, nor of those taking it to ever
step back again.

2. The harmlessless of the proposed oath is not a protection
when a principle is involved. A harmless oath formula which con-
ceals the true issue, is always the most dangerous one because it
baits even the old and experienced fish. It is the harmless oath
that hooks; it hooks *before* it has undergone those changes that

will render it, bit by bit, less harmless. Mussolini Italy of 1931, Hitler Germany of 1933 are terrifying and warning examples for the harmless bit-by-bit procedure in connection with politically enforced oaths.

3. History shows that it never pays to yield to the impact of momentary hysteria, or to jeopardize, for the sake of temporary or temporal advantages the permanent or external values. It was just that kind of a "little oath" that prompted thousands of non-conformists in recent years, and other thousands in the generations before ours, to leave their homes and seek the shores of this Continent and Country. The new oath, if really enforced, will endanger certain genuine values the grandeur of which is not in proportion with the alleged advantages. Besides, this oath, which is invalid anyhow because taken under duress, may cut also the other way. It may have the effect of a drum beating for Communist and Fascist recruits.

4. The new oath hurts, not merely by its content, but by the particular circumstances of its imposition. It tyrannizes because it brings the scholar sworn to truth into a conflict of conscience. To create alternatives — "black or white" — is a common privilege of modern and bygone dictatorships. It is a typical expedient of demagogues to bring the most loyal citizens, and only the loyal ones, into a conflict of conscience by branding nonconformists as un-Athenian, un-English, un-German, and — what is worse — by placing them before an alternative of two evils, different in kind, but equal in danger.

The crude method of "Take it or leave it" — "Take the oath or leave your job" — creates a condition of economic compulsion and duress close to blackmail. This impossible alternative which will make the official either jobless or cynical, leads to another completely false alternative: "If you do not sign, you are a Communist who has no claim to tenure." This whole procedure is bound to make the loyal citizen, one way or another, a liar and untrue to himself because any decision he makes will bind him to a cause which in truth is not his own. Those who belong, de facto or at heart, to the ostracized parties will always find it easy to sign the oath and make their mental reservation. Those who do *not* sign will be, now as ever, also those that suffer — suffer, not for their party creed or affiliations, but because they defend a superior constitutional principle far beyond and above trivial party lines.

5. I am not talking about political expediency or academic freedom, nor even about the fact that an oath taken under duress is invalidated the moment it is taken, but wish to emphasize the true and fundamental issue at stake: professional and human dignity.

It is a shameful and undignified action, it is an affront and a violation of both human sovereignty and professional dignity that the Regents of this University have dared to bully the bearer of this gown into a situation in which — under the pressure of a bewildering economic coercion — he is compelled to give up either his tenure or, together with his freedom of judgment, his human dignity and his responsible sovereignty as a scholar.[36]

A substitute motion was offered to modify the Tolman resolution somewhat by adding to it the Senate's willingness to accept a *revision of the oath rather than only its deletion.* After extended debate, a compromise resolution was passed, reading as follows:

RESOLVED: That the Academic Senate, Northern Section, requests the President to communicate to the Board of Regents the following:

The members of the Academic Senate, Northern Section, although unaware of any conduct which warrants doubt about their loyalty and zeal, have no objection to declaring again their loyalty to the Nation and State of which they are citizens and their determination to discharge their duties faithfully.

But the speed with which the new oath is being imposed, and the form of the second half of it raise serious questions in our minds as to a possible conflict with accepted principles of academic tenure and academic freedom.

We, therefore, request that the second half of the oath beginning with the words "That I do not believe in" and ending with the words "By any illegal or unconstitutional methods," be *deleted or revised* in a manner mutually acceptable to the Regents and the *members* of the Academic Senate before the signing of the new oath is required for the obtaining of 1949–50 contracts by members of the faculty or by other employees of the University; and further, that the *Advisory Committee be instructed to consult with the President of the University with a view to working out such a solution* [emphasis added].[37] (The southern section passed an identical resolution on June 20, 1949.)

The authority of the members of the Senate and of the Advisory Committee — a standing committee of the Senate responsible for advising the President on matters of general interest to the University — to commit the faculty was unclear under the terms of this resolution. The Senate had asked either for deletion of the oath or for its revision "in a manner mutually acceptable to the Regents and the members of the Academic Senate," but at the same time had instructed its Advisory Committee to work with the President to the same end. It was customary for the Advisory Committee to consult with the President but not necessarily to report to the Senate the results of those discussions. The resolution, however, as read by some, was not implicitly reliant on custom, but was, rather, explicitly dependent on the acceptability by the Senate of whatever agreements were struck between the President and the Advisory Committee.[38] The ambiguity later was to aggravate relations among members of the faculty and between the Senate and the Board of Regents. Nevertheless, the Senate was on record as willing to accept something in addition to the long-required oath of allegiance. The stronger Tolman resolution — which unqualifiedly called for deletion of the added disclaimer — had failed of support. Although there had been strong and critical opposition to the oath voiced by individual members of the faculty, the Senate itself had expressed only a modest objection; and it was this formal opinion that was to be given the greatest weight in the negotiations that followed.

V

The Advisory Committee, northern section, was composed of three men: Professors Joel H. Hildebrand, chairman, and Benjamin H. Lehman of the Berkeley campus, and H. B. Walker of the Davis campus.[39] Members of the Advisory Committee, southern section (which represented the campuses at Los Angeles, Riverside, and La Jolla, with Santa Barbara in informal association) were Professors Martin R. Huberty, chairman, and John W. Olmstead and Gordon S. Watkins, all of UCLA.[40] Professor Walker of the northern committee left for the East shortly after the Senate meeting, June 14, and did not personally participate in the discussions between the committee and the President. Before leaving, however, he advised Hildebrand of prevailing attitudes on the Davis campus. "Practically all faculty members at Davis are willing to sign the oath," Walker reported, and although some rewording of it might be regarded favorably, "a more affirmative statement regarding Communism would not be objectionable. . . ." And Walker concluded, no one at Davis believed that the President or the Regents "had any thought of curbing true academic freedom or civil rights, nor do they feel their tenure is in jeopardy."[41]

The Advisory Committees' responsibility was to represent the faculty position to the President. The position represented was the June 14 Senate resolution, supplemented by other written and oral suggestions from individual faculty members. In conference with the President, the Advisory Committees urged Sproul to follow all normal procedures with respect to privilege and tenure, to separate the oath from the contract of employment, and to consider the oath once taken as having continuing binding force.[42] On June 18, the Advisory Committees forwarded their formal recommendations to Sproul.[43] A fundamental assumption buttressed the proposals: *"We assume at the outset that Communist commitments and affiliations are inconsistent with that freedom of mind which is indispensable to the scholar, scientist, and teacher* [emphasis added]." The report unqualifiedly affirmed the University's nine-year policy on the non-employment of Communists and gave no hint that the issue was in active dispute or that several members of the faculty, not to mention the AAUP, patently rejected the notion that Communists, in the absence of demonstrable professional unfitness, should be barred from University teaching. The committees argued, however, that the constitutional prohibition against oaths raised grounds for questioning the legality of the disclaimer in question (Article XX, Section 3, of the California State Constitution specified the oath of allegiance that public officers were expected to take and declared that no other oath could be required as a condition of service. The oath of allegiance, taken by University employees since 1942, was identical in wording to the constitutional oath), and asked if normal intramural procedures in regard to charges against members of the faculty were not compromised in view of the requirement that the oath be notarized.[44] Finally, in commenting on the intentions of some respected and distinguished members of the faculty not to sign, the committees stated their preference for deletion of the oath in favor of another solution: "The oath prescribed in Article XX, Section 3 [constitutional oath], plus a statement of policy which members of the faculty could either approve or acquiesce in." (The suggested statement affirmed the University's rule that members of the Communist party were unacceptable as members of the faculty.) Finally, to be considered only if the public relations of the University made it indispensable, it was suggested by the Advisory Committee that the following clause added to the constitutional oath would prove to be almost universally acceptable: " '. . . ; that I am not under any oath, nor a party to any agreement, nor as a member of any party or organization am I under any commitment, that is in conflict with my obligations under this oath.' "

The evidence suggests that the Advisory Committees represented fairly the position taken by the Senate. If there was bias, it was in their effort to urge deletion of the disclaimer rather than its revision. Moreover, Hildebrand reported that Tolman had approved the Advisory Committees' recommendations before they were sent to Sproul; and with Tolman's backing, the committees very likely were confident that their recommendations would enjoy general faculty acceptance.[45]

VI

The President, of course, was working not only with the Advisory Committees, but with the Hutchinson committee as well. Since early June, he had had responsibility to prepare a resolution which the Regents' committee could recommend to the Board on June 24. Earlier drafts by members of the committee made no reference to the oath, although Hutchinson's coupled the University's policy on the use of facilities to the employment policy barring Communists. On June 21 Sproul sent the rough draft of a resolution to members of the committee for comment. The proposal was essentially an elaboration of the 1940 policy on the non-employment of Communists, but included the oath the Advisory Committee had recommended to the President as an alternative to deletion. The President, presumably, included the oath in response to instructions given him earlier in the month by the Committee on Finance and Business Management. (At a meeting of the Regents' Committee on Finance and Business Management, held shortly after the June 14 Senate meeting, the matter of the oath came up for prolonged and heated discussion. Following a review of the situation and how it had come about, "Regent Neylan then expressed the opinion, in which all present concurred, that the Regents' policy on Communism, which is presumably to be adopted at the June meeting, *should be coupled with whatever oath*, if any is to be required [emphasis added]. Personally, he [Neylan] does not favor an oath.")[46]

Upon receipt of Sproul's draft, Regent Neylan met in San Francisco to review it with Regent Farnham Griffiths, a local attorney prominent in the city's civic, charitable, and cultural life and a Regent of one year, having been appointed in 1948 by Governor Earl Warren. Anxious that no misunderstanding should occur between the faculty and the Regents, Neylan, late on Thursday afternoon, June 23, wired the following message to Sproul in Los Angeles, with copies to Regents Hansen and Hutchinson: "I suggest that invitation be extended immediately to Advisory Committees of both Northern and Southern sections of Academic Senate to attend meeting of special committee of Regents [Hutchinson committee] at Los Angeles tomorrow." Although Hansen and Hutchinson received their wires by dinner time, Sproul did not receive his until just before midnight, well after the members of the Advisory Committee had departed Los Angeles following their discussions with the President.

On the eve of the Regents' meeting, the *Westwood Hills Press*, under dateline of June 23, 1949, reported Regent Hansen as saying that opposition to the oath was the same as "making a mountain out of a molehill," and that "it is ridiculous to say that the loyalty oath is the result of political pressures." Regent Hansen was correct in asserting that the oath was not a result of political pressure, such as the Tenney bills and ACR 47, but he was wrong in calculating the extent and intensity of faculty opposition. His feelings, however, may be attributed to an underlying optimism and hope that on the following day action would be taken to settle the dispute. For had not the President secured a firm expression of opinion from the Senate's representatives, concurred in by those most critical of the oath? Had not the recommendations of the Advisory Committees confirmed the Regents' policy that members of the Communist party were unfit for employment in the University? Had not both sections of the Academic Senate expressed by formal resolution their willingness to accept some elaboration of the oath of allegiance, even though its deletion may have been preferred? Seemingly all that remained was to agree on the wording of the oath. Yet there was some uneasiness, as is evidenced by Neylan's wire requesting that the Advisory Committees be present and by Hutchinson's earlier apprehensions about timing and reasons. But as the Regents met in Los Angeles the morning of June 24 there was more hope than pessimism.

When the Hutchinson committee met on the Los Angeles campus, Regents Hansen, Hutchinson, Neylan, and Sproul were in attendance. Also present was Regent Dickson, chairman of the Board, who, though not an appointed member of the committee was, as chairman, exercising his prerogative of attending any and all committee meetings. Attorney for the Board, Jno. U. Calkins, Jr., Secretary and Treasurer Robert M. Underhill, and Assistant Secretary Marjorie Woolman completed the roster. Sproul read the Academic Senate's resolution which called for the oath to be either deleted or revised. He then read the recommendations made by the Advisory Committees: the first being that the faculty be asked to approve or acquiesce in a statement of policy that in substance affirmed the Regents' employment policy barring Communists, that the disclaimer be deleted, and that the oath of allegiance as worded prior to March 25, 1949, be continued as a requirement. Sproul then read the second proposal that suggested a revision to the oath adopted in March should the public relations of the University require it.

To the second proposal Regent Neylan responded: "This oath thing — I don't think much of it at all." [47] He then took up and supported the argument advanced by the Advisory Committees on the possible conflict between the disclaimer and the constitutional prohibition against any oath for a public officer other than the one provided in Article XX, Section 3, of the State Constitution. Said Neylan: "I do not conceive a member of the faculty as a public officer, but in any event, he is a servant of a public trust. . . . It seems to me that the [constitutional] prohibition of any other text or oath is certainly deserving of some consideration." [48] Calkins, attorney for the Regents, agreed that Neylan's point had merit but that from the legal aspect the oath could be required. [49] The Regents then turned to the impression given by the press that the President and the faculty were at odds with the Regents — an assertion denied with some vigor by Neylan: "There is no war between the faculty and the Regents. There has been none. This Board has been proud of the faculty and proud of the fact that the greatest faculty in the world has been assembled here. To say we are at war when we are bursting with pride is a farce and untrue." [50] Sproul denied with equal force that there was any division between the President and the Board.

Two resolutions had been drafted by members of the committee and brought to the meeting: the one prepared on June 21 by Sproul and the one drawn up jointly by Neylan and Griffiths the day before in San Francisco. The two resolutions differed in wording but agreed in principle. The resolution drafted by Neylan and Griffiths, however, made no reference to the oath, whereas Sproul's draft included the oath suggested by the Advisory Committees. [51] For Neylan, the policy was the all-important consideration. If the policy statement were to be issued jointly by the Regents, the President, and the Advisory Committees, then, Neylan said, he did not care what was done with the oath, for there would then be a united front. [52] As there was sympathy for this view among members of the committee, discussion centered on the wording of the policy statement. It appeared for a time that the Hutchinson committee would recommend to the Board that the oath be deleted. However, the following discussion led to its reconsideration and adoption as part of the resolution to be submitted to the Regents later that day (italics added for emphasis):

DICKSON [reading the Neylan draft which did *not* include the oath]: Do you want to say that the President is hereby authorized and instructed to dismiss such persons [those persons whose employment was inconsistent with the terms of the resolution]?
NEYLAN: No.
PRESIDENT: I don't think so.
DICKSON: There will be those who say the Regents have capitulated [referring to omission of the oath].
NEYLAN (to the President): Are you empowered to say that

the Academic Senate will *agree* to this [refers to inclusion of the oath in Sproul's draft]?

PRESIDENT: Yes. [Sproul's response would have been more accurate had it been qualified by stating that the Advisory Committees had recommended the oath included in the resolution *only* if the public relations of the University required it, and in fact *preferred* that no oath be required in addition to the oath of allegiance; and by pointing out that the Advisory Committees' proposals were only recommendations which had not enjoyed discussion and debate in the Academic Senate].

NEYLAN: The important part of this statement is the introductory paragraph that the Regents, the President, and the Advisory Committees, representing both the Northern and Southern Sections of the Academic Senate today issued the following statement — or the following statement was issued today by the Secretary of the Regents on behalf of the Regents of the University of California, the President of the University, and the Advisory Committees of the Northern and Southern Sections of the Academic Senate. *If agreed on I will go along with you on the oath.*

HUTCHINSON: The proper way would be to reconsider the resolution of March 25th.

PRESIDENT: The faculty wants the requirement of the oath to be tied to a declaration of policy. Otherwise they think it [the oath] is a reflection on their patriotism.[53]

Hutchinson asked Sproul if the faculty would object to stating that "they are not members of the Communist Party" and expressed his preference that this specific denial be included. The President's unqualified response was that the faculty would not object. (There is no written evidence confirming that the Advisory Committees in fact had approved the additional words "I am not a member of the Communist Party.")[54] The committee then voted to recommend the following resolution to the Board that afternoon (italics added for emphasis):

That, reaffirming the position of the University on the subject of Communism, the following policy be adopted and that a statement of said policy be issued by the Secretary of the Regents on behalf of the Regents of the University of California, the President of the University, and the Advisory Committees of the Northern and Southern Sections of the Academic Senate:

At its birth the University of California was dedicated to the search for truth and its full exposition.

The primary obligation of the Regents of the University of California has been to stand steadfastly for that freedom of the human mind and spirit which has enabled the assemblage of distinguished scholars constituting the faculty to continue to pursue these objectives.

The Regents gladly share with the faculty the responsibility to keep the University free from those who would destroy this freedom.

Today this freedom is menaced on a world-wide basis by the Communist Party through its determination by fraud, or otherwise, to establish control by the State over the thoughts and expressions of thoughts by the individual.

Therefore, the Regents reaffirm their declaration of policy adopted in 1940 that membership in the Communist Party is incompatible with objective teaching and with search for the truth.

Pursuant to this policy the Regents direct that no member of the Communist Party shall be employed by the University.

Any person who is or shall become a member of the Communist Party or otherwise undertakes obligations or advocates doctrines inconsistent with this policy shall, after the facts have been established by the University Administration, and after the traditional consultation with the Committee on Privilege and Tenure of the Academic Senate in cases of members of the faculty, be deemed to have severed his connection with the University.

and to *implement* the above stated policy, that the following oath be subscribed to by all members of the faculty, employees and administration of the University:

"I do solemnly swear (or affirm) that I will support the Constitution of the United States and the Constitution of the State of California, and that I will faithfully discharge the duties of my office according to the best of my ability; that I am not a member of the Communist Party or under any oath, or a party to any agreement, or under any commitment that is in conflict with my obligation under oath." [55]

The statement of policy and the oath recommended by the Hutchinson committee were considered by the full Board that afternoon in executive session (emphasis added):

AHLPORT: Do I understand that the Academic Senate has already approved this?

PRESIDENT: The Advisory Committees have already approved this, not the Senate. With regard to the oath they have said if the Regents deem an oath necessary this form is satisfactory. [The President here made the qualification he failed to make when asked much the same question by Neylan that morning. Also see n. 54.]

JORDAN: In that respect, if we pass this can we assume that there will be no flareback from the Academic Senate?

PRESIDENT: None from the Advisory Committes which have been authorized to negotiate with me on the problem. You can assume that there will be no likelihood of considerable flareback from the Senate.

GRIFFITHS: If the faculty now wants to fight and leave us out, that's all right. *This whole matter started because the Provost invited the expelled Communist member of the University of Washington to speak.* In some draft you had a phrase saying that the facilities would be denied to Communists.

NEYLAN: It would seem that this had taken a turn which warranted handling the matter in this form and leaving the matter of use of facilities to another time. To meet this existing situation, we voted to adopt this policy. It was deemed appropriate to leave the other for further action. I think the thing to meet is the present and imminent threat [the oath].

GRIFFITHS: I agree with that unless the President feels that he does not presently have authority by virtue of previous resolutions of the Board to see that the Provost cannot invite Communists to speak on campus but I hope we can wind this Communist imbroglio up.

TEAGUE: He must not allow the use of the facilities.

NEYLAN: *The happy part of this is that it brought the Board, the President, and the faculties in agreement on the issue.*

HELLER: I think the Committee should be congratulated. I would like to offer a resolution congratulating the Committee.

(The resolution [recommended by Hutchinson committee] was adopted).[56]

The Regents returned to regular session and by unanimous vote adopted the resolution.

The same day, four hundred miles to the north, the Assembly of the State of California moved to kill the Tenney bills. Leading the floor fight against the bills was Regent Sam L. Collins, speaker of the Assembly. Collins had argued that the constitutional oath was adequate and that the Tenney bills only added confusion to the law.[57] And for SB 280 (the bill to require a disclaimer of all state employees) Collins reserved his sharpest criticism: "When you substitute this mumble jumble of meaningless phrases, words, periods, commas, colons, etc. [the disclaimer], you accomplish naught. Naught except the tinkling of cymbals and the sounding of brass."[58] Ironically, Collins' fellow Regents in Los Angeles had just voted unanimously to require a disclaimer of University employees of the sort Collins had successfully opposed in the Assembly. Incredibly, Speaker Collins soon found himself supporting in the University the very kind of requirement he had helped defeat in the legislature.

"While many members of the faculty will feel sad that any oath is regarded as necessary," said Hildebrand when hearing of the Board's decision that evening, "they recognize that the present state of public opinion may make it seem expedient. At the same time," he continued, "I am sure that the willingness of the Regents to adopt a solution proposed by the authorized committees of the Academic Senate will go far to restore the mutual confidence between the Regents and the faculty which we have long enjoyed."[59]

The optimism was short-lived.

Chapter Three

The Opposition Forms

I

Several members of Berkeley's faculty gathered on the evening of June 24, 1949, to discuss the action of the Board earlier that day. They were critical of the Advisory Committee for having committed the faculty in negotiations with the President without first inviting Senate discussion and ratification of the position taken. Certain procedural questions unanswered by the Regents' resolution were also reviewed, such as the role of the Senate's Committee on Privilege and Tenure, and the relation of the oath to letters of appointment. As the evening ended, the group designated one of its number to invite a discussion of these matters with the President on July 6.[1] Similar criticism of the Advisory Committee was evident three days later when sixty members of the Berkeley faculty, among whom were thirty-five senior professors, met at the Faculty Club on the Berkeley campus. The majority believed that the members of the Advisory Committee had been given no authority to act for the Senate and that the committee had been remiss in failing to secure Senate ratification of the proposals made to Sproul.

The northern Advisory Committee, in response to these charges, circulated a memorandum to the members of the Academic Senate, which quoted in full and commented on the committee's report to the President (of June 18, 1949), the letter of concurrence signed by the southern Advisory Committee, and the statement made by Hildebrand on the evening of June 24. The circular concluded: "There remain certain matters of procedure growing out of the action of the Board of Regents in connection with which we are endeavoring to the best of our ability to represent to the President the questions and views of our colleagues."[2]

Professor Hildebrand followed the committee's circular with a memorandum of his own to members of the Senate. The Senate's resolution which instructed the Advisory Committee to meet with the President, Hildebrand stressed, made no provision for Senate ratification of the proposals made; and, he continued, as the Senate had voted to negotiate either for the oath's deletion or for its revision, the Advisory Committee had proposed an alternate to the oath in the event the Regents felt it necessary to retain the oath but in a revised form. "For the influence of the faculty with the President and the Regents to be maintained," he concluded, "we must endeavor to select as advisors to the President, in whatever capacity, men whom it [sic] can trust and who can speak with reasonable assurance of faculty backing."[3] Otherwise, Hildebrand believed, such committees might as well be abolished.

Members of the Regents' Committee on Finance and Business Management met in San Francisco on June 30. Word of the faculty's opposition had come informally to their attention. In acquainting the committee with the extent of this criticism, Sproul reported that there were about thirty-five persons on the faculty who had grave doubts about the situation and among them were distinguished men who, he believed, would temper their contrary attitude "provided we do not push them about."[4] Sproul recommended that the oath requirement not be coupled, for at least a year, with the employment contract and that there be no change in the procedure for mailing salary checks for July and August to members of the faculty and staff, even though the oath might not in some instances have been signed.[5] The recommendation proposed to separate the oath from the appointment letter to avoid the impression of duress.[6] The plan was for the President in mid-July to send the oath to members of the faculty and request their signature. Salaries for July and August were to be paid irrespective of individual signature, but appointment letters were to be withheld pending receipt of the oath signed and duly notarized. Although members of the Committee on Finance and Business Management approved Sproul's recommendation, they did so only after rather severe questioning (emphasis added):

GRIFFITHS: Supposing one of our eminent men and distinguished professors of the conservative trend concerning whom no one would even suggest he had Communist views would say "I do not care to sign the oath." Are you going to dismiss him because he has not signed the oath which is *not* part of the contract? [Regent Griffiths' son, Gordon, was an assistant professor of history on the Berkeley campus and later one of the leading protagonists among those on the faculty who most opposed the oath.]

NEYLAN: That is not our primary problem. (1) There is virtue in not coupling the oath with the contracts. (2) *If Mr. X, an eminent man, should say "I do not care to sign that oath," I do not think that is a primary problem of ours. It is a problem of Hildebrand, Lehman, and Walker. They represented the faculty and we, in good faith, accepted their suggestion. If they cannot keep their men in line that is too bad.*

PRESIDENT: They will agree with you on that.

NEYLAN: We will make a mistake if we are at loggerheads with the faculty.

PRESIDENT: *I would suggest that the appointment letters not be sent out until the oaths come in.* We have plenty of time. I will get an overwhelming majority or I am a bad guesser.

GRIFFITHS: But if you have one, I see no way out of this.

PRESIDENT: *I want to handle it in the way that will antagonize the smallest number of men. Then I can talk to those dissenters.*

NEYLAN: *I would not sign the oath. I would fight it but if I were committed by the Advisory Committee I would go along.* If they want to repudiate their representative that is the step they should take first. We should not engage in that. I think a small measure of resistance is stimulated from outside.

GRIFFITHS: I gather there is a good deal of feeling of compulsion and disapproval among the faculty. Unless you are satisfied now that we are not going to get to the point where we will have to take the decision against a man whom we know to have no taint of Communism merely because he will not sign the oath. I do not want to be put in that position. *I would rather, right now take the oath out, in spite of all we have gone through.*

PRESIDENT: You cannot do that. You are assuming the worst possible situation.

GRIFFITHS: I do not think that you can dismiss a man for not taking that oath.

HELLER: How did they take the old oath?

PRESIDENT: As a part of the contract.

GRIFFITHS: *Except for the fact of saving face, do we want this oath?*

PRESIDENT: *I think the Board does. Also, a majority of the faculty. They want to put themselves on record.*[7]

Regent Griffiths was also critical of the President's recommendation that the oath and appointment letters be separated. He pointed out that the oath of allegiance formerly required was a part of the contract and, without any change in this procedure having been discussed with the Board on June 24, the proposal now was to separate the two. Griffiths' argument did not prevail, however, and the President's proposal was accepted. (It is unclear why Sproul so insisted that the oath be kept. Later in the meeting, in response to further criticism by Griffiths, Sproul said: "We are in midstream and have a substantial majority of the faculty going along with us and to back down now would put us in a most difficult position." Apparently, Sproul was confident that only a very few would in fact resist the oath to the point of not signing and that by persuasion those few could be won over.)

II

The President lunched with Hildebrand and Lehman the next week.[8] They urged the President to word moderately the letter he was to prepare transmitting the oath to members of the faculty for signature. If this were possible, they agreed, opposition would wane.[9] Sproul suggested the following wording: " 'It is hoped that the form [oath] duly signed may be returned not later than October 1.' This met with the complete approval of Lehman and Hildebrand. Lehman said he would take it to the 'dissidents' and would hope to report to me [Sproul] very shortly that all is quiet for the summer." [10]

As Sproul preferred not to meet personally with the group opposed to the oath, he asked that Lehman and Hildebrand do so. Consequently, on July 6, Lehman and Hildebrand consulted with six representatives of the group to work out an acceptable solution to the procedural questions. The six representatives responded favorably to the separation of the oath from the contract, to the payment of July and August salaries irrespective of individual signature to the oath, and to the moderate wording the President had agreed to use in requesting signatures.[11] Because of these concessions, reported Lehman, the six representatives agreed to withhold a letter prepared by them and signed by twenty-three other faculty members, which invited Senate members to defer signing until after the September Senate Meeting.[12] The representatives also agreed that thereafter the opposition group would not meet as a whole, but rather in such small committees as were to be made responsible for preparing materials for the Senate meeting. No sooner had agreement been reached, however, than Hildebrand read from the letter sent by him on June 30 to members of the Senate. "This event produced consternation," Lehman observed, as "the representatives . . . immediately pointed out that the Senate was being circularized from one camp in the very hour in which the other had agreed not to circularize. I spare you [Sproul] the subsequent conversation." [13] Further discussion, however, led to reconfirmation of the agreements made earlier.

The oath was mailed by Sproul to members of the University's faculty and administrative staff in mid-July. The addressee was to sign, notarize, and return the oath by

October 1. To avoid the impression of duress, no reference was made to the appointment letter for the 1949–50 academic year or to the fact that it would be withheld pending receipt of the oath.

Professor Harry Hoijer, chairman of the Senate Committee on University Welfare, southern section, on July 15, 1949, sent to members of that section a memorandum urging the faculty not to sign the oath until the Senate had had an opportunity to consider it.[14] The preceding day, the executive council of the UCLA chapter of the American Association of University Professors mailed to its members a proposed memorial to the Regents which called for the Board to abolish the oath. A meeting of the chapter membership was called for July 26. The President, feeling that his agreement with those on the faculty who were opposed to the oath had been violated, responded quickly with a letter of his own to members of the southern section asking that they sign the oath and explaining that "The naming of October 1 as a date by which it is hoped all replies might be received was intended merely as a convenience to the faculty and was predicated upon 'no electioneering' by opponents or proponents of the oath in the meantime."[15] (George R. Stewart reports in his book that on July 8 the first meeting of "non-signers" was held in Los Angeles; and that this group and its counterpart in Berkeley kept in touch during the summer months.[16] It is not clear whether the southern group was aware or unaware of the July 6 agreements between Hildebrand, Lehman, and the six representatives of the northern opposition; whether or not the southern group, if aware of the agreement, failed to advise Professor Hoijer and the AAUP chapter of it; or whether the southern group and the AAUP chapter, as an organization independent of University control, did not feel bound by Berkeley's commitments.)

Sproul had relied heavily for the success of his plan — to reduce to an absolute minimum the number of non-signers — on the agreement struck on July 6 by Hildebrand

and Lehman with the representatives of those most opposed to the oath, that is, that during the summer no general effort would be made to encourage members of the faculty not to sign. The President's plan was thwarted initially by the Hoijer letter to the southern section and by the UCLA chapter of the AAUP. Once the "silence" was broken, however, and as it became clear that only those who had returned signed oaths were in turn receiving appointment letters, members of the non-signers group at Berkeley moved also to represent their views more widely when six of them wrote the Senate's northern section inviting the membership not to sign until the matter had been considered by the faculty in September.[17]

III

The calm of midsummer fell on the campus as the dispute and August came together and provided a month's respite. For the President, however, the calm was shattered on August 25 when Professor Lehman apprised him of a more general hostility toward the oath than had been earlier anticipated.[18] The withholding of contracts from non-signers, Lehman advised, was viewed by increasing numbers of the faculty as a form of duress. (Interestingly, the opposition at this point laid stress more on the possibility that non-signers would be dismissed for refusing to sign than on criticisms of the oath as a requirement. The elaborate rationale for objecting to the oath per se, other than what had been pointed out in Tolman's and Kantorowicz's remarks to the Senate in June, would only later be refined and articulated with any precision.) Lehman predicted that the Advisory Committees' earlier representations to the President would not be sustained by the Senate and urged Sproul to take the lead and seek deletion of the oath, and to do so before the formal call for the September meeting of the Senate. Otherwise, Lehman pointed out, the President's move to delete the oath would espouse the cause of the dissidents. If Sproul's announcement were to be made after Senate reconsideration, Lehman concluded, the President would have lost the initiative.[19]

The delicate truce negotiated on July 6 had been broken and in its wake members of the faculty were to be urged by their colleagues not to sign until after the Senate meeting in September. To avoid just such electioneering, Sproul had agreed to allow until October 1 for signature, and to separate the oath from the contract. The President's earlier hope of offending only a small number and then working personally with those few no longer proved tenable, as by the end of August only half the oaths had been signed and returned. Moreover, the Advisory Committee was narrowing its support from the broader representations made earlier to the President, who, in his understanding of those representations, had felt confident in urging the Regents to the action they took in June. If Sproul were to recover and regain the initiative, new ground must be secured — and quickly.

Upon his return to Berkeley from an August vacation, Sproul called a meeting of the Advisory Committees for the afternoon of September 6, 1949. The Advisory Committees agreed — in a two-hour meeting that morning — that the withholding of letters of appointment for the 1949–50 academic year from non-signers of the oath had been the chief factor in creating hostility and decided to urge the President: to preside at Senate meetings, to clarify how non-signers would be dealt with, to report on the number of signed oaths received, and to respond to the suggestion made earlier by Lehman that the oath be deleted.[20] The President agreed to preside at the meetings of the Senate and to elaborate on the responsibilities of the Senate's Committee on Privilege and Tenure in dealing with non-signers. He reported the return of signed oaths from the various campuses as being: Berkeley, 50 percent; Davis: 70 percent; Los Angeles, 40 percent; Mt. Hamilton, 100 percent; La Jolla, none; Riverside, 100 percent; and San Francisco, indeterminate. Sproul refused, however, either to comment publicly before the next meeting of the Regents (September 23) about the possibility of deleting the oath or to make any announcement which would create the impression that he had deserted the Regents in favor of the faculty point of view.[21]

It was clear to Sproul that the Advisory Committees had receded from their earlier position. This shift, coupled with Regent Griffiths' willingness as late as July to abandon the oath, and Regent Neylan's earlier opposition to it, probably encouraged Sproul to believe that the oath could and should be deleted. Also, the circumstances that gave rise to the oath in March were not altogether relevant in the late summer of 1949. The Board might prove willing to delete the amendment to the oath of allegiance, Sproul thought, if he and the Senate representatives were to urge it and if, in exchange, the Senate would unequivocally endorse the Regents' policy on the non-employment of Communists. The strategy proved acceptable to the Advisory Committees, and the tactics to achieve it were put into motion. Sproul suggested that the committees draw up a resolution for action by the Senate in which the Regents would *be requested now to accept in lieu of the presently required oath an affirmation by the Senate of the Regents' policy on communism, and that the faculty be not required to take any oath beyond that which they have taken for the past eight or ten years* [emphasis added]."[22]

Meanwhile, those members of the faculty who earlier in the summer most opposed the oath had prepared a resolution of their own to submit for Senate consideration in September. The resolution asked the Regents to rescind the oath and detailed the injury it had already inflicted on the University:

It [the oath] has impaired the morale of the faculty by implicitly segregating them from other public servants in the State.

It has injured the University's reputation in the academic world, setting it in contrast with universities of comparable distinction, such as Harvard, Yale, Chicago.

It has handicapped the University in attracting a continuous flow of young scholars. In this connection, the Senate calls to the attention of the Board the fact that nowhere has the morale of the faculty been more seriously damaged than among the younger members of the teaching staff who do not have tenure.

Most especially the Senate calls to the attention of the Board of Regents the serious doubt which the imposition of this oath, and indeed any unilateral change in the conditions of employment in a university, casts upon the principles of tenure. *It seems evident that, if the terms under which tenure of faculty members is secured are liable to unilateral or arbitrary change, tenure itself ceases to be a fact* [emphasis added].[23]

As the proposed resolution failed to include any statement affirming the University's policy on communism, it met only partially what the President on September 6 had agreed to support. Consequently, on September 13, following approval by Sproul of a separate resolution drafted by the Advisory Committees,[24] Professors Lehman and Will R. Dennes (Walker's replacement) of the Advisory Committee, northern section, and Professor Hildebrand as advisor met with the representatives of the opposition. The Advisory Committee persuaded the representatives to withdraw their resolution in favor of the one proposed by the Advisory Committees and endorsed by Sproul. In exchange, the President was to clarify the role of the Senate's Committee on Privilege and Tenure in hearing the cases of non-signers and was to seek the release of letters of contract and letters of salary rate irrespective of signature to the oath.[25] Rather good success was enjoyed during the next few days in persuading men to support the Advisory Committee's resolution.

IV

Some six hundred fifty members of the Senate assembled in the largest hall on the Berkeley campus on September 19 to consider the loyalty oath. Sproul presided. The large, unattractive, dimly lit hall was only two-thirds full, but it was alive and vital, with the movement of men about it persuading, cajoling, listening, and with a sense of tenseness and expectation prevailing throughout. The Advisory Committee sat together and "operated as a team with four or five of the converted members of the dissident groups close by to be signalled into argument as occasion arose." [26] Sproul, in the form of answers to questions, commented on what was of principal concern to those opposing the oath (emphasis added):

Q: Exactly what is meant by paragraph 7 of the Regents' resolution of June 24, reading "Any person who is or shall become a member of the Communist Party, or who otherwise undertakes obligations or advocates doctrines inconsistent with this policy, shall, after the facts have been established by the University Administration, and after the traditional consultation with the Committee on Privilege and Tenure of the Academic Senate in cases of members of the faculty, be deemed to have severed his connection with the University"?

A: While I am not sure that I can tell you "exactly" what is meant by this paragraph, I can assure you (1) that the paragraph is aimed at the Communist Party alone and that the qualifying words are designed solely to meet the well-established Communist Party tactics of operating as a party under a variety of names; (2) *that the paragraph does not mean that a member of the faculty who regards the adoption of the Regents' policy as unwise will "be deemed to have severed his connection with the University."*

Q: Will a faculty member who fails to sign the oath, *ipso facto*, "be deemed to have severed his connection with the University," and cease to receive salary?

A: My answer is that the words "after the facts have been established by the University Administration and after the traditional consultation with the Committee on Privilege and Tenure of the Academic Senate" apply to those who fail to sign the oath, as well as to members of the Communist Party *et al.*, *and the facts to be established will have to do with more than such failure to sign.*[27]

Then, following some prefatory remarks, Professor Lehman moved adoption of the resolution proposed by his committee. Extended discussion ensued, during which several amendments were offered but failed to pass. Finally, after the committee agreed to include endorsement of University Regulation Number 5,[28] the Senate adopted the following resolution which in its critical portions read:

1. The faculties assembled in the Senate, Northern Section, wholeheartedly concur in the University policy as set forth in University Regulation Number 5 which *prohibits the employment of persons whose commitments or obligations to any organization, Communist or other, prejudice impartial scholarship and the free pursuit of truth* [emphasis added].

(2) The members of the Senate request the privilege of affirming their loyalty to the principles of free constitutional government, by subscribing voluntarily to the oath of loyalty sworn by officers of public trust in the State of California.[29]

The meeting had gone reasonably well, though not without some rather sharp debate. The goals established on September 6 by the Advisory Committee and the President, however, had been realized only in part. Although the Senate had preferred wording of its own to that of the Regents' resolution of June 24, the spirit and intent were coincident — at least so thought the President and the Advisory Committee. A careful reading of part (1) of the Senate resolution, however, suggests that the prohibition against those whose commitments prejudice free scholarship does not admit explicitly to members of the Communist party per se. The wording of the Regents' policy of nine years' standing, as reaffirmed in their June 24 resolution, named the Communist party and denied University employment to any member thereof without further qualification. The resolution passed by the Senate, on the other hand, did not mention membership in any organization as ground for disbarment but only "commitments or obligations to any organization, Communist or other, which prejudice impartial scholarship and the free pursuit of truth." It was not membership in an organization per se but commitments prejudicial to scholarship that the Senate agreed to proscribe, the implication being that the latter need not necessarily follow the former. (The wording of the Advisory Committee's resolution — except for reference to University Regulation 5 — had been agreed to by the President in conversation on September 13 with Lehman, Dennes, and Hildebrand, who had persuaded Sproul from his earlier position of a more specific designation proscribing members of the Communist party to a more general designation on the ground that the party worked under several names. It does not appear that in so arguing Lehman, Dennes, and Hildebrand had intended to exempt members of the party, but rather, to extend the prohibition to those fronting for it.[30] This element of equivocation was later to cause considerable dispute within the faculty itself and to create hostility and confusion between the Senate and the Board of Regents.)

There was also a residue of concern that the bare resolution taken by itself might appear hostile to the Regents, and in order to avoid any possibility of misunderstanding, Hildebrand suggested to Sproul that a direct conference between representatives of the Senate and the Regents might furnish a complete basis for agreement. Hildebrand felt encouraged by what he regarded as "the reasonable and responsible and conciliatory attitude on the part of the leaders of the originally dissident group. . . ."[31]

The Senate's southern section met on the UCLA campus on September 22. After nearly two hours of debate, members of the southern Advisory Committee succeeded in securing adoption of the resolution approved three days earlier in Berkeley, with but one amendment to part (1) of the resolution, which substituted for that portion immediately following University Regulation 5 the following: "They also believe that the University should prohibit employment of any person whose commitments or obligations, Communist or other, *demonstrably* [emphasis added] prevent objective teaching

and the free pursuit of truth." [32] The change in wording grew
out of a lively discussion prior to the vote during which two
principles were stressed, namely, one's associations ought
not to be the sole ground for judging the commitment or
character of an individual; and guilt should be demonstrable.
The southern section had taken a harder line than the
northern.

V

The Senate's resolutions were reported by President
Sproul to the Board the following day. In view of these
resolutions and the low rate of return of signed oaths (53
percent), the President expressed his conviction that the

> . . . present enforcement of the requirement of a special loyalty
> oath, in the form specified on June 24, is neither practical nor
> wise, at least without conference between Regents and faculty.
> Therefore, it seems to me that the Regents should relieve the
> present tension by authorizing their officers, in the spirit as well
> as the letter of instruction that the *requirement of the loyalty
> oath should not be coupled with the contracts of employment, to
> release now the 1949–50 appointment letters, and pay the sala-
> ries for which they call* [emphasis added]. What is next to be
> done could then be considered deliberately by a special com-
> mittee, and reported to the next meeting of the Board.[33]

Sproul commented on the element of duress inferred by the
faculty from the withholding of appointment letters and
the sense of coercion felt by some owing to announcement
of the requirement late in the academic year. The President
concluded by emphasizing that the faculty was not challenging the Regents' policy on communism, but the form of the
oath and the implication of duress it carried. (While the Senate may not have directly challenged the Regents' policy on
communism, neither had it approved it.)

A number of the Regents were concerned that the integrity of the Board and the confidence of the people of the

State in it had by this time become a very real issue. Neylan pointed out that the Board had assumed the full responsibility for the oath when it had acted only in response to the wishes of the President and his academic advisers. He moved that the record of the previous six months be opened to the public and that a special committee of the Board be appointed to meet with the President and members of the Senate. Several Regents, while unwilling to open the record to public view, agreed with Neylan that direct negotiations between the Board and the Senate would be advantageous. The President opposed any public pronouncement that would compromise his relations with the faculty, and at the same time reserved judgment on the facts Neylan had offered to the Board for public release, that is, that the Board had acted only in response to the wishes of the President and the Advisory Committees. Acting on Neylan's suggestion, the Regents appointed a five-man committee to meet with the President and representatives of the Senate on September 29, and called a special meeting of the Board for September 30.[34] The Regents authorized the release of September paychecks to non-signers and instructed the secretary to issue a statement to the press which read in part as follows:

On June 24, 1949 at a meeting of a subcommittee of the Regents [Hutchinson committee] held on the Los Angeles campus, President Sproul reported that he had had several meetings with the Advisory Committees of the Northern and Southern Sections of the Academic Senate and had agreed with these committees on a revised form of oath which would be acceptable to the faculty.

On the basis of this representation, the subcommittee reported to the Board that same afternoon, and the Regents unanimously agreed to the form of oath presented by the President and the Advisory Committees of the Academic Senate.

The Board is now advised that the Northern and Southern Sections of the Senate have failed to sustain the representations made to the Regents by their respective Advisory Committees [emphasis added].[35]

Although the President had secured release of September salary checks to non-signers, he had failed in his purpose to convince the Regents to separate the oath from the 1949–50 contract. The resolution passed by the Regents reflected their concern for the prestige of the governing Board among the people of the state, and probably a sense of resentment toward the President and the Advisory Committees for not seeking more aggressively Senate approval of the representations they made to the Board in June. The resolution also asserted that the Senate had failed to sustain the representations earlier made to the Board by the Advisory Committees. Of course, some members of the Senate felt that the Advisory Committees were given no authority by the Senate to represent faculty opinion either to the President or to the Regents. Others felt that the committees had enjoyed that right. The significant point, however, is not the authority of the Advisory Committees but simply that what they had proposed to the President in June had never been referred to the Senate. Instead, in early September, the President and the committees had decided to seek abolition of the oath in return for an unequivocal approval by the Senate of the Regents' policy barring Communists from University employment. However, at the September meetings of the Senate, the Advisory Committees had proposed that the Senate adopt a resolution asking the Regents to delete the oath *and* that the Senate approve a policy statement equivocal in meaning as to its endorsement of the Regents' policy on communism. Thus, it was not accurate to assert as the Board did in its resolution that the Senate had failed to sustain the position taken by the faculty representatives. Rather, it would have been more correct to have stated that members of the Advisory Committees had changed their minds and had decided against putting their June proposals to a test on the floor of the Senate. And it would also have been more accurate to have said that the Senate had reversed itself, as it no longer regarded a revised oath to be acceptable.

The distinctions here are significant, for as the controversy evolved it was said often and with bitterness, although inaccurately, by some members of the Board of Regents that the Senate had repudiated its own committees, thus unfairly putting the Regents in a bad spot. Although this particular assertion is not true, it is certain that both the Advisory Committees and the Senate had taken positions in September far narrower than what they had led the President and the Regents to believe were acceptable three months earlier and on the basis of which the Regents had acted.

Nevertheless, the Board on September 23, 1949, was not yet ready to dismiss any member of the faculty or administrative staff simply for refusing to sign.

VI

On September 28, 1949, Sproul met with members of the northern Advisory Committee. The President stressed that "the Regents feel that they have been, in a sense, led to the slaughter by the failure of the Academic Senate to sustain the recommendations of its Advisory Committees, on the basis of which the regents acted. I [Sproul] told them also, that while I could understand the attitude of some of the faculty, and was tolerant, as they are, of its views, I nevertheless would stand firm with the Regents for the Communist policy which has been announced, and would be willing to reconsider only methods of implementation."[36] (Sproul's views on the unfitness of Communists to teach were shared unanimously by the members of the Board of Regents and by several of the nation's leading university presidents including Conant at Harvard, Eisenhower at Columbia, Sterling at Stanford, and Seymour at Yale — although the view contradicted the position of the AAUP. Sproul was never to waver in his support of the thesis that Communists, by reason of their membership in the party, had relinquished not only their intellectual freedom but their right to teach as well.)

The meeting the following day between the special com-

mittee of the Regents, the President, the Advisory Committees, and Professor Hildebrand represented a sharp break
with tradition. For a quarter of a century no direct formal
negotiations had occurred in the University of California
between representatives of the Academic Senate and the
Board of Regents. Rather, during that time, all academic
and administrative matters had been represented to the Board
by the President. The departure reflected the severity of the
situation.

Regent Maurice Harrison, well-known San Francisco attorney, former dean of Hastings College of Law in San
Francisco, and Regent since 1944, was in the chair. The
meeting proved mutually respectful and cordial. Following
a brief review of the oath matter, Harrison reported that the
Regents had been shocked the previous week when the President reported enactment of Senate resolutions in conflict
with what had earlier been represented to the Regents as
faculty opinion and on the basis of which the Regents had
acted. Harrison wondered whether the representations made
to the Board by the Advisory Committees on June 24 were
true, and if so, what efforts had been made to sustain that
position.[37]

Professor Lehman spoke to Harrison's question and indicated that the announcement of the oath requirement late
in the academic year had prevented the Senate from fully
and deliberatively considering the question. Consequently,
at the June 14 meeting of the northern section, the Senate
had asked the Regents either to delete or to revise the oath
with the preference in discussion favoring the former alternative. This expression of Senate opinion, Lehman continued,
was clearly reported to the President by the Advisory Committees on June 18 when two proposals were made, one in
preferential relation to the other. The changes in faculty
opinion that had occurred during the summer, as reported
to Sproul in late August, were then reviewed by Lehman. He
stated in conclusion that "the faculty is composed of men
given to examining things carefully and slowly. . . . In the

present situation, however, on a matter of the highest importance the Senate was forced into quick action, since the members were not aware of the oath requirement until late in May. After more leisurely consideration of the problem they saw the whole thing in a different light." [38]

Professor Martin Huberty, chairman of the southern committee, reported that section's resolutions and the reasoning behind them. Elaborating, Professor Hugh Miller stressed the section's preference for faculty self-regulation and assured the Regents that they could "rely upon the faculty to implement the policy and to keep from the campuses not only members of the Communist Party but also persons whose activities gain communist objectives." [39] Miller was supported by Lehman, who argued similarly for faculty self-government in the appointment, promotion, and dismissal of members of the faculty. Professor Olmstead detailed the thinking of the southern section. In June, he said, the issue had been mostly the wording of the oath itself, but during the summer the faculty had realized that the oath was not the only element involved; rather, many of them were more disturbed about the University's policy on communism. [40] Olmstead went on to report the "majority" feeling of his colleagues that a man should not be barred from teaching until he had been heard, and that in implementing the policy the establishment of facts should in any event be an individual matter. Miller put it best:

It is their [faculty] thought that if the oath is a requirement, it cannot be voluntarily affirmed; and if the oath is a condition of service, the faculty could be accused of not having reached its conclusions by impartial logic and thought. If it is understood that communism is incompatible with truth and impartial scholarship, then the faculty would agree 100 per cent on the exclusion of communists on the theory that they are not seekers of the truth. . . . If there is a blanket political disqualification of service with regard to communism, a precedent will have been established which may lead in the future to the disqualification of other minority groups; which . . . would be the destruction of the University.

Neylan responded to this by asserting that "Communism is not a political party but a criminal conspiracy and . . . that the disqualifying of a person for membership in the communist movement would [not] set a bad precedent any more than the dismissal of members of Murder, Inc." [41]

The faculty was walking a taut tightrope. On the one hand, it was arguing for self-governance in implementing the University's policy on the non-employment of Communists, and on the other, qualifying its acceptance of that policy to a point that bordered on its rejection. The inconsistency did not escape Neylan. He moved quickly to commit the faculty representatives to support the University's policy that Communists would not be employed. Neylan proposed that the Board adopt a statement worded to point out that the Regents had not forced the oath on the faculty, that the oath had originated on the academic side of the University, that the Senate after mature study now questioned the soundness of the requirement, and that the Senate subscribed to the statement of policy as issued by the Regents on June 24. If the Advisory Committees would agree, then Neylan was willing to extend for sixty days the deadline for signing, with the understanding that the faculty during that period would formulate its own plan for implementing the policy. The Advisory Committees supported this proposal but excepted their concurrence in the policy, which they felt obligated to refer back to the Academic Senate for further consideration. As the faculty representatives left the meeting they expressed again their belief that fitness for appointment should be on the basis of "honesty, integrity and freedom from bias." Also, that any oath imposed on the faculty other than the one taken since 1942 "will be taken as reflecting a suspicion of their [faculty] loyalty." [42]

After the Advisory Committees had withdrawn, the Regents decided not to retreat from the requirement of the oath until the faculty proposed a better means of implementating the policy than the disclaimer offered. The following statement was voted unanimously for submission to the Board the next day:

Your Special Committee to discuss the oath requirements with the faculty committees recommends that the following statement be adopted as the action of the Board, and that the Secretary be authorized to release it to the Press:

The Board of Regents of the University of California reaffirms its announced policy that no member of the communist party shall be employed by the University.

In implementing this policy, the Board heretofore has adopted a form of oath which was formulated by the President and the Advisory Committees of the Academic Senate.

The Advisory Committees of the Academic Senate now advise the Board that after more mature consideration, the Senate would like to have a portion of that oath deleted.

In the absence of a better method of implementing its policy, the Board stands on its requirement of the oath.

The Board, however, will be glad to consider any method which the faculty may deem to be a further or better implementation of the policy and requests that such suggestions be made within sixty days.[43]

VII

Members of the Advisory Committees, north and south, and Professor Hildebrand were invited to attend the Regents' meeting the following afternoon. After Regent Harrison had read the statement adopted the previous day by his committee, Professor Miller proposed to substitute for it one prepared by the Advisory Committees reading:

Complete agreement upon the *objectives* of the University policy excluding *Communist teaching and influence* [emphasis added] from the campuses of the University was disclosed at today's meeting of the Regents with representatives of the faculty. Discussion turned upon the means most effectively implementing the policy.

The Regents and the Faculty will continue their close and active cooperation to the end that this policy be given its fullest effect. It was agreed that, pending the conclusion of these discussions, members of the Faculty should make affirmation of their loyalty either by signing the oath issued by the Regents on June 24, 1949, or by other acceptable affirmation.[44]

Neylan believed that there was considerable merit in what Miller proposed, and wondered if the statement were meant to include members of the Communist party, and if so, whether there be objection to making that particular point unequivocally clear. Miller said that in his personal opinion the statement implied prohibitions against members of the party, but he would object to a more specific reference than he had suggested as "this was the underlying issue of the whole discussion by the faculty."[45] Miller emphasized that "the faculties are agreed and as heartily determined as the Regents to exclude Communist influence and teaching and Communists from the campuses, but they questioned the ground on which the policy is based. *Their view is that the ground should be that Communist membership or Communist thought and belief is incompatible with impartial scholarship and objective teaching* [emphasis added]. They felt that the determining grounds for exclusion should be based on a man's thought, ideas and teaching."[46]

Hildebrand then recalled that the first oath as proposed to and accepted by the Regents on March 25 did not mention the Communist party, but placed the matter on a broader basis.[47] The President answered Hildebrand, however, by expressing his unqualified support of the Regents' policy of barring from employment members of the party and said he "could not see that anything would be accomplished by dodging that issue." His view was that the statement should exclude both Communists and those under the influence of their doctrine. In answer to Sproul, Hildebrand expressed the view that the vast majority of the faculty would support the position just enunciated by the President.

Neylan asserted that the faculty by a majority of 90 percent to 95 percent would support the Regents' policy on communism and that the argument advanced against it was "not a solution to the problem at all, but a surrender to a small minority."[48] For him, the faculty effort at unity had weakened its position and compromised the earlier representations of the Advisory Committees. Moreover, he continued, the Senate had blundered in failing to acknowledge the part its representatives had earlier played in the actions of the Regents, a failure which had caused the Board to be placed in an awkward position both with the public and with large numbers of the faculty.

A compromise resolution was finally agreed to by all parties present and was released to the press. As much of the controversy later that fall evolved from the several conflicting interpretations of this resolution, it deserves to be quoted in full:

The Board of Regents of the University of California reaffirms its announced policy that no member of the Communist party shall be employed by the University.

In implementing this policy the Board heretofore has adopted a form of oath or affirmation which was formulated by the President and the Advisory Committees of the Academic Senate.

The Advisory Committees of the Academic Senate have advised the Board that after more mature consideration, the Senate would like to have a portion of that oath deleted.

In the absence of a better method of implementing its policy, the Board stands on its requirement of the oath or affirmation.

The Board, however, will be glad to consider any method which the faculty may deem to be a further or better implementation of the policy.

Complete agreement upon the objectives of the University policy [emphasis added] excluding members of the Communist party from employment and Communist teaching and influence from the campuses of the University was disclosed at today's meeting of the Regents with the Advisory Committees of the

Academic Senate. Discussion turned upon the means of most effectively implementing the policy.

The Regents and the faculty will continue their close and active consideration to the end that this policy be given its fullest effect. It was agreed that pending the conclusion of these discussions members of the faculty and employees of the University should make oath or affirmation of their loyalty either by signing the oath approved by the Regents on June 24, 1949, or by other equivalent affirmation acceptable to the Regents.[49]

In order to meet the conditions of close cooperation just pledged and to remove the element of duress implicit in the October 1 deadline, by which date all University employees were to have signed the oath, the Regents voted to mail immediately to all non-signers their letter of appointment for the 1949–50 academic year. Professor Hildebrand, as the senior faculty member present, at the close of the meeting expressed for the faculty representatives their satisfaction with the session and their appreciation of the Regents' patience and understanding.[50]

VIII

In June, the President and the Board of Regents had been led to believe by resolutions of both sections of the Senate and in private conference with the Advisory Committees that the faculty would be willing to accept a revised oath. The willingness to accept a revision was in no way qualified either by the Senate resolutions or by the proposals of the Advisory Committees. Of course, deletion rather than revision had been preferred by some members of the Senate during the course of debate in Berkeley on June 14 and in Los Angeles on June 20, and by the Advisory Committees when they submitted their proposals to Sproul. Nevertheless, a revision of the oath was represented to be an acceptable alternative to its deletion. Three months later, the President and the Regents had been told both by the Senate and the

Advisory Committees that not only was any revision of the oath unacceptable but that the policy it implemented was questionable as well. The antecedent events of the past three months were not that easily disregarded, however, and as the dispute moved well into fall the Regents, the President, and the faculty fell victim to their prior inconsistencies and inabilities to communicate one with another.

Chapter Four

A Retreat From Civility

I

The statement issued jointly by the Advisory Committees and the Board of Regents, September 30, served as a point of departure for further negotiations. The Regents' decision to mail 1949–50 letters of appointment to nonsigners had removed the immediate cause of tension between the faculty and the Board and had freed the Advisory Committees to work for a solution unhindered by the immediate prospect of colleagues being dismissed for refusing to sign. While the Regents had reaffirmed their policy of prohibiting the employment of Communists in the University, the Advisory Committees had joined the Board *only* in agreeing upon the *objective* of that policy, namely, to secure in the University an impartial, unbiased search for truth. But the committees had not agreed on the *policy*, per se, namely, exclusion from University service of members of the Communist party. It was more than semantics for some, and the tactics that fall turned on the distinction. The Advisory Committees undertook the delicate task of reconciling the two views without compromising either.

The southern section of the Senate met in special session on October 7 with approximately two hundred voting members present. The Advisory Committee reported its deliberations with the Regents. A motion was made and carried to refer the Regents' resolution to the Advisory Committees for further study.[1] Although the section agreed easily to inaction, a fundamental split in the faculty developed later

when a motion was put asking each member of the Senate
who had signed the oath to request its return. The motion
was tabled but only after heated discussion. Other disagree-
ments arose, and as the situation deteriorated a motion to
adjourn carried by a vote of 74 to 71.[2]

Anxious for a more deliberative effort toward solution
than had been evinced in Los Angeles, the northern Advisory
Committee prepared carefully for a Senate meeting on October 10. The committee's objectives were to make clear
that the Regents had not acted without advice from the
Advisory Committees (the purpose was to invalidate asser-
tions then being made by some members of the faculty that
the Board had violated tenure rights in the University by
unilaterally altering the conditions of employment, and to
give rise in the Senate to a sense of obligation toward the
work of its committees) ;[3] to secure ratification by the Senate
of the area of agreement (in other words, to reconcile the
opposing views on the University's non-Communist policy
without at the same time destroying the integrity of the principles in conflict) ;[4] and to secure appointment of a special
Senate Committee on Conference to negotiate with the
Regents.[5]

Some four hundred members of the Senate's northern
section met at Berkeley on October 10. Professor Lehman
reported his deliberations with the Regents and offered three
resolutions for the Senate's consideration. The resolutions
admitted faculty participation in the antecedent actions of
the Regents; evidenced faculty agreement with the Board
on the objectives sought by the University's policy on communism, and expressed the Senate's willingness to implement that policy; requested deletion of the oath; and assigned
to a special Senate committee responsibility to negotiate a
settlement with the Regents within the terms of the resolutions just proposed.[6] The section resolved itself into a committee of the whole and for two hours debated without
consensus the resolutions offered by Lehman, as well as two
others introduced and urged on the Senate. The committee

of the whole finally instructed the vice-chairman and the secretary to call a special meeting at an early date to continue the discussion.

The recommendations of the Advisory Committee had not been acted on by the Senate. The Regents' policy on the non-employment of Communists had been subjected to increasing attack, and one resolution expressly made the point that the Senate was not agreeing to the policy but only to the objectives the policy sought, that is, impartial scholarship and the free pursuit of truth. The unity that the Advisory Committee had so earnestly sought to achieve in the Senate was fast becoming improbable.

II

During the month of October the Regents remained silent, feeling, perhaps, that the Advisory Committees could best bring about a solution if left to their own devices,[7] and consistent with that opinion did not much discuss the dispute at their Board meeting on October 21. The single action of the Board that day with regard to the oath was to instruct the President to mail a letter to all non-signers quoting the statement issued September 30 by the Regents and the Advisory Committees and requesting signature to the oath or an equivalent affirmation.[8] The first letters were mailed October 22. Faculty reaction was immediate.

Lehman promptly wrote to the President and reported the adverse response brought about by the letters and urged that no more be sent. He pointed out that "the difficulties arise largely from the inference made by members of the faculty from the President's letter that the following words 'should make oath or affirmation of their loyalty either by signing the oath approved by the Regents on June 24, 1949, or by other equivalent affirmation acceptable to the Regents,' are mandatory."[9] Should such be the President's understanding and the Regents' intention, Lehman wished Sproul to know, he along with the other members of the Advisory

Committee, in agreeing with the Regents on September 30 "that members of the faculty *should* make oath, etc., understand a clear differentiation between 'shall' as constituting requirement and 'should' as denoting propriety or experience." [10] Consequently, "this distinction leaves members of the faculty free to withhold oath or letter pending the conclusion of the discussion." [11] Although the President sent no more letters, the incident served to strengthen the suspicion of motives and intentions, and very likely served to cast doubt on the integrity of the already tenuous wording of the Advisory Committee's resolutions then pending.

III

On November 1, 1949, in fulfilling a speaking engagement of long standing, President Sproul addressed a national conference of the American Bankers Association convened in San Francisco. Sproul selected for the burden of his remarks one of the questions then under dispute at the University, namely, whether academic freedom entitles Communists to be faculty members. His answer was unequivocal:

Nowhere is the philosophy of communism more harmful than in a university, for it is a philosophy of ironclad orthodoxy, which circumscribes every field of the intellect, whether in science or economics or art, with an adamantine authoritarianism. In such barren soil there can be no flowering of the human spirit; it can only wither and die. Four hundred years ago, Galileo shook the world with the question: Who is willing to set limits to the human intellect? Well, the Communist Party is not only willing to do it, they are eager to do it. What place in a university can be given appropriately to such purblind fanatics as those who use a false and brutal hope to persuade the young and gullible to sign away their American birthright? . . .

I am not thinking, of course, of men who merely hold unorthodox political or economic views, but of members of that close knit, rigidly controlled conspiracy mislabelled Communist Party, every member of which is thoroughly indoctrinated, and cannot possibly be ignorant of the obligations he has undertaken, and the discipline to which he has committed himself. No man can be a member of this subversive organization without taking on the coloration of its leaders and sharing in their guilt.[12]

The statement was Sproul's first major public pronounce-ment of his unqualified support of the Regents' policy that denied faculty appointment to members of the Communist party. The President's remarks were widely reported in the press, and in the reporting the statement somehow was made out to be an endorsement of the oath by Sproul. "Bankers Hear Defense Of Loyalty Oath By Sproul" asserted the *San Francisco Chronicle* in headlining its account of the speech;[13] and a similar twist was given to it by other California news-papers. In reading the original text, however, it is clear that the President had taken care to omit any direct or indirect reference to the oath and had confined his observations to the policy — not the method of implementation. The inter-pretation given the statement, however, that Sproul in back-ing the policy was also favoring the oath, served to hamper, as had the letters to non-signers the previous week, the strenuous efforts Lehman and his colleagues were making to ensure favorable Senate action on the Advisory Com-mittee's resolutions.

IV

In late October, the Advisory Committee, northern section, on advice that the first of its three resolutions pro-posed October 10, 1949, reading: "(1) the faculties convened in the Senate, Northern Section, informed by representatives who conferred with the Regents, recognize that the Regents did not act without advice of the President or the Senate or its agencies," would be opposed by a large number of the faculty on the ground that it implied a lack of confidence in the President, withdrew the resolution from the others offered by it for Senate action in November.[14] Withdrawal of the resolution, out of respect for the President, lost for the Regents a public admission by the faculty that its representatives had participated in the discussions that led to the Board's action the previous June. The Board regarded this recognition to be important, and its removal from the series of resolutions offered to the Senate by the Advisory Committee irritated several Regents, who felt that the faculty had quite unfairly refused to bear its rightful share of responsibility for the controversy. (The author fails to understand the logic that led to the withdrawal of its resolution. The Board of Regents was well aware of the part played by the President and the Advisory Committees, and for the Senate to have recognized it could hardly have weakened the President's position. In fact, on September 23 the Board itself had issued a public statement calling attention to the representations made to it both by the President and by the Advisory Committees. The Academic Senate too was aware of the role played by the Advisory Committees and the President in June, as the Committees themselves had reported it to the Senate by letter [June 28 in the northern section and July 25 in the southern section]. Withdrawal of the resolution, it seems, served no purpose other than to aggravate already delicate relations between the Regents and the faculty.)

V

On November 7, 1949, four hundred members of the northern section of the Academic Senate met in special session on the Berkeley campus. The business of the day was the loyalty oath, and the gravity of the decision to be reached was early apparent. Sproul introduced the business at hand by reading a three-page statement explaining his personal role in the dispute and his view of the President's responsibility:

I have kept in mind always the dual role I must play as executive officer of the Regents, and as presiding officer of the Senate. Consequently, my contribution to the debate has been confined to the answering of questions, and I have taken almost no part in the arguments. Because this has been my conception of the duty I owed both to the Regents and to the Senate, my lot has not been a happy one. I have been damned by some members of the Board of Regents for not defending their position, and by some members of the Senate for not espousing the cause of the faculty. Indeed, even my answers to questions, concerning which I could hardly plead ignorance, such as how many signed oaths have been received, I am informed, have been resented by the more dedicated opponents of the Regents' policy and its implementation.[15]

Sproul made passing reference to the origin of the oath, to its legality,[16] to his letter to non-signers of October 22, and to his address the previous week before the American Bankers Association — explaining in each instance causes and motivations. His remarks concluded with a plea "to accord to those who differ with you in this company, and especially to the Regents, the same recognition of worthy motives, and the same willingness to consider points of conflict with open minds. Only so can we serve the University as she deserves to be served."

For two hours the Senate debated the resolutions that had been introduced during its October 10 meeting and then passed the two remaining resolutions proposed by the Advisory Committee.[17]

The resolutions were substantively identical to the ones proposed to the Senate on October 10. They had been amended to improve their specificity, but not their purpose or meaning. In passing them, the Senate agreed with the Regents on the objectives sought by the University policy excluding Communists, agreed to implement that policy in ways consistent with Senate resolutions passed on September 19, and agreed to explore with the Regents the means of attaining those objectives other than by the oath. The Senate had not, however, approved the policy that members of the Communist party should *automatically* be barred from faculty appointment. Neither, however, had it challenged that policy. Rather, in adopting the Advisory Committee's proposals the Senate had chosen not to mention the policy at all. It seems most likely that had the matter rested with the passage of the Advisory Committee's resolutions, the controversy would have been resolved shortly, for the Board could have pointed to the Senate as a partner in the University's purpose to ensure honest scholarship and unbiased and unprejudiced instruction and to the Senate's willingness to implement University policy that proscribed Communists because of their inability to seek the truth freely. Once the Board and the Senate had agreed to that point, implementation would have followed, probably with little difficulty. Whatever hope Lehman and his colleagues held for the successful conclusion of the controversy was soon shattered, however.

With the passage of the Advisory Committee's resolutions, a large number of Senate members, in view of the lateness of the hour and supposing that the Senate had taken final action, left the meeting. They did so prematurely, for what then transpired essentially compromised the deliberately worded language of the resolutions just passed. Those on the faculty most opposed to the oath and the policy it implemented had introduced, on October 10, through resolutions offered by two of their number, proposals in conflict both with the spirit and intent of the Advisory Committee's resolutions. Earlier in the meeting on November 7, these resolutions had been discussed but not adopted. After the Advisory Committee's resolutions had passed and attendance had thinned, the two resolutions, somewhat amended, were reintroduced. The first was moved for adoption by George P. Adams, a senior member of the Berkeley faculty and Mills Professor of Mental and Moral Philosophy and Civil Polity. The critical portion of the Adams' resolution, which gained Senate approval, read as follows:

a. The Senate approves the agreement between the Advisory Committees and the Board of Regents upon the "objectives of the University Policy excluding members of the Communist Party from employment" in this University, *but emphasizes that it is the objectives of "impartial scholarship and the free pursuit of truth" which are being approved, not the specific policy barring employment to members of the Communist Party solely on the grounds of such membership* [emphasis added].

b. The Senate, Northern Section, notes with pleasure that the Regents have authorized the release of so-called "contracts" to all members of the faculty and interprets this action to mean that, while further discussions are in progress, no employee of the University stands in any danger of losing his position through failure to sign the present oath or an equivalent satisfactory to the Board of Regents.[18]

Additionally, by a vote of 148 to 113, the section adopted a motion of Professor Gordon Griffiths (a young historian who was closely associated with the group most opposed to the oath and whose father was Regent Farnham Griffiths) to instruct the Senate's Special Committee on Conference that the first three paragraphs of a resolution first offered on October 10 by Professor Jacobus ten Broek (also a member of the group most critical of the oath) be represented to the Regents as the views of the Senate (emphasis added):

Because the State of California is a community of free men it values the spirit of free inquiry and encourages the vigorous search for truth. It therefore cherishes and supports a University. The People of the State in establishing their University have placed it under the legal authority of a Board of Regents, entrusting to them a task of great delicacy recognizing that the fostering of a University's life requires an administration sensitive and restrained in internal affairs and vigorous and determined in protecting the University from external political or partisan pressures. The purpose and spirit expressed in the establishment of the University guides, defines, and limits the exercise of administrative power.

The public responsibility of the Regents is to create and maintain the conditions necessary to the University's life. The power of the Regents must accordingly be exercised not only with due regard for those principles of freedom of thought and association which constitutionally limit the power of all public officials but also with deep respect for the essential nature of a University as an institution peculiarly dedicated to freedom of mind.

A University has its own Constitution expressive of its purposes, its functions and its obligations. That constitution, cherished under the name of "Academic Freedom," is a system of government which cannot be violated without frustrating the purpose for which Universities are created. The principles of academic freedom are the rules and procedures protecting the academic community against any attempt, however well intentioned, to hinder it in the pursuit of truth or to "protect it from error." These principles, including the principle of Tenure, provide not only a high degree of independence for individuals of attested competence but also a significant degree of faculty self-government. Experience has demonstrated that the security of the former depends upon the strength of the latter. The area of faculty self-government is, of course, limited. *But it includes full faculty participation in the making of decisions affecting the conditions crucial to the work of teaching and research and a high degree of deference to faculty judgment in matters, such as qualifications for membership, which are peculiarly within the competence of the faculty.*[19]

The Senate finally adjourned at 7:00 P.M.

With the passage of the Adams and ten Broek resolutions, the Senate shifted away from the more conciliatory position taken by the Advisory Committee to ground more directly and explicitly at odds with the Regents. The Senate made clear in the Adams resolution that it was not approving the University's policy barring Communists; and, in passing the ten Broek resolution, set forth what it regarded to be the proper sphere of authority in the administration of the University, both for the Regents and for the faculty. Passage of the Adams and ten Broek resolutions late in the meeting, after they had been earlier discussed and rejected, not only created resentments among members of the faculty who regarded the tactics as improper and irresponsible but, more important, also engendered hostility among the Regents toward the Senate. The resolutions were viewed by many of the Regents as a challenge and were principally responsible for turning a sharp disagreement between the faculty and the Regents into a very real and bitter controversy. That is not to say that passage of these two resolutions was unjustified, unwise, or improper; or that the reaction to them by members of the Board was justified, wise, and proper; or the reverse. Rather, it is simply an observation that, given the history of the dispute to that point, the two resolutions turned an argument into a controversy of a very different kind.

VI

By this time Neylan had succeeded Harrison as chairman of the Regents' Special Committee on Conference, owing to the latter's ill health. Neylan's reaction to the Adams and ten Broek resolutions was hostile. Not only, Neylan believed, had the Senate gratuitously lectured the governing board on its duties, but it had repudiated its own Advisory Committee and claimed that the oath was now without purpose, as the policy it implemented had been rejected.[20]

Two hundred and fifteen voting members of the southern section met in Los Angeles one week following the northern Senate's adoption of the Adams and ten Broek resolutions. As at Berkeley, Sproul read his three-page statement, and the Advisory Committee offered resolutions which affirmed support for the objectives of the University's policy on communism, authorized the appointment of a committee to work with that of the northern section in negotiating with the Regents, and provided that the report of the negotiating committee be submitted to the Senate's membership for approval or rejection by mail ballot.[21] Far less complex than the resolutions offered to the northern section, the resolution presented in Los Angeles was worded simply so as to attract the widest possible support, to reduce the probability of amendment, to move discussion off the floor and into committee, and to remove the likelihood of a repetition of the Berkeley incident by providing for mail ballot when voting on the Special Committee report. An amendment was offered immediately by Professor John Caughey of history, a leader among the more active opponents of the oath and the policy it implemented. Caughey's amendment combined the critical portions of the resolutions proposed by Lehman and Adams in Berkeley on November 7. The amendment lost by a vote of 102 to 101. The vote was challenged and a written ballot called. The results showed that the amendment had lost by a vote of 110 to 103.[22] The Advisory Committee's resolution, unamended, was then passed by voice vote. Next, by a vote of 90 to 75 the Senate appointed a committee to conduct an anonymous poll among members of the southern section to ascertain faculty opinion toward the loyalty oath and the University's policy on communism. Although the southern Advisory Committee had enjoyed a slim vote of confidence, the Senate in Los Angeles was too badly split to allow its representatives the measure of support necessary for effective bargaining.

The waning influence of those with whom the President had been negotiating in both sections of the Senate, coupled with the increasing hostility of Regent Neylan, left the President without the immediate means of securing the initiative. Consequently, those on the Board and in the Senate, who, above all else, were willing to fight for principle, gained the advantage, found their ground, and dug in for battle.

VII

The Regents gathered on Friday, November 18, for their regular monthly meeting. The Senate's resolutions were reported to the Board in executive session by the President. Regent Fred Jordan, a UCLA graduate and Los Angeles advertising executive who was appointed a Regent in 1938 by Governor Frank Merriam, expressed the feelings of several members in being disappointed that the Senate resolutions failed to endorse the University's policy on the non-employment of Communists. He also wondered how the faculty had gained the impression that disciplinary measures were not to be taken by the Regents against non-signers (Adams resolution). Jordan "stressed the fact that the oath was agreed upon by the Board and the Advisory Committees, and the employees were told that in the absence of a better implementation of the Regents' policy, they were to sign it." [23] Neylan successfully urged that any further implementation of the policy await negotiations between the Regents' Special Committee and the Senate's Combined Special Committee on Conference. [24] Sproul reported that as of November 17, 1949, 84½ percent of all employees had signed the oath. In the Senate itself, 75 percent had signed and 2 percent had chosen some substitute oath or affirmation. And at Mt. Hamilton and Davis, Sproul reported, 100 percent of the staff had signed. [25]

Regents Edward Heller and Farnham Griffiths lunched with Sproul at the Palace Hotel in San Francisco four days following the Regents' meeting and told the President of their fear that the situation was rapidly deteriorating, and that "decisions harmful to the University are likely to be made prematurely and on an emotional basis. . . ." [26] The two Regents were convinced that current developments were not only harmful to the University but harmful to Governor Earl Warren's political prospects as well. Sproul, fearing offense to the Board, opposed the suggestion that they personally visit the Governor. He agreed, however, to call Warren and apprise him of the situation. Regents Heller and Griffiths, in their concern for Warren's political position, probably feared that if the controversy became more severe, the Governor could not very well remain aloof from it, and in a volatile and widely noticed dispute, Warren could be expected to make enemies regardless of the position he took. That Warren was increasingly disaffecting the more conservative elements of the Republican party in California, among whom Regent Neylan was numbered, may have been a relevant concern as well. The governor of the state of California was ex officio president of the Board of Regents. Like his predecessors, Governor Warren did not often attend meetings of the Board. Rather, it was for the chairman of the Board, elected annually by the members, to exercise the continuing leadership. Warren attended no Regents' meetings during the controversy until January, 1950. The Governor — later appointed Chief Justice of the United States Supreme Court by President Eisenhower — and Sproul had been close personal friends since their days together as students on the Berkeley campus. In fact, it was Sproul who the previous year had nominated Warren for the presidency of the United States at the Republican Convention. When Warren two months later publicly entered into the controversy, he was allied on principle with Sproul, and his unwavering and unqualified support of the President throughout the controversy was probably the most important single factor in enabling Sproul to remain as president. Regent Heller, appointed to the Board by Governor Olson in 1942, was not only prominent in the state's business and financial circles, but was also an important patron of the Democratic party, influential in California's political life, and a member of a family that had given generously to the University. He was a grandson of I. W. Hellman, Regent of the University from 1881 to 1918, who was one of its greatest benefactors and the founder of one of California's pioneer banking families.

VIII

During the next few weeks the dispute drifted. Little was done to turn its course. Positions were consolidated. Many of the Berkeley non-signers, joined by some signers who were nevertheless sympathetic to the principles motivating the non-signers, decided to organize more formally. This group met on the evening of November 30, 1949, and appointed an eight-man steering committee to direct its efforts. Frank Newman, a young professor in the School of Law, was appointed acting chairman.[27] During the fall, win-

ter, and spring, members of the group, with attendance rang-
ing from fifty to two hundred, met early every Friday night
at the Faculty Club to review the course of events and to
discuss and decide strategy and tactics recommended by the
steering committee. This group of non-signers formed the
backbone of faculty opposition to both the Regents' policy
and the oath, and of its support for the concept of University
governance as expressed in the ten Broek resolution. Professor Edward Tolman was regarded as the titular head of the
non-signers, and the strength of his influence was to prove
very great indeed.

IX

In early December, the Senate's Special Combined
Conference Committee was appointed by the Committee on
Committees. From the south were chosen Professor J. A. C.
Grant of political science as chairman, and as members,
Professors John W. Caughey, history, Martin R. Huberty,
engineering, and Robert V. Merrill, French. From the north
were selected Professor Malcolm Davisson of economics as
chairman, and as members, Professors Wendell Stanley, vi-
rology, Joel Hildebrand, chemistry, and R. Aaron Gordon,
economics. Huberty and Hildebrand had each served as
chairman of the Advisory Committee for the south and north
respectively in the early stages of the dispute. Grant and
Davisson were among the more promising younger men in
their respective sections for both Senate and University positions of leadership. Caughey and Gordon for their sections
were, from the first, prominent among the group most opposing the Regents' actions. Stanley, a Nobel laureate and internationally renowned scientist, although opposed to the oath,
was not willing to allow that opposition to turn into open
conflict with the Regents.[28] Merrill was among those at
UCLA most opposed both to the oath and to the policy.

The Regents' Special Committee on Conference was
chaired by John Francis Neylan and included as members

Earl J. Fenston, San Francisco attorney, Victor R. Hansen, Los Angeles attorney (had taken Neylan's place on the committee when Neylan replaced Harrison as chairman in late October), Fred M. Jordan, Los Angeles advertising executive, and Sidney M. Ehrman. Ehrman, appointed a Regent in 1930 by Governor C. C. Young and again by Governor Warren in 1948, was Regent Heller's uncle and the son-in-law of I. W. Hellman. He was a highly successful and well respected attorney in San Francisco. Ehrman was held in esteem by his fellow Regents and enjoyed, as had Heller, the friendship of many members of the Berkeley faculty. He, as other members of his family, had given generously to the University, and in memory of their son who passed away in England as a graduate student at Cambridge, Regent and Mrs. Ehrman had endowed the Sidney Hellman Ehrman Professorship of European History at Berkeley. Ehrman's role in the controversy proved to be ambivalent and, consequently, highly significant as each side strove for his support. Sitting with the Regents' committee, but not serving as members, were Chairman of the Board Edward A. Dickson and President Sproul. The Senate's committee was as fairly biased against the oath as the Regents' committee was for it, although less of a single mind on the policy than the Regents, who were unanimous in its support.

A meeting of the chairmen of the Senate committee and the chairman of the Regents' committee was considered a necessary first step in preparation for a joint meeting of the two committees. Consequently, on December 13, Professors Davisson and Grant spent four hours with Regent Neylan as the latter's guests for lunch at the Pacific Union Club atop Nob Hill in San Francisco. During the course of the discussions, Davisson and Grant report, Neylan took great pains to make certain that the professors knew that "the oath was conceived by the President, and the faculty played at least as important a role as the Regents in its birth." [29] Neylan argued that the statement issued jointly by the Regents and the Advisory Committees on September 30 obligated the faculty to support the policy. To hold otherwise, he believed, was to commit a breach of good faith. Responding, Davisson and Grant urged that the resolutions of the Senate, passed in September and reaffirmed on November 7, provided a broader and sounder basis of attack, namely, barring persons whose commitments or obligations to any organization prejudice impartial scholarship and the free pursuit of truth. The rejoinder was that this wording dodged the issue and that the Regents' policy required no evidence as to the character or quality of a man's teaching or research, but only as to his membership in the Communist party. The professors called Neylan's attention to the absence of Communists on the faculty as evidence of a system of faculty self-selection that screened out those not intellectually free; and that should there be members of the Communist party on the faculty, "Aren't they so quiet that they are doing the C.P. [Communist party] no real good?" Neylan's answer was that as a member of the Nimitz screening committee (the Atomic Energy Commission committee charged with hearing and reviewing security cases in connection with the work of the Radiation Laboratory on the Berkeley campus), he had information that he could not disclose "but that would shock us." (Earlier in the afternoon Neylan had expressed his doubts that there were more than twenty Communists in the entire faculty.) It was clear to Davisson and Grant that Neylan expected from the faculty a plan of action to locate and dismiss Communists. Neylan would not comment on the possibility of dismissing non-signers against whom no other charge was made than refusal to sign. For Regent Neylan, those on the faculty most opposing the Regents had as their objective the driving of a wedge between the faculty and Regents. The leadership, Neylan continued, was "leftist" and the followers were "dupes." Davisson and Grant made no headway against this view.

As Neylan ended the meeting, he agreed to arrange for his committee to meet with the Senate's only after the faculty committee had prepared a plan designed to implement the Regents' policy. Of this luncheon Professor Davisson has said: "I came away from the lunch meeting with Regent Neylan firmly convinced that as far as what the Davisson–Grant committee would be able to do the answer was that we couldn't do anything. I felt that we might as well have disbanded right then." [30]

Although disheartened, the Senate committee worked hard during December in an effort to devise some plan to bring new light to a fast darkening scene.

X

The Regents met in Los Angeles on December 16 for their final meeting of the year. In the morning executive session, Regent Neylan reported the discussion he had had with Davisson and Grant three days earlier. They proposed an agenda for a meeting of their committee with the Regents' committee, said Neylan, which "would consist of the discussion of another statement of policy, ignoring the loyalty oath and substituting nothing for it." [31] And, he continued, it was the hope of Davisson and Grant that the whole matter would be dropped. [32] For the first time Neylan put himself on record with the Regents that for him the oath was a secondary problem. The University's policy on communism, on the other hand, was a gravely important matter, and a mistake on it, Neylan continued, "might be disastrous to the University." [33] As the session continued, a division of opinion arose on the issue that was later to split the Board sharply. The difference was best stated by Regent Heller, who said that, although he agreed with the policy, he opposed discharging any faculty member for refusing to sign the oath and he would publicly and privately contend against any such move on the part of the Board. [34] The morning session ended with the Regents voting unanimously to affirm the September 30 joint statement. [35]

XI

A teaching assistant in physics named Irving David Fox was employed at this time on the Berkeley campus. Fox had appeared on September 27, 1949, as a witness at hearings in Washington, D.C., of the House Sub-Committee of the Committee on Un-American Activities. The hearings had been called to investigate Communist infiltration of the Radiation Laboratory (Berkeley) and atomic bomb project where Fox had been employed in 1942 and 1943. Fox had been cooperative in every respect except when questioned about communism and his relation to it, when, on recommendation of counsel, he had been uncooperative.[36]

The hearings had been noticed by the Regents, and on September 30, 1949, Sproul had been asked to investigate. Following some preliminary inquiry, the President and Fox met on November 25. Sproul told Fox that his work as a teacher and his academic record generally were satisfactory to his department and were not an issue. However, in view of his previous testimony and past association with communism, Fox was invited by Sproul to present his case to the Board personally. Fox agreed and was in Los Angeles for the afternoon session of the Board on December 16, 1949.

When questioned in open session, Fox attested to the accuracy of the transcript reporting his appearance at the House hearings and volunteered further information to the Regents. He told the Board that in the late 1930's he had been a member of certain organizations "which might be considered communist front organizations" but gradually lost interest in and contact with them. Subsequently, in Berkeley, his interest in communism was rekindled and he "for all intents and purposes was a member of the party" during much of 1942 and 1943.[37] Fox professed no personal knowledge of any espionage at the Radiation Laboratory either on the part of the Communist party or among his colleagues.

His refusal in Washington to answer questions concerning

FORSYTH LIBRARY
FORT HAYS KANSAS STATE COLLEGE

his affiliations, Fox said, were based upon consideration for onetime friends whose membership or nonmembership in the Communist party he did not wish to discuss, and on recommendation of his counsel, Clifford J. Durr. Fox admitted that his testimony very likely embarrassed the University and, although he regretted that, he supposed that his presence on the stand would have embarrassed the University even had he testified in full. Fox left the room as the Board went into executive session.

Neylan moved immediately for dismissal and commented: "I do not believe he [Fox] has been frank with this Board, and I do not believe he has repaired the damage he did to the University. I do not believe he measures up to the minimum requirements for the honor of membership in one of the greatest faculties in the world." [38] Discussion subsequently centered on the legality of dismissal on these grounds and the implications the motion carried for the controversy over the oath. Sproul thought that a vote for dismissal would complicate and perhaps jeopardize the negotiations between the Board and the faculty but said he would "vote on the merits of this case and with no regard to expedience." [39] Neylan retorted that "by the wildest stretch of logic" dismissal could not jeopardize anything, as the Regents and the faculty remained well apart and without any basis for optimism as regards a settlement, particularly in view of the conference he had had with the faculty the previous week.

As the Board prepared to vote, Regent Heller indicated his intention to vote against the motion for dismissal: "I do not understand what the minimum standards are [sic] we have set for employment on the faculty, and that is the ground on which we are going to dismiss this man. I am not sure we have set any standard. I do not believe we have. I certainly think this man was at one time — but I do not think it was proven that he is now — a communist." [40] Regent Arthur McFadden responded: "This man admits that he was a communist, and he is still sticking to the people who were communists along with him. He is not willing to cast them overboard."[41] On a roll-call vote only Heller voted against dismissal.

The Non-Senate Academic Employees (NSAE), an informal organization at Berkeley of teaching assistants, lecturers, research assistants, and other members of the academic staff not eligible for membership in the Academic Senate, quickly condemned the decision. The Regents' action strengthened the resolve of this group to organize more actively its opposition both to the oath and to the policy in order to protect its members more effectively. As it became increasingly clear that the Senate would take no steps to urge reconsideration of the Fox case, but, in fact, would take little official cognizance of it, the NSAE appealed to the Senate to declare minimum requirements for membership in the faculty in which political tests for teachers had no part; to demand from the Regents authority to determine the fitness of individual members of the faculty; and to urge the immediate reinstatement of Fox.[42] The appeal went unheeded. The Senate refused to take formal and official recognition of the Fox case, for it did not consider him to be a member of the faculty. As Fox was a teaching assistant, and did not enjoy faculty rank, he was not subject to the same procedures for appointment as were members of the faculty and, therefore, the Senate did not consider him eligible to enjoy the protections inherent in such an appointment.

The Fox "case," nevertheless, was a factor that fall in negotiations between the Regents and the faculty. When members of the Board pointed to the Fox case as evidence of Communist influence on the faculty, the Senate representatives responded by making a distinction between a member of the academic staff with Senate rank, and one of non-Senate rank. For Neylan, however, it was a distinction without a difference, at least as it related to the desire of the faculty to police its own members in lieu of the oath. The Fox "case" meant for Neylan a clear reason for turning away from faculty self-government as a reliable alternative to the oath in implementing the University's policy on communism.

On the other hand, Fox had signed the oath—a circumstance causing some to wonder if the method of implementation as determined by the Regents might be less effective than was earlier assumed.

As the Fox "case" paradoxically proved publicly embarrassing to both adversary parties, neither pursued it with much enthusiasm or vigor, but preferred to call it to the other's attention only when the situation in private conversation commended it.

XII

During Christmas recess, the Senate Conference Committee was at work drafting its case in anticipation of a January 4, 1950, meeting with the Neylan committee. A first draft of "Issues Raised by the Special Oath and Proposals for Their Solution" had been put together in November by Professor Malcolm Davisson, cochairman of the Senate's committee. As Davisson was away from Berkeley during the last days of December, the final draft was completed by Professor R. A. Gordon and mailed by him to members of the Neylan committee on December 29. The twelve-page document was organized into three main sections, titled General Principles, Implementation, and Appendix, respectively.

The section on general principles began by recalling that until the previous spring the Board had not considered it necessary, even during the war years, to impose any special test beyond the standard oath to support the federal and state constitutions, and concluded by asserting that the framework for maintaining a loyal faculty existed before the new oath was adopted.[43] The oath, it argued, had done violence to the conditions that nurture greatness in a university—the faculty's devotion to teaching and research, the faculty's pride in the University, and the University's reputation in the academic world — by creating suspicion where there had been trust, by causing disunity where there had been harmony, and by engendering doubt where there had been confidence — both within the University and between the institution and the country's scholarly societies.

The argument then shifted to the matter of a notarized oath. The committee stressed that the implication of perjury for falsely swearing contemplated the possible intervention of the state's attorney, a condition less desirable, it was thought, than maintaining internal control over disciplinary matters. Far better, it was argued, that the University return to its long-recognized system of evaluation and screening. (Here the committee referred to the Appendix, titled "Memorandum on the Procedure Whereby Faculty Members are Selected and Appraised." See Appendix C below for full text.)

The section on implementation made clear the unacceptability of the oath because of the unacceptability of the policy (barring Communists from teaching posts) and proposed, therefore, the substitution of common objectives (objective scholarship and impartial teaching) for the policy and faculty self-government for the oath:

> *There is no disagreement about the objectives. What is in dispute is the best means of attaining them* [emphasis added]. This Committee is convinced that the exclusion of members of the Communist Party *per se* from employment is not the best means. On the contrary it may make their attainment more rather than less difficult. So far as the requirement of a special oath is concerned, this is inadequate to implement the *policy* aimed at Communists, and it actually conflicts with the *objectives* on which all are agreed. So far as we can see, attainment of these objectives must rest on (1) the ethical standards of the faculty and (2) an improved use of existing procedures.[44]

The faculty, it was said, was sharply divided over the policy, but the "larger number" shared with the American Association of University Professors the position "that evidence must be produced to show that the individual in question himself shares the faults which have brought the Party into disrepute." Therefore, the committee continued, the ultimate objectives should be sought through the broader, more fundamental, and more realistic policy favored by the faculty. (The committee gave no evidence in support of its conviction that the "larger number" of the faculty agreed with the AAUP and disagreed with the Regents. The author knows of no poll or sampling of opinion in the northern section that would lead to this conclusion. True, the Senate votes during the fall clearly opposed the oath and in the case of the Adams resolution on November 7 refused explicitly to approve the policy. It should be remembered, however, that no Senate meeting enjoyed the attendance of even 50 percent of the Senate membership, and all votes had been taken at Senate meetings in Berkeley. In the south, however, a mail poll had been taken, with a 77 percent return. The results of this poll were known on December 21, 1949, and the results, in combination with the southern section's resolutions, clearly gave, at least to the southern half of the Senate committee, a solid base for its assertion.)[45]

The Committee further observed that the oath requirement had created an artificial offense, namely, that of not obeying Regents' orders. Consequently, it was contended, the oath would permit a Communist to hide behind members of the faculty who were guilty of nothing more than not signing.

In arguing the merits of faculty self-government, the committee pointed out that, during the ten years the University's policy on communism had been in effect, the Regents had intervened in only two cases, both involving teaching assistants (Kenneth May in 1940 and Irving David Fox in 1949); was this not evidence that existing procedures had on the whole been operating effectively? (For Neylan, who believed there were Communists on the faculty, this was proof that the procedures didn't work at all.) The committee was clearly sensitive to the matter of teaching and research assistants, and in reacting to the Fox case (without, however, referring directly to it) concluded its presentation with two pages of suggestions for improving procedures for the appointment of non-Senate academic staff, all the while taking pains to emphasize the differences between these appointments and those of faculty rank.

The committee presentation was forthright, honest, and cooperative. It was courteous in its wording. It was also wholly unequivocal with regard to its criticism of the oath and the policy it implemented. It was equally unqualified in its support of what the committee considered to be a more enlightened and preferable plan for ensuring honest scholarship and teaching in the University. At issue was not only the Regents' policy expressly prohibiting the employment of members of the Communist party, but also a question of regental authority. Both were to come in for hard debate when the Davisson–Grant committee and the Neylan committee met the following week.

XIII

The meeting of the Senate's and Regents' committees was held on January 4, 1950, at the Crocker Building in downtown San Francisco. Regent Neylan presided and opened the discussion with a review of what had occurred since the oath was first adopted in March of 1949 and then moved to narrow the range of discussion to the oath or some other alternative method of implementing the policy. The job, he said, was to seek a joint implementation of the policy barring members of the Communist party from employment; "that is my interpretation of what we are delegated to do here." [46] As members of the Senate committee had come prepared more to discuss the weaknesses of the policy than methods of implementing it, no real headway was made for some time. As rational discussion turned to emotional response, and principal issues to irrelevant or peripheral considerations, Professor Grant quite accurately observed: "We are not getting very far." Discussion then shifted to the "Detailed Proposals" which constituted the Senate committee's hope for solution.

The three-page set of "Detailed Proposals" by omission refused to approve the Regents' policy barring Communists from employment, proposed to rescind the Communist disclaimer, agreed formally to recognize character and loyalty in the appointment and promotion procedures for members of the Senate and for teaching and research assistants, and asked the Regents to recognize that standards of competence for membership in the faculty were a responsibility jointly of the Regents and the faculty and that the testing of individuals for fitness must rest primarily with the faculty. The proposals were unsympathetically received, as Regent Neylan's reaction and subsequent dialogue suggest (emphasis added):

The Regents are going to be shocked that after the meeting of September 30 there was not a clear and distinct understanding between the faculty committees and the Board. If we had broken up after the committees [Advisory Committees and Regents' committee] had met on September 29, there might be some basis of confusion, but when you have in mind that because of the importance of the matter we asked the Advisory Committees to meet with the Board that next day — I know that the Board is going to be shocked when it is told for a second time that not only the construction of the action of the Senate [November 7] is a repudiation of the meeting of September 30, but in fact is —

Here the Board, since this was agitated — in the beginning there was some question about it. The President conferred with the faculty. The Board adopted an oath [June 24] and gave a statement to the public. To the Board's amazement later that was *repudiated* [has reference to September Senate meetings]. The Board met again and gave another statement to the public [September 30]. You suggest that the Board proceed to protect the University. Who do you think has been defending the University all these years? *I would not hesitate for one minute tearing up this oath and forgetting the whole thing.* In the beginning I was against it and fought it and did not accept it until it was adopted by the faculty [meant agreed to by the Advisory Committees]. Now then, having made that statement to the public and the statement of September 30, and then to come out now and tell the public some nebulous thing like this, it would be a disaster and I would not share the responsibility. *You have to realize this Board had a right to stand on what it understood was complete agreement with representatives of the faculty.* If you go behind these agreements constantly you create a situation of irresponsibility. It means that an aggressive minority of that faculty, stressing unity — an aggressive minority constantly can exercise a veto power embroiling this faculty and the Regents in constant turmoil. I beg of you to look at this thing in a realistic light. *You cannot make agreements and abandon them as if they were a nullity.* I know the Regents will be shocked that there is no agreement.

I would like to get the President's view. Am I wrong in my estimate of the situation?

PRESIDENT SPROUL: You report the position of the Board. As to my own position, that is based on the agreement reached between the committees representing the Regents and committees representing the faculty which were announced in June and September, and I understood the latter of those agreements, which was announced to the public in a statement agreed upon [September 30], to include a clear understanding of what the objectives were. *I thought the statement had in mind — the objectives had to do with keeping the University free of those who would destroy its freedom, and among those were members of the communist party*, and I am quite sure I stated that and unless that was understood we had not made any advance at the two meetings.

.   .   .   .

DR. STANLEY [responding to Neylan]: *I simply cannot come to the conclusion that there has been repudiation on the part of the faculty.* You time and again have stated that the faculty has repudiated an obligation. That is completely false to any understanding I have as a faculty member. The President already has indicated that, assuming you were as far apart as north and south in agreement with the Advisory Committee, the committee could not bind the Senate. It has to go back always to the Senate. That is important to the honor of the Senate.

As the dialogue deteriorated Professor Davisson moved for a much needed recess.

(It should be remembered that what the Advisory Committees represented to the President in June was never referred to the Senate for discussion and therefore could not have been repudiated by the Senate. The statement issued September 30 by the Advisory Committees and the Regents, of which Neylan makes such a point, did not commit the committees to the University's *policy* barring Communists, but only to the *objectives* that policy sought to achieve, that is, impartial scholarship and teaching. On September 29, the Advisory Committees had made it clear to the Regents' special committee that they could not represent the Senate's view on the policy without first returning to the Senate for further discussion. However, when the issue arose before the full Board the following day, the Advisory Committees failed to make as clear a statement as they had the previous day, namely, that they must perforce return to the Senate before purporting to represent the faculty to the Regents on this point. Furthermore, on September 30 Hildebrand said, in response to Sproul's contention that nothing would be accomplished by avoiding the policy question in the statement to be issued, that he agreed and that the vast majority of the faculty would agree as well. Apparently, Sproul, Neylan, and other Regents took this to mean that the objectives had to do with keeping the University free of those who would destroy its freedom, and among those were members of the Communist Party. When the northern Advisory Committee offered its resolutions to the Senate on November 7, it asked for approval of the objectives sought by the University policy on communism but made no mention of the policy per se. The committee also invited the Senate to implement the policy with due regard for earlier Senate action [the somewhat equivocal statement adopted September 19]. These proposals were enacted by the Senate. However, their effect was compromised soon after by adoption of the Adams resolution. The author is unable to say, in view of the events just noted, whether or not the Advisory Committees agreed with the Regents on the meaning of the statement issued September 30, much less whether or not whatever was agreed to was repudiated later by the Senate. The author does conclude, however, that the protagonists in the controversy selected from the antecedent events what gave credibility to their particular positions, and as the controversy continued, along with the confusion, so too did the adversaries continue to improve upon and strengthen the believability of their several and conflicting claims.)

Although Davisson offered further alternatives to the Regents following recess, they were received no more warmly than the ones earlier suggested, and as the conversation threatened again to move to the periphery, the issue was joined (emphasis added):

REGENT HANSEN: I would like an expression on this one vital issue — whether the faculty is adamant that a person shall not be dismissed merely because he is a member of the Communist Party.

MR. GRANT: . . . We are faced with this concrete factual situation. We might just as well face it here. *Our committee is convinced that we cannot go back to the faculty and request approval of anything which carries a specific approval of the Regents' policy of dismissal for communist party membership per se. We are not saying that would not be a good thing if it could be done, but we are saying to you because the faculty had confidence in us, we are saying to you that could not be passed by the Senate.* Therefore, the issue is this: If the policy is to remain settled, what use would it be for this committee to agree with you and take back to the Senate an implementation which would carry with it approval by the faculty of the Regents' policy, when we are telling you in advance, as honestly as we can reflect the opinion of the Senate, gentlemen, we would fail. We would not get approval.

REGENT NEYLAN: *I think that is the answer. I want to thank you for being frank about it. Anything else is nonsense.*

MR. HILDEBRAND: Even if the faculty approved it by a large majority, you cannot prove that the Committee on Privilege and Tenure would take that view.

REGENT NEYLAN: Dr. Grant has stated it very well. I think we are in a situation here where this Board adopted a policy nine years ago, which it has reaffirmed. I think the Board has properly had the right to assume that, not once, but twice, the faculty through its representatives has agreed to a restatement of that policy. I do not believe this Board out of decent respect for public respect in California can abandon its position. I think you are utterly unrealistic, and I think you are theorizing despite the fact——

MR. DAVISSON: These proposals do not require the Regents to retreat from that policy.

REVENT NEYLAN: Dr. Grant stated that it was so. He said the Academic Senate will not accept this policy.

PRESIDENT SPROUL: Oh, no — will not approve it.

REGENT NEYLAN: All right, not approve it, the Board has adopted that policy for nine years.

MR. DAVISSON: The proposals do not require the Board to retreat from the position it took a decade ago. It is perfectly clear that the Board is not asked to retreat. [While the Regents were not being asked to retreat publicly from the policy, they were being told that the faculty would not approve it.]

REGENT NEYLAN: Have you given any consideration to what would happen if the people of California were told that the faculty of the University of California refuses to agree to the policy, which has been the policy for nine years?

MR. GORDON: We are asking you not to lead to a situation in which the faculty might do that. The situation is grave. It is grave, not in the sense that communism does raise a real threat outside the University. Over and above that threat there is the real danger and real threat to the welfare of the University over the fact that things that were under the surface have been brought to the surface and have become aggravated. If this goes on, and if this communist policy thing is served to the faculty and it is told to stand up and be counted and it makes more headlines, I do not see how the reputation of the University would not suffer.

Following further unrewarding dialogue, the two committees finally agreed to explore a plan which would eliminate the oath and would place on the back of the contract

of employment the first three paragraphs of the statement
of principles adopted in June by the Regents, reading:

> At its birth the University of California was dedicated to the
> search for truth and its full exposition.
> The primary obligation of the Regents of the University of
> California has been to stand steadfastly for that freedom of the
> human mind and spirit which has enabled the assemblage of dis-
> tinguished scholars constituting the faculty to continue to pursue
> these objectives.
> The Regents gladly share with the faculty the responsibility
> to keep the University free from those who would destroy these
> objectives. . . .

and University Regulation 5 — both statements having already been accepted in full by both sections of the Academic
Senate. Each member of the academic and administrative
staff would be required to subscribe to these statements in
accepting University employment. As the meeting adjourned,
it was agreed that the Regents' committee should meet prior
to the January 13, 1950, meeting of the Board, and a dinner meeting for that purpose was scheduled for Thursday,
January 12, at the Pacific Union Club in San Francisco.[47]
    The meeting of the two committees had lasted four hours
and had been fundamentally unproductive. The Senate committee had sought without success to persuade the Regents
to regard both the oath *and* the policy it implemented as
means, thus enabling the faculty to substitute means of its
own to attain mutually agreed upon *ends*, that is, impartial
scholarship and teaching and freedom to pursue the truth.
The Regents had been told unqualifiedly that the Academic
Senate would refuse to approve the policy barring Communists from teaching posts but very likely would be willing
to accept it if implementation did not derive specifically
from it. Conversely, the Senate committee had been advised
by the Regents that the Board would in no way alter or
qualify that policy. Both the faculty representatives and
members of the Regents' committee had agreed that a con-

tinuation of the dispute would do great harm to the University, although each party had in mind a harm of a different sort. For the faculty the damage would be done by the lowering of the University's prestige in the view of colleagues at other universities and colleges, and for the Regents the hurt would be inflicted by an aroused citizenry. The single constructive result of the meeting was the agreement to explore further the plan to abolish the oath and place on the back of the contract of employment University Regulation 5 and the first three paragraphs of the statement of principles adopted by the Regents the previous June.

Three weeks earlier the *New York Times* had reported in an article on the controversy that "despite its refusal to retract the oath requirement, the Board of Regents would like to find a way out of its predicament without losing face." [48] Although the statement may have been valid for some Regents, Neylan was playing for much higher stakes. He had sought in conference with the Senate committee to put the faculty representatives on record, in the presence of other Regents, as being clearly opposed to the 1940 policy on the non-employment of Communists and to have them contend, as had Davisson and Grant in their conversation with Neylan on December 13, that this was a view shared by most members of the Senate. Once he obtained this admission, clearly and unequivocally, Neylan then was in a position to convince other members of the Board of the need to retain the oath as an inducement for the Academic Senate to approve the policy. Neylan believed firmly that the Davisson–Grant committee represented not the majority but the minority view of the faculty, and that if invited to approve the policy, members of the Academic Senate by secret ballot would do so overwhelmingly. Only after the policy had been endorsed by the Academic Senate would Neylan be willing to discuss alternate methods of implementation. Neylan dedicated the next two months to the purpose of securing the faculty's endorsement of the University's policy on communism.

XIV

Autumn of 1949 had been a period of retreat from the stability of common resolve, harmony of purpose, and respectful goodwill which had for so long characterized relations within the University. Mutual confidence and personal civilities had withered. Each succeeding session of the Regents, each succeeding meeting of the Senate, each succeeding conference between the President and the representatives of the two bodies had perceptibly shifted the principal point of dispute from the oath to the policy. By late fall the oath had become a secondary consideration, utilized by the contending parties as a wedge to pry apart unyielding positions and to exact concessions. The oath had come to be utilized by the several adversaries in the furtherance of their respective strategic objectives. The condition of the dispute was clear enough to those whose position or influence intimately involved them, but the situation was not perceived generally either by the faculty, the public, or for that matter, by several of the Regents. Almost inevitably, in light of this circumstance, confusion as to methods, issues, objectives, and civilities was to capture the deliberations of the larger constituency.

Chapter Five

The Ultimatum

I

Professor Hildebrand wrote to Regent Neylan on January 6, 1950, urging him to accept the proposals advanced by the Davisson–Grant committee two days earlier and criticizing the Board for contemplating the dismissal of members of the faculty who refused to sign the oath. "You cannot expect the faculty to retreat from this position," Hildebrand said, for "we have been the target of too many unjust, irresponsible accusations to be willing to abandon any of our means of legitimate defense."[1] Neylan should know, Hildebrand continued, that men who would not think of defending a Communist would, however, vigorously defend any colleague who was guilty of nothing more than a spirit of independence against a demand which he regarded as an indignity. The next morning, in a telephone conversation with Sproul, Neylan expressed "weariness and disgust over the Regent–Faculty conferences about the loyalty oath . . ." and suggested that the matter be returned to "normal channels from faculty, through President, to Regents." Sproul agreed.[2]

As previously arranged, the Neylan committee met in San Francisco the evening of January 12. Members of the committee, although disagreeing sharply over methods of implementation of the policy that forbade the employment of Communists, were, nevertheless, united in their support of that policy. The full Board met the following day.

The meeting was presided over by Governor Earl Warren.

On January 4, 1950, Warren had been contacted by Frank L. Kidner, a professor of economics on the Berkeley campus who later in the year was to play an important role in the faculty's fight against the oath. In 1948, during the course of the presidential campaign, Kidner had been an economic consultant to the Governor and had come to know him personally. His purpose in visiting the Governor in Sacramento was to brief him fully on the controversy and urge him to attend and preside when the Regents met the following week. Warren did decide to attend and attended regularly thereafter until the controversy ended.[3] During the Regents' executive session, Neylan reported that on January 4 the Davisson–Grant committee had proposed that the oath be abolished. Moreover, Neylan continued, the committee had refused to approve the Regents' policy on communism, and had claimed a like position for the Senate itself. "They sought," said Neylan, "to have the matter solved by referring everything back to the Academic Senate or the Committee on Privilege and Tenure. In other words, I think it is fair to say that the substance of their position was that the faculty committees should have enlarged powers in relation to the employment and retention of people on the academic side of the University."[4] Also, "I think it is fair to say that on January 4 they were dealing with us at arms length in an adversary position." The proposals offered by the Senate committee, Neylan continued, were an attempt to enlarge at least by implication the authority of the Academic Senate in the selection and retention of faculty members and to circumscribe the President's power. For Neylan an "irreconcilable minority of the faculty [the non-signers group] had ruthlessly maneuvered the situation," and the Regents should clearly understand that "we are up against here a situation in which there is a great reluctance to recognize the fact that there can never be unity on this thing, except by abject submission on the part of the Regents, the President and the Senate to a minority of that faculty."[5] As partial evidence that a dissident few were at the heart of the controversy, Neylan pointed to the fact that 86 percent of the staff had signed the oath.[6] Regent Heller observed that to infer that impression from the percentage of oaths returned was to misunderstand the attitude of the faculty completely. "I have discussed this with a number of the faculty, and practically all of them have signed the oath. They all hate the oath. They disagree with the oath itself, even though they think Communists should be kept off the campus." (Regent Heller enjoyed the personal friendship of many members of the Berkeley faculty. During the controversy, at the invitation of Professor Lawrence Sears of nearby Mills College, Heller several times met socially with some faculty members at Sears' home in Berkeley, gave them encouragement about the eventual defeat of the oath and said he thought the oath could be fought better by signing it than by not signing it or by leaving the University. He urged them to stay on.)[7]

Neylan reported that the Regents' special committee had met the evening before, and while it had rejected unanimously the Davisson–Grant committee's proposals, it had divided sharply over the wisdom of retaining the oath and on the matter of counterproposals. The committee was willing, however, Neylan concluded, to put on the contract of employment some as yet unspecified statement of policy. (Both Sproul and Neylan were to draft statements.)

Little by little, as the discussion continued, the point that was to become the final issue in dispute between the faculty and the Board emerged: the government of the University itself and the authority of the Regents and the Senate in it. Regent Mario Giannini, president of the Bank of America, the nation's largest banking system, who the previous June had been appointed by Governor Warren to fill the vacancy on the Board left by the death of the senior Giannini, articulated the issue clearly:

They [Regents] have been pussy-footing around and now are reaping the results of what they sowed. No organization can be run without course and direction. You must have that to get somewhere. This organization is drifting, and it needs to have a little more course and direction. *This is one of the issues which tells whether the Regents are going to run the University or whether the staff is going to run it* [emphasis added]. I, for one, am very much opposed to pussy-footing any further to trying to work out a compromise where you stick something on the back of a contract, and it doesn't answer the question. It is a back down by the Board of Regents, and it is bad business. If you let these fellows take hold of the situation and get away with this, I am of no further use to the Board and neither will any other member [be].

Giannini espoused an essentially managerial view of University government. He regarded the relationship between the Board and the faculty much as one would the common connection between management and labor. The concept was in nearly diametric opposition to the ten Broek resolution and to the proposals advanced by the Davisson–Grant committee — each having stressed the essential role of faculty self-government and the principle of shared responsibility. The conflict between these divergent views grew gradually to equal in importance and eventually to surpass the University's policy on communism as the chief inhibitor to a peaceful solution of the controversy. Regents concerned with the influence of communism in the University plus those holding the Giannini concept of University governance constituted a majority of the members of the Board; and the alliance proved adequate to reject any plan proposed to the Regents which infringed upon the integrity of either commitment.

As the meeting closed, Neylan proffered his resignation as chairman of the Regents' special committee "because I do not feel that I can serve any useful purpose in going ahead with it. It has got to the stage where I have no hope." Subsequently, he moved that the committee be dissolved. The motion secured unanimous consent. With the dissolution of the Neylan committee, the Regents asked the President to make a recommendation to the Board at its next meeting, February 24, 1950, and agreed that any further meetings between the Senate's committee and the Regents be with the Board as a whole.

For the first time in four months the initiative rested with the President. Negotiations between the Regents and the faculty had failed. Not since the 1920's had representatives of the governing Board and the Academic Senate met officially to bargain. The decision to break with custom had served little purpose other than to allow the protagonists to emphasize personally the essential incompatibility of their respective views. Sproul confronted a far less fluid situation in January than he had faced the previous September. In the interim, some members of the Board and non-signers among the faculty had committed themselves to principles regarded as elemental to their own integrity and to that of their respective constituency. The dedication was total and unyielding. The President's task was to seek ground between the two extremes where a majority of the Board and faculty would find it possible to stand without seriously offending either the conscience or prestige of the principal adversaries.

II

Sproul reported the Board's action to Davisson the following week and was told in response that no further proposals could be expected from the faculty, and that the faculty committee believed that final Board action would not be taken without further conference.[8] The apparent unwillingness of Davisson to compromise further, coupled with the Board's seeming intransigence, left Sproul little choice but to seek options from the less committed elements of the faculty. Consequently, he met on January 23 with Professors Lehman, Dennes, and Walker (the northern section's Advisory Committee).

The committee was of the view that a statement of the full Regents' policy on communism placed on the contract of employment would be accepted by the faculty committee on conference and by the Academic Senate.[9] Acting on this advice, the President offered no new proposal of his own but awaited a "crack" in the Davisson–Grant committee's position. For nearly two weeks the dispute simmered. Finally, as the Advisory Committee had predicted, the Davisson–Grant committee told Sproul that it would compromise its earlier proposals to the extent of allowing on the reverse side of the contract a full statement of the Regents' 1940 policy on communism along with University Regulation 5, and on the face of the contract a statement that the individual in accepting appointment acknowledged "notification of the conditions of employment stated on the reverse side of the contract." The offer, however, was hedged about with the following qualifications:

(1) The Communist disclaimer was to be rescinded.

(2) The Regents were to accept University Regulation 5 as official University policy.

(3) The right to tenure was to be abrogated for proved members of the Communist party.

(4) The Regents were to reaffirm in all other cases involving tenure the traditional role of the Senate's Committee on Privilege and Tenure and accord to the committee the same respect for its judgment as in the past.

(5) The Regents were to agree not to dismiss any member of the academic staff without the Committee on Privilege and Tenure having heard the case.[10]

The proposal was to abolish the oath; to secure regental cognizance of University Regulation 5; to prevent the University's policy on communism from coming to the Senate for approval by stating it on the contract of employment where individual members of the staff would acknowledge it in accepting University employment; to maintain for the tenured staff their traditional rights to tenure by refusing to proved members of the Communist party any claim to tenure but without approving University policy that such persons should be automatically subject to dismissal for reason of their membership; to obtain regental recognition of the traditional role of the Committee on Privilege and Tenure, that is, acceptance of the committee's recommendations by the Board; and to prevent the Regents from again unilaterally dismissing non-Senate academic employees (Fox) by establishing procedures to guarantee the competency and fitness of such persons by the faculty. The President made no commitment to support the plan.

III

The following day Sproul and Neylan met for two hours in San Francisco to review the draft of a statement prepared by Neylan for inclusion on the contract. For Sproul, Neylan's statement was little more than justification of the position the Regents had taken with no yielding to views presented by the faculty. When reminded by Sproul that the Board on September 30, 1949, had agreed to pursue with the faculty other ways of implementing the policy, Neylan answered that the faculty had enjoyed sufficient time to propose such an implementation but had failed to do so; and, therefore, the Regents had no further obligation.[11] The President made no mention to Neylan of the compromise proposals offered the previous day by the Davisson–Grant committee. Sproul most likely felt that they would clearly be unacceptable to the Regent, both on the basis of Neylan's draft and because of his then apparently unyielding position. Sproul realized also that Neylan's proposal would prove equally unacceptable to the faculty. The President prepared a plan of his own and tested it out on the members of the Davisson–Grant committee on February 20 — four days prior to the Regents' monthly meeting. The draft proposed to retain the oath as an alternative to signing an acceptance of the policy stated on the contract of employment. The faculty committee found this proviso unacceptable, although with certain minor modifications the remainder of the statement was approved.[12]

Sproul was keenly aware, however, that the Neylan draft which he had earlier referred to Davisson for comment was utterly without hope of faculty acceptance, and he probably felt that his more moderate position would enjoy greater faculty support than Neylan's could ever hope to gain. It is not known how Sproul assayed the relative strength of his draft and Neylan's among the Regents themselves.

IV

The President introduced his statement to the Regents in executive session on February 24 by reading letters recently received from members of the faculty opposed to the oath:

These letters were to the effect that the signers believed a solution to the problem would be reached which would be acceptable to the faculty; that the faculty's opposition to the oath took time to crystallize and the Regents had grounds for complaint that the faculty's position was not clear at the beginning; that the opposition to the oath was not led by a small minority nor was it communist led or communist inspired; that there will be a number of faculty members with tenure who will refuse to sign the oath, and among them will be men of national and international reputation whose integrity and loyalty to the state and nation are beyond dispute.[13]

The President then offered a seven-paragraph resolution for the Board's consideration. The first three paragraphs dealt with the history of the University's policy on communism, and referred to actions of the Regents on October 11, 1940, June 24, 1949, and September 29 and 30, 1949. Paragraph four asserted that a member of the Communist party had violated the terms of his employment, was not entitled to tenure, and was to be dismissed after the facts had been established by the University administration and by the Committee on Privilege and Tenure of the Academic Senate. Paragraph five endorsed University Regulation 5 and, with the exception of members of the Communist party, assured full rights and privileges of tenure to all members of the faculty otherwise eligible, reserving to the Senate Committee on Privilege and Tenure responsibility for full findings and recommendations as in the past on all other questions regarding tenure.[14]

Through paragraph five, Neylan and Sproul were in complete accord. In paragraph six they disagreed. Sproul proposed:

> The Regents, in the light of facts herein stated, give notice that a condition precedent to employment or renewal of employment in the University shall be the execution of an oath in the form prescribed on June 24, 1949, or the equivalent affirmation that the appointee *accepts his position subject to the policy excluding Communists from membership in the faculty of the University, as stated in the Regents' resolutions of October 11, 1940, and June 24, 1949* [emphasis added]. Such oath or affirmation shall accompany the letter of acceptance of appointment and shall be a part thereof.

Neylan asserted that the President's resolution called for no statement to be made by an appointee that he was not a member of the Communist party. Further, in view of the Senate committee's representations to the Regents' special committee on January 4, that the faculty would not approve the Regents' policy excluding members of the Communist party from employment and Communist teachers and influence from the campuses of the University, a retreat at this time by the Regents on the oath requirement would be disastrous. Neylan proposed, therefore, to substitute for Sproul's paragraphs six and seven the following (emphasis added):

> The Regents, in the light of the facts herein stated, give notice that a condition precedent to employment or renewal of employment in the University shall be execution of an oath in the form

prescribed on June 24, 1949, or the equivalent affirmation that the appointee *is not a member of the Communist Party, or under any oath or commitment, or a party to any agreement that is in conflict with the policy of the Regents excluding Communists from membership in the faculty of the University.* Such oath or affirmation shall accompany the letter of acceptance of appointment and shall be a part thereof.

Each appointee will be notified that if an acceptance of appointment on the terms stated is not received by the Secretary of the Regents on or before *April 30, 1950,* he will be deemed to have served his connection with the University as of June 30, 1950. [Sproul's paragraph seven was identical except that he would have allowed until May 31, 1950, for acceptances to be filed.]

The President, previously aware of the Neylan proposal, indicated to the Board that he had discussed the Neylan amendment with many of the soundest men on the faculty and was convinced there would be no Senate backing for an affirmation that merely repeated the words of the oath. Moreover, the President's proposal to substitute for the oath an affirmation calling for acceptance of the policy, was a preferable change in words with no substantive change in understanding. Regents Warren, Fenston, Heller, and Hansen agreed with the President. Governor Warren asked the Board's attorney whether the oath could be required under the State Constitution.[15] It was the attorney's opinion that the oath could be required legally as a condition of appointment but that an affiant could not be prosecuted for perjury for falsely swearing to it. Furthermore, the use of the words "Communist Party" in the oath to some meant a subversive element in the body politic and to others merely a political party. In relation to the constitutional provision that the University was to be kept free of political and sectarian influence (Article IX, Section 9), the attorney offered no opinion pending further study of the matter. He concluded by saying, in regard to the Sproul and Neylan resolutions, that legally the Regents could do as much under one as the other.

The Board found Neylan's proposal the more persuasive and on a roll call the Regents voted twelve to six in favor of it.[16] As the session ended, Regent Heller "announced that he thought the action taken by the Regents would be ruinous to the University and he gave notice that he would do everything he could to defeat it."

Prior to February 24 the Board's ultimate intentions toward the non-signers had remained uncertain. Adoption of the Neylan resolution, however, introduced a new and critically urgent issue, namely, that non-signers, against whom no other charge was laid, would be dismissed regardless of tenure and without reference to the traditional procedures governing privilege and tenure in the University of California. Whereas among the faculty there was and continued to be disunity on the principles previously in conflict, there was at least near unity of opinion that loyal members of the faculty should not be dismissed only for failure to sign the oath or the statement on the contract as specified by the Regents on February 24. *It was a violation of the principle of tenure that provoked the faculty and finally galvanized it into action.*

(The right to tenure — thought generally to mean the continuing right of a member of the faculty to his position during good behavior and efficient service — had been understood to exist in the University since 1920 for associate or full professors and other officers of instruction whose length of service exceeded eight years. By the time of the oath controversy, it was the expectation both of the administration and of the Academic Senate that these rights were in force through custom even if not explicitly a part of the University's controlling legislation — the Standing Orders of the Regents. The indefiniteness of tenure in the University was called into question, therefore, when the Board proposed to dismiss, for not signing, tenured members of the faculty against whom no charge of unfitness had been laid, and to dismiss them without a hearing of the case by the Senate's Committee on Privilege and Tenure. Tenure rights were finally given legislative force by the Regents in December of 1958.)

Paradoxically, faculty unity which the Senate committees had for months sought unsuccessfully, was achieved by the Regents in a single stroke. The irony was that Regent Neylan desired an aroused faculty. He believed that the Adams and ten Broek resolutions passed the previous November and the proposals and positions argued by the Davisson–Grant committee were unrepresentative of the opinion held generally among members of the University's faculty. Only by actively involving a greater proportion of the academic staff in the controversy, could he expect the Senate to overturn, in favor of the University's policy on communism, the November resolutions of the Senate and thus refute the representations made by the Davisson–Grant committee. By proposing to violate tenure rights, Neylan and those on the Board who shared his belief apparently hoped to engender widespread interest and active participation in the controversy by a larger segment of the faculty. Once that purpose was realized, the next step Neylan intended, as will be seen, was to seek the Senate's unequivocal approval of the University's policy on communism. With Senate endorsement of the policy a reality, the Board could then attempt, in negotiations with a more "representative" Senate committee, to find a mutually acceptable alternative to the oath and thus conclude the controversy.

V

"Loyalty Oath Or No Job, Cal Professors Are Told," read the banner headline on the front page of the *San Francisco Chronicle* the morning following the Board's decision.[17] "The Regents of the University of California, headed by Governor Earl Warren," the paper erroneously reported, "laid down a flat policy yesterday to reluctant professors:

Sign the anti-Communist oath or no job."[18] Said Warner Brown, professor of psychology, a member of the Berkeley faculty for twenty-nine years and a well-known scientist, "I think the Regents have been derelict in their duty and should be thrown out."[19] The sign-or-get-out ultimatum, as it was to be popularly called on campus, catapulted the controversy into the front pages of nearly all the state's newspapers and was carried across the country by the several news services. Since early fall, the press had mentioned the dispute only when reporting formal meetings of the Regents and Senate and when the Fox case was prominent. The private negotiations and bartering had not been publicly noticed in any great detail. Thus, the decision of the Board to dismiss non-signers by April 30 jolted not only the public but large numbers of the faculty as well. Publicly reported accounts of the Regents' vote, later corrected, conveyed the impression that the Board was united, when in fact it was bitterly split and would never again unite on this issue.

The Davisson–Grant committee by this time was in a very awkward position. The faculty had united, not on the principles argued by the committee in its negotiations with the Regents, but rather on what was regarded by the faculty to be a violation of tenure. Several of the Regents, who voted with the minority on February 24, called the members of the Davisson–Grant committee and expressed concern that the Board's decision would do the University serious harm. These Regents urged the committee to take the lead in securing Senate recognition of the Regents' policy barring Communists and its willingness to abide by some reasonable and equitable means of implementing the policy.[20] Some members of the faculty, on the other hand, applied pressure on the committee to coordinate and lead the opposition to the Regents' action, while still others urged the committee to support mass faculty resignations, resignations of faculty members from administrative posts, legal proceedings to test the legality of the Board's action, return of oaths to the signers, and a public meeting of the Regents where representatives of the faculty could appear.[21] With authority from the Senate to negotiate only specific issues and with an obligation to return to that body with the results of its negotiations and recommendations, the Davisson-Grant committee faced a very real dilemma as to the part it could legitimately continue to play. The committee decided it had no choice but to consult with as many members of the faculty as possible to gain some broad consensus as to course and direction.

The committee's first step was to call an emergency meeting of the deans and department chairmen of the Senate's northern section for Sunday, February 26. These administrative officers gave a vote of confidence to the Davisson–Grant committee and asked it to work for a reversal of the Board's action, and in particular, to draft a statement setting forth a faculty position which would have the support of signers and non-signers alike.[22]

The following evening the committee met with some one hundred fifty members of the faculty, chiefly non-signers. This group of faculty members, the more adamant opponents of the oath, had believed that the break between Regents and faculty was open and irreparable and had expressed their intention to accept dismissal rather than sign.[23] The principles unifying the non-signers, however, did not form the basis of general faculty unity. Professor John Hicks, respected American historian and a senior member of the Berkeley faculty, soon to play a highly significant role in the controversy, had attended the meeting and was disturbed by it. "I wonder," he wrote in a letter the following morning to Frank Newman, chairman of the Non-signers Steering Committee, "if I could not communicate through you some of my misgivings, arising from attendance in your meeting at the Faculty Club Monday night." The non-signers, Hicks continued, seemed "bent on insisting that the rest of the faculty, the overwhelming majority, must come over to its (the minority's) position, and that without compromise." The position Hicks referred to was the University's policy barring Communists from employment — a policy at least some of the non-signers hoped to overturn along with the oath. "Our area of agreement," said Hicks, "is strictly limited. We agree (1) that the oath was a foolish business which would in no way accomplish the end it appeared to seek, and (2) that no faculty member should be dismissed for failure to sign it as it now stands." Only on those points, argued Hicks, could there ever be full faculty agreement. On the other hand, he continued,

If your group insists on bringing other and controversial issues into the discussion, we shall eventually part company again. *In particular, many of us totally disagree with the premise expressed Monday night that discrimination against members of the Communist Party, as such, constitutes an infraction of academic freedom* [emphasis added]. If your group insists on fighting for the right of Communist Party members to be members of this faculty, our present very impressive unity will soon evaporate.[24]

The intensity of feeling among the non-signers as to the strength of their position and the weakness of those who would yield may be shown in a letter from one of their number to another. Professor Ernst H. Kantorowicz, a close colleague of John Hicks's, wrote Professor Edward Strong (later the third chancellor of the Berkeley campus) and proposed that there be immediately circulated among the faculty a declaration reading:

We, the undersigned, hereby solemnly declare that unless at the next meeting of the Regents on March 27 the proposed special oath of loyalty is revoked, we the undersigned shall immediately and automatically discontinue to discharge our duties in offices and classrooms.

If any member of the teaching staff, including teaching assistants, be dismissed on or by July 1, 1950, for the sole reason of not having signed the oath, section 2, the resignation *in corpore* will follow immediately and automatically.[25]

The faculty, as a body corporate, asserted Kantorowicz, should meet ultimatums with ultimatums, alternatives with alternatives, deadlines with deadlines: "We have to stop building treacherous 'golden bridges' which can only lead to defeat and disaster." Although the proposal gained little support, the fact that it was made at all and by a scholar of international repute, was indicative of the gravity of the situation.

Meanwhile, the Davisson–Grant committee had drafted a formal statement of the faculty's position. The oath, it was claimed, reflected adversely on the loyalty and integrity of the faculty and impaired the meaning of the oath of allegiance already willingly sworn to by every faculty member. The statement stressed the effectiveness of the Senate's committee system in preventing subversive and disloyal persons from gaining membership on the faculty, and pointed to the fact that no member of the faculty during the effective period of the Regents' policy had been accused of membership in the Communist party. The document stressed the principle enjoying the widest faculty support and treated it as follows (emphasis added):

Academic Freedom does not exist where the right of tenure is not inviolate. If competent and loyal scholars can be dismissed solely for preferring the Constitutional oath to a special oath, they are obviously not free to pursue truth wherever it may lead them. At least, they are not free to pursue it in this University. The Regents can claim, and rightly so, that they make no attempt to influence or interfere with the research and teaching of the faculty. This is also an essential ingredient of academic freedom. But the whole no longer exists if one part is taken away. *The Regents propose suddenly to take away the right of some men to engage in any kind of research or teaching at this University for a reason totally unrelated to their competence, character or loyalty.* This is not freedom as it is understood by the scholar or any believer in democratic principles and fair play.[26]

Should the Regents persist in the requirement, the statement concluded, the results were predictable. Loyal and competent members of the faculty would be dismissed, and

out of sympathy many others would resign; morale would
be shattered and men would look to other universities for
more attractive opportunities; and the University would suffer in its failure to attract new men to its ranks for want of
an environment hospitable to scholarship and protective of
academic freedom. The statement ended:

> The faculty is not trying to defend Communism or Commu-
> nists. It abhors all totalitarian beliefs and has said so repeatedly.
> It has not challenged the *right* of the Regents to fire Communists.
> But virtually to a man, the faculty protests the Regents' right to
> wreck the University by firing men for no other reason than
> non-signing of a particular oath, created by the Regents, *with-
> out the Regents ever bothering to investigate whether these men
> are in fact Communists or otherwise disloyal* [emphasis added].[27]

The document had been drafted for the express purpose
of publicly setting forth the faculty's opposition to the February 24 action of the Board and had been worded to enjoy the
greatest possible support from the faculty itself. That more
than eight hundred members of the faculty affixed their
names to the document is a credit to its authors. However, the
document wholly omitted reference to the "rock" upon which
negotiations had earlier foundered, namely, disagreement
with the policy of the Regents that the University would not
employ members of the Communist party, *ipso facto*. The
closest the document came to mentioning this fundamental
issue was in the final paragraph when reference was made
to the right of the Regents to fire Communists. The right to
fire Communists and the policy of not employing them, of
course, were two quite separate matters. The decision not to
include arguments against the policy was made presumably
for fear of failing to obtain general faculty acceptance of it,
or for fear of aggravating further the estrangement then
existing between the faculty and the Regents, or for fear
extended debate on this issue would serve only to complicate
further an already confused situation, or for fear of adding

greater harm to the general welfare of the University, or for some or all of these reasons.

At a second meeting of the deans and department chairmen, held on February 28 at Berkeley, an Operating Committee of Seven was appointed to work with the Davisson–Grant Committee in coordinating faculty opposition to the Regents' action.[28] Professor John Hicks, who had not been officially involved earlier in the controversy and who had attended the meeting only on the urging of his colleague Professor Raymond Sontag, who held Berkeley's Sidney Hellman Ehrman Chair of European History, was elected chairman of the Committee of Seven. The other six members included Dean Morrough P. O'Brien of engineering, and Professors Griffith C. Evans of mathematics, Francis A. Jenkins of physics, Stephen C. Pepper of philosophy, Lesley B. Simpson of Spanish, and Raymond J. Sontag of history. Pepper and Simpson were non-signers, and the former was to serve as liaison between the Committee of Seven and the non-signers.

On March 1, 1950, a press conference was held in the Directors' Room of the Men's Faculty Club on the Berkeley campus. Representing the faculty were Professors Davisson, Gordon, Hildebrand, and Stanley (the four northern members of the Davisson–Grant committee), and Professor Frank L. Kidner, chairman of the publicity committee for the Committee of Seven. The faculty would fight to reverse the action taken six days earlier by the Regents, members of the press were told, and a Committee of Seven had been appointed to carry the faculty's hopes for a successful conclusion of the controversy. The committee was organized as follows:

(1) A publicity committee, chaired by Professor Frank L. Kidner of economics. (Kidner, it will be remembered, had been since early January in rather close, but informal and unofficial, communication with the Governor.) Within this committee were operative (a) Professor Lloyd Fisher, who was to organize a speakers' bureau of men both within and

without the University to respond to requests then being received from business and civic groups for speakers on the controversy; (b) Professor Philip F. Griffin (a member of the Non-signers Steering Committee) who was to work with the public media; and (c) Professor James R. Caldwell of English, who was to organize support for the faculty position among other universities, principally by securing statements favorable to the faculty and unfavorable to the Regents. Caldwell was to enjoy the help of Professors Clark Kerr (later Berkeley's first chancellor and then president of the University succeeding Sproul), Van Deusen Kennedy, and Lloyd Fisher in obtaining from labor leaders statements supporting the faculty view, and from Professor Jacobus ten Broek (a member of the Non-signers Steering Committee) assistance in gaining the backing of the California State Bar. Others at the Medical Center in San Francisco were in like fashion to seek endorsement of the faculty view from the California State Medical Association and the California State Dental Association.

(2) A financial assistance committee, chaired by Professor Frank C. Newman of the School of Law (the same Newman who was chairman of the Non-signers Steering Committee). This committee was to secure gifts to aid the Committee of Seven in meeting its financial requirements. As will be noted later, this fund received contributions both from within and without the University, including at least one member of the Board of Regents. Professor Robert Brode was to act as custodian of the fund, ensuring its safety and the legitimacy of the demands made on it.

(3) A legal committee, chaired by Professor Richard W. Jennings of the School of Law. The committee was to investigate legal remedies open to non-signers.[29]

As had been the pattern previously, the southern section followed the northern's lead, and the following day, at a meeting of deans and department chairmen in Los Angeles, an Activating Committee was appointed with responsibility to elects its own chairman and appoint committees. Professor

Paul Dodd of economics was elected chairman and to serve with him were appointed Joseph A. Brandt of journalism, Cordell Durrell of geology, Carl Epling of botany, Neil Jacoby of business administration, E. L. Kinsey of physics, and Marion A. Wenger of psychology.[30] The Activating Committee was organized essentially on the northern pattern and substantially for the same purpose, namely, to mount an effective public and private effort to defeat the position taken by the Regents on February 24.

VI

For the first time in the controversy, the principals chose to take the dispute consciously and deliberately into the public arena. Governor Warren started it off when he released to the press a statement of his opposition to the action of the Board on February 24. "Governor Earl Warren broke silence yesterday," reported the *San Francisco Chronicle*, "and lambasted the loyalty oath imposed on the University of California faculty."[31] It was an "oath any Communist would take — and laugh about it," Warren was reported as saying.[32] The demand for a special oath, Dean William Prosser of Berkeley's School of Law was quoted as saying in the same newspaper report, is viewed by the faculty in much the same way as they would view "a demand that each individually sign an oath he is not a bigamist and is not operating a house of prostitution." During the next few days the dispute was front-page news in all principal California newspapers: "Indignation Rises," "Profs Call for Public Support," "Loyalty Oath Stirs Ire of U. C. Professors," "Berkeley Big Guns See Mass Resignations," "U. Profs Threaten Loyalty Oath Bolt," were among headlines appearing in California newspapers in reporting the charges and countercharges made by Regents Neylan, Dickson, Teague, Warren, and others, and by Professors Stanley, Davisson, Hildebrand, Grant, Caughey, Hicks, Prosser, Birge, along with many others.

James H. Corley, Vice-President of the University, comptroller and business manager, told the press on March 3 that it was he who in January of 1949 had recommended to Sproul a special loyalty oath to "save the State University from being wrecked by possible political influences."[33] Corley made reference generally to the Tenney bills pending in the legislature in the spring of 1949 and particularly to Senate Constitutional Amendment 13 which proposed to take from the Regents and give to the legislature the power to ensure the loyalty of University employees. This piece of legislation, Corley said, was not pressed in the legislature "on assurance from University officials that we would reaffirm our 1940 declaration of policy, pledging to keep our institution free of Communistic influences. . . ."[34] Davisson responded by giving credit to Corley for his statement, but emphasized that the admission in no way changed the situation or lessened the damage that had been done.[35]

The same day Monroe Deutsch, Vice-President and Provost Emeritus of the University, for the first time in the course of the controversy, made his sentiments known publicly. His influence, born of forty years of dedicated service to the University, could not be discounted by any party to the dispute. Thus, when he unqualifiedly joined forces with the faculty and the minority faction of the Regents in opposing the February 24 action of the Board, the press paid his words special attention. For Deutsch the principle of tenure was at issue and with it the authority of the faculty in the appointment, promotion, and dismissal of colleagues. Deutsch was in the fight to stay.

The President released a statement on March 4, 1950, and in summarizing the history of the controversy, ended with an account of his reasons for opposing the resolution enacted by the Board on February 24.

The original motion made by me, which did not come to a vote, my arguments in the debate which followed, and my negative vote on the substitute motion [Neylan resolution] were all predicated upon a belief that the welfare of the University would not be served by insisting upon a special form of oath as the single method of implementing, through the faculty, the Regents' policy of excluding Communists from University employment.

This belief is re-enforced by my knowledge that this method is regarded as a violation of both privilege and principle by many members of the faculty in whose loyalty I have complete confidence and for whom I hold the deepest respect and affection.[36]

Sproul had broken publicly with the Board and had taken issue with a policy which he, as the University's chief administrative officer, was responsible for executing.

The Corley, Deutsch, and Sproul statements are noted as evidence generally of the issues held up to the public as in dispute, namely, the oath itself, tenure, and to a lesser extent the authority of the faculty in matters of appointment and promotion. The public utterances of the principals conspicuously omitted reference to the dispute over the policy the oath was meant to effect.

The charges and countercharges hurled publicly about during the hectic early days of March, 1950, probably hindered more than helped the faculty's cause. The essence of the faculty's opposition to the oath was never articulated wholly by the press but rather in parts and sections. The continuity of the argument, therefore, vanished in a maze of selected quotations which served better the rather sensational character of the reporting than the hopes of the faculty for public support. The intemperate character of the public utterances provide ample grist for the editorial mills and worked severely against the faculty's best interests. The Hearst papers in California's two major metropolitan centers, including the *San Francisco Examiner*, the *San Francisco Call-Bulletin*, the *Los Angeles Evening Herald Express*, and the *Los Angeles Examiner*, and the independently owned *Los Angeles Times* all unqualifiedly editorialized in support of the Regents' and against the faculty's view. Of all of California's major dailies, only the *San Francisco Chronicle* consistently and unqualifiedly, since the previous June, had urged the Board to rescind the oath.

Moreover, when the controversy burst into public debate, it confronted at the same time a national mood fundamentally more hostile toward those whose actions or interests appeared friendly to the "Red" cause than had been true a year earlier. The nation's international posture had been threatened in the fall of 1949 with the explosion of Russia's first atomic bomb and with Generalissimo Chiang Kai-shek and his Nationalist government being pushed off the Chinese mainland on December 8, 1949, by Mao Tse-tung's Communist armies. Internal security had been dealt a severe blow with the arrest in early February of Dr. Klaus Fuchs in England for transmitting atomic secrets of both the United States and Britain to Russia. His conviction and sentencing for espionage was widely reported in the nation's press in early March of 1950. Alger Hiss had been convicted of perjury in January of 1950 for denying that he had given State Department papers to Whittaker Chambers; and, Judith Coplon was found guilty on March 7 of spying for Russia. And Senator Joseph McCarthy, feeding on the country's disquietude, boldly attacked, in the late winter and spring of 1950, both Secretary of State Dean Acheson and the department he administered, and others whose activities McCarthy regarded as inimical to the nation's best interests. The atmosphere pervading the nation's political consciousness those months proved unreceptive to dissent and, as the faculty of the University of California was to discover, particularly unsympathetic to those unwilling publicly to assert their loyalty. The *San Francisco Chronicle*, in a front-page editorial March 2, 1950, stated rather clearly its reasons for sympathizing with the faculty view and put the dispute into national context:

This thing— this frantic, self-crippling retreat — is not unique in today's international climate. You have seen other manifestations of the stampede in this country and around the world. It is an outgrowth of the cold war, and one that must be pleasant for the Kremlin to behold. For if the totalitarians can scare us out of our prized freedoms — if they can frighten us into the limitation of intellectual horizons and the fettering of imagination and initiative — that is one phase of their victory that has cost them nothing.

If they can dry up the sources of philosophical leadership and scientific achievement at this great university, they can forget about boring from within; the job will have been taken care of by other simpler means.

In brief, this is no private struggle over at Berkeley; some part of the welfare of each of us is at stake. We suggest that all of those who believe that academic freedom is essential to democracy take off their gloves and step into this fight.[37]

VII

While the Committee of Seven in the north and the Activating Committee in the south carried the fight in the public media and gathered both moral and financial support, members of the Davisson–Grant committee both in Berkeley and in Los Angeles struggled to word a resolution for Senate action on March 7, which at the same time would stay within the boundaries of consensus and yet satisfy the more individual or pronounced opinions of their colleagues. The precariousness of this task may be evidenced by quoting from a letter written by Professor Frank Kidner to Provost Grayson Kirk of Columbia University. Kidner wrote, hoping for support from Dwight D. Eisenhower, then president of Columbia, and indicated that "we are doing all we can to bring together support for the moderate expression" of view proposed by the Davisson–Grant committee "from a small group who desire more drastic statements of program and policy. . . ." And Kidner concluded, "We shall be able to do so provided that the dispute does not remain unsettled for too long a time."[38]

March 6 was a day of intense activity. Under auspices of the Associated Students of the University of California

(Berkeley campus) a meeting was called to acquaint the students with the controversy. Several key members of the faculty had been invited to represent their views, and Regent Neylan had been asked to speak as well. Neylan was ill in Arizona, however, and declined the invitation, but in sending his regrets he asked that the following message be read to the eight thousand students who had assembled in Berkeley's Greek Theater:

> As a constructive step toward the solution of this situation, why does the Academic Senate not adopt a resolution in plain English unequivocally endorsing the policy excluding Communists?
> Let us find out who objects to a resolution of the following form:
> RESOLVED: that the Academic Senate approve without qualification the policy of the Regents adopted October 11, 1940, and reaffirmed June 24, 1949, excluding Communists from employment in the University."[39]

Neylan's statement was widely noticed in the public media. It hinted publicly for the first time of disagreement between the faculty and the Board over the University's policy barring members of the Communist party from employment. The Neylan statement was strategically exact as it was given generous coverage in the state's newspapers on the morning of the day the Senate's northern section was scheduled to meet in Berkeley. Earlier in the week Neylan had arranged to have excerpts from the January 4 meeting of his committee with the Davisson–Grant group privately circulated among the more influential, moderate, and conservative members of the faculty. By March 6, word had passed among the Berkeley faculty that earlier negotiations between the Senate and the Regents had failed more because of a challenge to the policy rather than to the oath. Principally through his intermediary, Ralph Chaney, professor of paleontology on the Berkeley campus, a member of the National Academy of Sciences and the American Philosophical Society, and former assistant director of Berkeley's Radiation

Laboratory, Neylan privately left the impression with men of influence that the oath requirement would be altered in a way satisfactory to the faculty if the Senate without equivocation would approve the University's policy on communism. Some of the faculty responded affirmatively to this proposition as a tactical means of breaking the deadlock. Others found the proposition wholly in line with their own principles and beliefs and, therefore, very much to be desired. Others, regardless of their feelings at that point were willing to do very nearly anything to put an end to the dispute. Still others considered the maneuver wholly lacking in merit and thought it would be destructive of the faculty's position. To many of those newly charged with responsibility of leadership in the controversy, the time had come to put the Senate on record in favor of the policy excluding Communists. "The time has come," wrote Professor Sontag, a member of the Committee of Seven, to Professor Davisson, "when those who oppose dismissal solely for refusal to sign the oath, but who also oppose the employment of members of the Communist Party must insist on a *clear, positive,* and *unequivocal* statement of the Senate position on the employment of Communists. . . ." Such a statement, Sontag concluded, was a condition precedent to his further active support.[40] Considerable effort was spent on March 6 to reach those of like persuasion and urge them to attend the Senate meeting the following afternoon.

Late in the afternoon of March 6, Davisson advised Sproul that part of his committee's report would be put to a vote on the floor of the Senate rather than by mail ballot without prior action.[41] And, Davisson continued, the Senate upon adjournment would sit unofficially as the faculty of the University to discuss a campaign to defeat the Regents' ultimatum.[42] In light of these intentions and for the reason that he could not be present without diminishing his later effectiveness in conferences between the Regents and the faculty Sproul decided against presiding at the Senate meeting the next day.[43]

The non-signers met that evening in the Unitarian Church adjoining the Berkeley campus. Discussion centered on means by which the Regents might be induced to alter their action of February 24 and how the Senate the following day might advance the prospects for a rapprochement with the Board — without, however, approving the Regents' policy barring Communists from employment.

VIII

Some seven hundred and fifty members of the Senate's northern section gathered in Wheeler Hall — the largest on the Berkeley campus — late on the afternoon of March 7. Professor Joel Hildebrand, vice-chairman, presided in Sproul's absence. Davisson proposed that the membership by mail ballot vote affirmatively on a resolution which in its prefatory portion declared the oath to be discriminatory against the faculty in relation to other public servants, ineffectual in its purposes, and a violation of established principles of academic privilege and tenure. The resolution concluded by proposing to substitute the following plan for the one approved by the Board on February 24:

1. All members of the Senate will subscribe to the constitutional oath of loyalty sworn by officers of public trust in the State of California, as prescribed in Article XX, Section 3, of the Constitution of the State of California.
2. All future letters of acceptance of salary and position will contain a statement that the person concerned accepts such position subject to the University's policies embodied in the Regents' resolutions of October 11, 1940, and June 24, 1949, excluding members of the Communist Party from employment in the University, and in University Regulation 5, endorsed in the Regents' statement of February 24, 1950.

The prefatory section of the resolution was moved by Davisson for immediate vote on the floor. Extended debate ensued during which the Senate gave "thunderous and loud applause" to the Davisson–Grant committee for the work it had done.[44]

Professor A. R. Davis, a senior member of the Berkeley faculty, offered two resolutions of his own, one worded precisely to meet the faculty's objection to the oath and the other to satisfy Neylan's demand for an unequivocal endorsement of the Regents' policy. A substitute motion was immediately offered by Professor Pepper (member of the Committee of Seven and of the Non-signers Steering Committee). Pepper's resolution proposed to accept the Regents' policy barring Communists by including a statement of it on the contract of employment. Professor Lawrence Harper of history next suggested separating the earlier Davisson motion into two parts, the first asking that the Senate submit the full resolution for mail ballot and the second asking for an immediate vote on the prefatory portion of it. Davisson agreed and moved that the full resolution be submitted to the membership for mail ballot. The motion carried.[45]

Discussion turned to the Davis and Pepper resolutions, particularly to those parts dealing with the Regents' policy. In the course of debate further resolutions were introduced by Professors Tolman and Kent — both prominent members of the non-signers group.[46] Professors John Hicks and Peter Odegard endeavored to put together, from all the proposals advanced, a resolution which would secure maximum faculty support and at the same time meet Regent Neylan's expectations. While thus engaged "amidst the tumult," Professor Wendell Stanley, a member of the Davisson–Grant committee, came to Hicks and Odegard with a prepared statement reading: "No person whose commitments or obligations to any organization, Communist or other, prejudice impartial scholarship and the free pursuit of truth will be employed by the University. *Proved members of the Communist Party, by reason of such commitments to that party, are not acceptable as members of the faculty* [emphasis added]."[47] The Stanley statement was identical to the first part of a resolution introduced earlier in the meeting by Professor Tolman except for the final sentence, which in the Tolman proposal read: "Proved members of the Communist Party *having such commitment* [emphasis added] are not acceptable as members of the faculty."[48] (In the Tolman version, guilt was necessarily demonstrable, whereas, in the Stanley proposal guilt was *a priori*.)

Davis was consulted by Hicks on the Stanley suggestion, agreed to the proposed wording, and withdrew the second of his earlier resolutions in favor of it. Thus, the Davis–Hicks–Stanley resolution, as it was to be known, was moved to the floor for debate. It secured passage as the second and final proposition to be submitted to the membership for mail ballot. The Senate then quickly adopted the prefatory portion of the Davisson resolution and the first of the two resolutions offered earlier by Professor Davis, the latter reading: "The members of the Academic Senate, Northern Section, without any reservation of any kind, pledge their loyalty to the Nation and the State. As an attest of this loyalty they stand ready to sign anew the Constitutional oath required of the President of the United States, the Governor of the State, and other state officials."[49]

The Senate adjourned into an informal assembly of the faculty. The Committee on Committees was asked to appoint a policy committee to direct the work of the faculty against the oath and, if necessary, to negotiate with the Board.[50] The northern members of the faculty would not meet again as a Senate for nearly two months. Their fight would be carried on unofficially and from a headquarters located off-campus.[51]

Similar resolutions were adopted the following afternoon by members of the southern section meeting in Los Angeles; and, as in the north, a steering and policy committee was appointed to carry the fight.

IX

Although the Senate and the Regents had publicly declared themselves adversaries on the question of the oath requirement, an affirmative vote on the Davis–Hicks–Stanley resolution had been thought by the faculty leadership to offer hope for reconciliation. To that end, the Davis–Hicks–Stanley resolution had been submitted to the members of the Senate. The morning of March 9, California newspapers carried the story of the Senate's actions and this encouragement from Regent Neylan: "With the Regents and faculty united and determined on . . . eliminating Communists . . . we shall solve all our problems."[52] In their private correspondence, however, some members of the Board, as a representative sample suggests, expressed an essentially unchanged and unyielding position: "We certainly have an insurrection on our hands in the Faculty," wrote Regent Charles C. Teague, Board member of twenty years and prominent in California agricultural circles and growers organizations and councils, and "as far as I am concerned I am not in favor of backing down."[53] Other members of the Board, like Roy E. Simpson, superintendent of public instruction, and Admiral Chester W. Nimitz, neither of whom had attended or participated in meetings of the Board during the previous months of dispute, sought information from their fellow Regents. Still others, who on February 24, 1950, had voted with the majority of the Board (like Regent Ehrman), were slowly persuaded to the faculty viewpoint by fellow Regents and by personal friends among the faculty. "I have reached the conclusion that we should eliminate the oath," wrote Ehrman to Neylan on March 18.[54] "We must remember," he continued, "that the moderates were able to force the submission of the anti-communist resolution and compel the resignation of the conference committee [Davisson–Grant]." Should the Regents not accept the Senate resolutions of March 7 and 8, Ehrman concluded, the position and influence of the moderates would be in great jeopardy.[55]

The end result of this "lobbying" among the Regents was a Board evenly divided. Paradoxically, the Regents split at the very time the faculty came together——a condition soon to be as untenable for the Regents as it previously had been for the faculty. A divided Board, however, gave the faculty little reason for optimism. On the contrary, it created consternation among the leadership who had labored under the illusion that the Board, in exchange for a Senate vote endorsing the Regents' policy, would agree to eliminate the oath. The immense falsity of this premise gradually dawned on the faculty only after the Senate had voted overwhelmingly its affirmation of the Regents' policy and finally severed the few remaining threads of confidence between the Board and the faculty.

The resolutions approved by the Senate for mail ballot were sent to the membership on March 13, 1950, with printed arguments for and against the Davis–Hicks–Stanley resolution. Supporters of the resolution quoted the arguments expressed in the Summer number of the *American Scholar*, 1949, p. 332, by Arthur O. Lovejoy, founder and first secretary of the American Association of University Professors:

Argument for Proposition No. 2
[The Davis–Hicks–Stanley Resolution]

1. Freedom of inquiry, of opinion, and of teaching in universities is a prerequisite, if the academic scholar is to perform the function proper to his profession.

2. The Communist Party in the United States is an organization whose aim is to bring about the establishment in this country of a political as well as an economic system essentially similar to that which now exists in the Soviet Union.

3. That system does not permit freedom of inquiry, of opinion, and of teaching, either in or outside of universities; in it the political government claims and exercises the right to dictate to scholars what conclusions they must accept, or at least profess to accept, even on questions lying within their own specialties — for example, in philosophy, in history, in aesthetics and literary criticism, in economics, in biology.

4. A member of the Communist Party is therefore engaged in a movement which has already extinguished academic free-

dom in many countries and would — if it were successful here — result in the abolition of such freedom in American universities.

5. *No one, therefore, who desires to maintain academic freedom in America can consistently favor that movement, or give indirect assistance to it by accepting as fit members of the faculties of universities, persons who have voluntarily adhered to an organization one of whose aims is to abolish academic freedom* [emphasis added].[56]

Those opposed argued the position of the AAUP's Committee A on Academic Freedom and Tenure:

Argument Against Proposition No. 2

Recommendation for a "no" vote on this resolution is based (1) on the belief that professional fitness to teach or engage in research should be determined by an objective evaluation of the quality of an individual's mind, character, and loyalty and not by his political or religious beliefs or lawful associations: and (2) on the belief that the proposed resolution, if passed, would contradict the above principle and would put the Senate on record as favoring a political test.

A statement of this same argument against a political test and for academic freedom was made by the Committee on Academic Freedom and Tenure for 1948 of the American Association of University Professors and published in the "Bulletin," 1949, 35, 1, 56–57. That statement read as follows:

". . . If a teacher, as an individual, should advocate the forcible overthrow of the government or should incite others to do so; if he should use his classes as a forum for communism, or otherwise abuse his relationship with his students for that purpose; if his thinking should show more than normal bias or be so uncritical as to evidence professional unfitness, these are the charges that should be brought against him. If these charges should be established by evidence adduced at a hearing, the teacher should be dismissed because of his acts of disloyalty or because of professional unfitness, and not because he is a Communist. *So long as the Communist Party in the United States is a legal party, affiliation with that party in and of itself should not be regarded as a justifiable reason for exclusion from the academic profession* [emphasis added]." [57]

By Wednesday evening March 22, 1950, the ballots had been tallied and the results posted.

	Proposition 1 (Davisson–Grant Resolution) Opposing Oath			Proposition 2 (Davis–Hicks–Stanley Resolution) Affirming Policy		
	For	Against	Abstained	For	Against	Abstained
NORTHERN SECTION	841	93	15	724	203	22
SOUTHERN SECTION	313	43	18	301	65	8
ACADEMIC SENATE	1154	136	33	1025	268	30

The Senate leadership, in announcing the vote, clearly and unequivocally related the Senate's support for the Davis–Hicks–Stanley resolution to the Davisson–Grant resolution which called for the elimination of the oath: "The proposal is that the Regents *repeal* [emphasis added] the requirement of the special oath and permit members of the faculty to declare their loyalty by taking the standard oath specified by the State Constitution, as they have done in the past. In addition, in signing their annual contracts faculty members will accept their positions subject to the University policy excluding members of the Communist Party." (Carl Epling, vice-chairman southern section, Academic Senate.) [58] The spokesmen also pointed out that the small negative vote was not to be interpreted as a vote sympathetic to communism. Rather, it stemmed from the belief that other and better means of reaching common objectives could be found. [59]

Those on the faculty, however, who most opposed passage of the Davis–Hicks–Stanley resolution were convinced that the vote had compromised the integrity of the academic profession, the prestige of the University of California in the academic world, and the civil and academic rights of the individual members of the faculty. The non-signers were greatly discouraged. [60] The vote unqualifiedly contradicted the position of Committee A and the Council of the American Association of University Professors on the fitness of a Communist to teach. Coincidentally, the AAUP, in Cleveland for its national convention on March 26–27, 1950, effected no change in its policy, but on the contrary more strongly enunciated it and criticized universities and colleges who would dismiss members of the teaching staff on the basis of guilt-by-association.[61]

During the period March 8 to 21, 1950, Regent Neylan had remained wholly noncommittal on the matter of how the oath requirement was to be modified — assuming Senate endorsement of the policy. Rather, he had encouraged the moderate and conservative leadership of the Senate to its then strong support of the Davis–Hicks–Stanley resolution, had maintained close contact with his allies on the Board, had communicated regularly with those on the faculty who had for most of the dispute kept him fully informed of the pulse of the faculty and its intentions, and had scrupulously avoided further substantive public statements. Neylan wrote to Sproul on March 21, and expressed his belief that there was hope for solving the oath problem if the faculty voted favorably on the Davis–Hicks–Stanley resolution.[62] When Neylan wrote this letter, the ballots had not been counted. There was a general belief, however, that the Senate vote on the resolution would be overwhelmingly affirmative.[63] Anticipating positive results, Neylan drafted, as a substitute for paragraph six of the Regents' resolution of February 24, the following:

The Regents in the light of the facts herein stated give notice that a condition precedent to employment or renewal of employment in the University shall be the execution of an oath in the form prescribed on June 24, 1949, or the equivalent affirmation on the Letter of Appointment reading as follows:

As a condition for the attached contract, the undersigned affirms that he is under no commitment in conflict with University policies embodied in Regents' Resolutions of October 11, 1940 and June 24, 1949, and in the Faculty Resolution adopted March 22, 1950, excluding members of the Communist Party from employment in the University.[64]

Through his intermediary at Berkeley, Professor Chaney, Neylan sought to arrange a meeting with Hicks to ascertain the acceptability of this proposition. Hicks, on the urging of other members of the Committee of Seven, decided against meeting personally with Neylan, but did agree to meet with Chaney and discuss the proposal. Hicks and Chaney met Saturday morning, March 25. Professor Sontag and Professor Prosser, dean of the School of Law, joined them. Hicks reported the conference to Sproul the following day (emphasis added):

The [Neylan] proposition was that the oath should be retained as now stated, but that the form of contract suggested by the Faculty, "with some modification by the Regents," should serve as an equivalent. *Members of the Faculty would be required to sign one or the other, thus establishing a permanent split between what might be called "first class citizens" and "second class citizens."*

Needless to say we rejected the "proposition" unanimously and emphatically. . . .

I may also add that if the Regents take the suggested action the faculty moderates who put over Resolution No. 2 [Davis–Hicks–Stanley] will be completely discredited. *We were given to understand from many sources, both public and private, that the real battle was not over the oath at all, but over the right of the Communist Party members to be accepted as members of the faculty. . . .*[65]

Paradoxically, the Neylan proposition was substantively identical to paragraph six of the resolution offered to the Board on February 24 by Sproul (see p. 114). One wonders what the faculty response would have been to the Sproul resolution had it passed the Regents. (The author believes that although there would have been objection to it — as the Davisson–Grant committee had in fact objected on February 20 — the faculty at that time would have gone along with it.)

Since February 24, however, the leaders of the faculty had worked hard to obtain a heavy endorsement of the Regents' policy for what they had regarded to be an "understanding" with Neylan that the oath would be *eliminated*. Now, having obtained this affirmation and discovering that the oath was to remain even as an alternative, the faculty's sense of fair play was violated. It may have been this offense more than the wording of the Neylan proposal that turned Hicks and his colleagues against it. (The author believes that the vagueness of the "understanding" was largely responsible for the schism here between Hicks and Neylan. Whereas Neylan had talked in terms of altering the method of implementation in a manner more acceptable to the faculty, Hicks and his associates, although using much the same language in expressing their "understanding," had in mind not a modification of the oath but its absolute elimination.)

Early the following week, Neylan was reported to the President by Regent Griffiths as being more fixed in his demand for an oath than before, having been adversely affected by the number of negative votes on the Davis–Hicks–Stanley resolution.[66] (The author believes that although the number of negative votes may have been a factor in Neylan's attitude, it can hardly be considered overriding, as he knew of the negative proportion of votes when he proposed his "compromise" to Hicks, Sontag, and Prosser on March 25. Moreover, it is unlikely that his proposal was merely a gesture which he knew would prove unacceptable, as it represented in substance what only one month earlier he himself had emphatically rejected, that is, Sproul's proposal to the Board on February 24. Whatever propensity Neylan had to "compromise" probably vanished with the rebuff he received from Hicks, Sontag, and Prosser.) The Board now had to decide either to eliminate the oath by adopting the Davisson–Grant resolution which had passed the Senate or to remain firm in its commitment to the Regents' resolution of February 24.

X

The March meeting of the Board of Regents was held the last day of the month on the Santa Barbara campus. Twelve months and one week following the enactment of the first oath, the Regents had returned to the place of its birth. In the week before the meeting three Regental appointments had been made by Governor Warren: Cornelius J. Haggerty, San Francisco labor leader, to replace Mortimer Fleishhacker, a Regent of thirty-two years and prominent San Francisco businessman whose term expired March 1; Jesse H. Steinhart, well-known San Francisco attorney, to succeed Charles C. Teague, who had died March 20, 1950; and L. Mario Giannini, president of the Bank of America, to a full term succeeding himself. The appointments increased the minority's vote by one (Steinhart's) and possibly by two (Haggerty's). The reappointment of Giannini probably seemed politically necessary in view of the other two appointments, but it was also consistent with the family's long history of involvement in the life of the University.

Sproul opened the discussion of the loyalty oath by reading the Davisson–Grant and Davis–Hicks–Stanley resolutions enacted by the Senate. Regent Jordan moved that they be received and filed. Dickson seconded. A substitute motion was offered by Regent Fenston to rescind the Board's action of February 24. When seconded by Regent Heller the substitute motion was open for discussion. At that point Professors Hicks and O'Brien of the Committee of Seven and Professor Dodd of the Steering Committee were invited into the meeting.[67] For better than an hour they sat listening without comment to a very heated discussion among the members of the Board which made it clear that positions were fixed. In the course of the debate, Neylan was unambiguous in manifesting his opposition to any change in the February 24 resolution:

Finally it kept coming back and coming back that evidently all these months this minority ["dissident" non-signers] was powerful enough to reject the President's original oath, this minority in the Academic Senate was powerful enough to reject the agreement of June 24, and even after that it was powerful enough on November 7 to repudiate the agreement of September 30, and finally last Saturday night [has reference to Chaney's report of his conversation earlier that day with Hicks, Sontag, and Prosser] I was told it was powerful enough that if we don't accept the program offered today the moderates, or those in control of the Senate, will lose control again and this minority will again take control. I say to you that if we have a minority in the faculty of the University of California which have been that powerful, it is time to find it out now. . . . I was convinced last Saturday night that the minority is still there and is still powerful enough to keep on doing what it has been doing during the last year. *Now is the time to find out if that minority is going by threat and menace to run the University of California* [emphasis added].[68]

The policy barring Communists from employment was no longer of principal interest to Regent Neylan. Members of the Senate by mail vote had approved the policy, and overwhelmingly. Neylan had turned his energies to the next and final point at issue, namely, the authority of the Board of Regents and the Senate in the governance of the University, particularly in relation to the appointment, promotion, and dismissal of members of the faculty. Allied were other Regents, who, if not in every respect agreeing with Neylan, shared, nevertheless, for their own reasons, his firm opposition to any action that would rescind the oath. Governor Warren led those Regents of the opposite persuasion who agreed with the principles expressed in the Davisson–Grant resolution or were amenable to some optional method of implementing the non-Communist policy. In the middle were men like Regent Ehrman who would argue for whichever course would do the University the least damage.[69]

When Professor Hicks was at last invited to speak, he argued that the Senate vote on the Davis–Hicks–Stanley resolution, passed by a majority of 79 percent, constituted new evidence of sufficient importance to warrant reconsideration of the oath requirement:

> From our reading of the minutes of the recent Senate Committee on Conference with the Regents [January 4, 1950], we are led to believe that there was a false assumption on both sides that a majority of the Senate favored exclusion of a Communist Party member from the faculty only when individual and personal misconduct, other than mere membership in the Communist Party, could be proved against him. Conservative members of the faculty were aghast to learn that any such assumption had ever been made. It is simply not true, and we believe that it has never been true. We therefore determined to obtain a straightout vote on the matter by mail ballot to ascertain the facts. The results of that ballot are conclusive.[70]

Hicks also stressed that the same Senate, by a majority of 89 percent, had voted to ask the Regents to abolish the oath in favor of including a statement of the University's policy on communism (Davisson–Grant resolution) on the contract of employment. The Senate had done its part in endorsing the University's policy on communism, Hicks contended, and now the Regents should do theirs by rescinding its resolution of February 24 and by substituting for it the Davisson–Grant resolution. Professors O'Brien and Dodd each added emphasis to what Hicks had said. "I hope, Dr. Hicks," responded Neylan, "that you did not mean that I ever intimated there would be any giving up of the oath. . . . I wanted to work with the faculty, the big majority of the faculty, to bring us into an agreement on the equivalent. . . ."[71]

As the question moved to a vote, Governor Warren asked to say a word, "not for the purpose of changing anyone's mind — because I am quite sure that everyone here knows how he is going to vote on this matter, and I don't impugn the motive of any member of this Board," but rather to put clearly into the record his reasons for voting to rescind. Of his rather full statement, the following at least deserves quotation:

I have an added interest in this University. I am an alumnus myself, and have three youngsters in the University today. God willing I will have two more in two or three years on one of the campuses of the University. I would cut my right arm off before I would willingly submit my youngsters to the wiles or infamy of a Communist faculty. I don't believe that the faculty of the University of California is Communist; I don't believe that it is soft on Communism, and neither am I. I believe that in their hearts the members of the faculty of our University are just as sincere on the things they represent against Communism as any member of this Board, and I want to say here and now that I have absolute confidence in the faculty of the University of California. I don't mean that they don't have a Communist piano player some place in there [72] and may have a Communist in other places, and you will find them infiltrated in business to a point where you know nothing about it. You may have some working for you, you men in business would be surprised to find out about. I don't believe there is any difference of opinion between the individual members of the Regents and between the Regents and the faculty in their desire to get rid of Communists. If I thought that my course would be entirely different. I believe we are having too much pride of opinion in this matter and there has been too much stated, it seems to me, about what the public expects us to do, because the public doesn't know what the facts of this case are. . . . The only thing the people of this State are interested in is our seeking to keep Communists out of the University and, believe me, I am interested in that too. [73]

On the vote to rescind, a roll call was requested. Regents Ahlport, Collins, Dickson, Giannini, Jordan, Knight, McFadden, Merchant, Neylan, and Sprague voting no; Regents Ehrman, Fenston, Griffiths, Haggerty, Hansen, Heller, Simpson, Sproul, Steinhart, and Warren voting aye: the vote was ten to ten. The motion to rescind lost and the February 24 resolution of the Board remained unchanged. After four and a half hours of hard, heated, and acrimonious debate, the session adjourned. In faculty circles, the vote that day was known as the Great Double-cross.[74]

XI

The Committee of Seven met on the evening of March 31 and agreed that efforts must be made to persuade the President to support actively, publicly, and aggressively the faculty position on the oath. His cooperation was regarded as imperative. On the afternoon of April 2, Sproul met with members of the Committee of Seven at their headquarters in Berkeley's Durant Hotel and was urged to come out strongly and publicly for the faculty position. The Committee of Seven felt that the President was now able to make known his views, as the ten-to-ten vote at Santa Barbara was thought to relieve him of the necessity of publicly siding with either the majority or the minority of the Board. Sproul's answer was that to do so would force his resignation and permit the appointment of a successor wholly responsive to the Neylan faction. The following day, Professor Dodd spoke with Sproul by telephone and urged him publicly to back the faculty's stance. The President advised Dodd that to do as he suggested "would be fatal to the ends the faculty has in mind, and that he [Dodd] and his colleagues would have to trust me to do at what I regard as an appropriate time the things that need to be done."[75]

The President worked on a plan of his own and on April 4 sent a draft of it to Regent Ehrman. The proposal was to make no change in the Regents resolution of February 24 but to interpret it for administrative purposes as follows:

1. Each signer shall be free to file with his oath or affirmation a statement of his opposition to test oaths as a means of implementing the Regents' policy excluding Communists from membership in the faculty, providing the wording of such protest does

not invalidate or negate the oath or affirmation to which he has subscribed.

2. *Failure to file the oath or affirmation will not be regarded as ipso facto evidence of membership in the Communist Party and no non-signer will therefore be dismissed* [emphasis added] "without referring the case through the President to the Committee on Privilege and Tenure of the Academic Senate for full findings and recommendations as in the past." [76]

Acting as intermediary for Sproul, Ehrman sent the President's proposal to Neylan and invited his reaction. Neylan responded the following day. Sproul's proposal, said Neylan, was designed to give the public the impression that the policy had been sustained, when it merely permitted the President to interpret it to do the very opposite. To accept the proposal, Neylan concluded, would be to surrender to the dissident minority of the faculty. [77]

Discouraged with the reply, Ehrman called Sproul and informed him of it. Sproul noted:

Regent Ehrman said that he was much discouraged by this reply [Neylan's] but that he did not know what further he could do. I asked him whether Neylan's reply was to be interpreted as evidence of determination on the part of his group in the Board to stand pat on the decision of March 31, or of unwillingness to have me play any part in the negotiations. He replied that he had no idea which of these possibilities the reply represents. *I told him that the exclusion of the President from any part in the present critical situation is a simply impossible arrangement* [emphasis added]. [78]

On Wednesday evening April 5 some sixty-five deans and department chairmen from the northern section of the Academic Senate gathered on the Berkeley campus. Hicks reported the work of the Committee of Seven and read to the group the statement he had made to the Regents at Santa Barbara. The reaction was reported to Sproul by Kidner. The statement was received unkindly by some of those present who had signed, Kidner said, because Hicks's statement appeared to discredit the Davisson–Grant committee and seemed to imply that immoderates on the faculty had previously been in control.[79]

The following day, in a letter to Kidner, Hicks submitted his resignation as chairman of the Committee of Seven. Hicks believed the criticism expressed the evening before was directed not toward the committee as a whole, but rather toward his own leadership. Hicks suggested that Kidner (then chairman of the Senate's Committee on Committees), on making the resignation public, ascribe it to "the fact that I shall have to be out of town over this week-end, and also from April 12 to 24 to attend two historical meetings in the east." Otherwise, Hicks feared, the members of the Board who must be persuaded to the faculty side "would see in my forced resignation a sign of weakening on the part of the faculty."[80] Moreover, Professor Sontag, a member of the committee, upon hearing of Hicks's resignation, threatened to quit as well. Hicks was most anxious that Sontag not resign in view of the latter's closeness to Regent Ehrman. (Hicks believed that Sontag's resignation would be disastrous. Sontag held the Sidney Hellman Ehrman Chair of European History and was on good terms with Regent Ehrman. Sontag's resignation would threaten the loss of Ehrman's vote — a circumstance nearly certain to negate all efforts to persuade other Regents to the faculty point of view, as Ehrman enjoyed considerable influence with his fellow Regents.) That evening some one hundred fifty non-signers and others associated with that group met at the Faculty Club and gave Hicks and the other members of the Committee of Seven a vote of confidence. The vote encouraged Hicks and he subsequently agreed to remain as titular head of the committee.[81]

Sproul's personal position as president of the University was increasingly of concern to all interested parties. Rumors of an impending resignation by the President were widespread among the faculty and reported in the press. In response, the President on April 11, 1950, issued the following public release: "The talk about my resignation comes from others, not from me. My participation in the loyalty oath discussion has been confined to efforts to clarify the facts and the issues, and to promote a decision in accordance with them upon which faculty and Regents might agree." [82]

The publicity of Sproul's supposed intentions prompted within the Board a response quite the opposite of what was then generally bruited about, namely, that the Board under the leadership of Neylan and Regents associated with him wished for the President's immediate removal. There is reason to doubt the veracity of these rumors, as the two following samples suggest. As part of a letter to Regent Sam Collins, speaker of the California State Assembly and member of the Neylan faction, Neylan expressed the view that it was extremely important to repair Sproul's prestige; [83] while Dickson wrote to Ehrman two days later, and told of his anxiety for the President's position: "This situation cannot be permitted to rage. You and I — and I believe the whole Board — love Bob Sproul. He has been placed in a most unfortunate position, and his reputation is badly battered. We must all endeavor to restore not only the University's own prestige, but that of our President as well." [84]

Hicks left on April 12 for eight days of meetings in the Midwest. In his absence Professor Pepper, liaison man for the non-signers, acted as chairman of the Committee of Seven. Kidner continued in his responsibilities at the committee offices in the Durant Hotel. It was Hicks's belief that the faculty must make a show of strength sufficient to persuade a majority of the Board to abandon the April 30 deadline for signing and reenter into direct negotiations with the faculty. As the Davisson-Grant committee was disbanded by action of the Senate March 7 and 8, and as the Committee of Seven enjoyed only limited powers and a rather indistinct relationship to the Academic Senate proper, Hicks hoped to reopen direct negotiations between the Regents and the Senate. [85] Hicks believed that if the majority faction of the Board was to be induced to reopen the issues, some compromise must be struck, and although he offered several possibilities in a letter to Kidner on April 13, none gained support.[86] With but one week before the next meeting of the Regents (April 21) the principal faculty committee was still groping for a means of obviating the April 30 deadline for signing.

Matters were no better with the faculty cause in the southern part of the state. The Steering and Policy committees were engaged in work in the south very much the same as that occupying the interests and energies of the Committee of Seven.[87] On April 10 the Steering and Policy committees released to the press a five-page document which gave the "facts" of the controversy, discussed the "issues," advanced the arguments against the oath, and predicted the "consequences" for the welfare of the University should the oath not be rescinded. The burden of the statement was that communism was not the issue. Rather: "(1) The Regents' action of February 24 threatens the maintenance of professional standards in the selection of faculty members. (2) The Regents' action of February 24 is a breach of moral contract. [Has reference to tenure.] (3) The Regents' action of February 24 violates the principle of faculty self-government."[88]

In other words, what was in dispute at that point was the authority of the Regents and the faculty in the selection and retention of members of the faculty; and this view was confirmed by Regent Jordan, an important member of the Neylan majority, who in a letter to Ehrman admitted that "the real issue has nothing to do with Communism, the Loyalty Oath or anything else." The real issue, Jordan continued, was "whether this faculty is to be permitted to select its own members and govern itself without encroachment or interferences by the Trustees of the State University."[89] Still, California and out-of-state newspapers continued during this time to set headlines reading "Students and Professors to War on Oath," "Faculty Leader Dislikes Being Pushed Around," "U.C. Oath Cold War Charges," "Three Regents

Denounce U.C. Foes of Oath," "Battle On U.C. Oath." The faculty's message never got across.

Time was running out. As each passing day brought closer to home the full meaning of the April 30 deadline, the faculty, rather than fully mobilizing its influence and strength, grew ever more resigned. A kind of paralysis set in.[90] If the faculty felt frustrated in its position and in its effort to seek a solution, so also did President Robert Gordon Sproul; and in consideration of the delicacy of his position, coupled with his singular lack of success in seeking a middle ground between the faculty and the Regents, Sproul turned to the University's alumni for help.

XII

The California Alumni Association's governing board, the Alumni Council, earlier in the year had authorized its president, Regent William Hale, to appoint a five-member committee to study the loyalty oath dispute and to report back with recommendations for Council action. Hale appointed the committee on March 7. The members included: Stephen D. Bechtel, president and director of Bechtel Construction Corporation, San Francisco, as chairman of the committee; Paul Davies, president of Food Machinery and Chemical Corporation, San Jose; Dr. William Deamer, professor on the Berkeley campus (Dr. Deamer was later succeeded by Dr. Donald H. McLaughlin, president of Homestake Mining Corporation and former member of the California and Harvard faculties); Milton H. Esberg, Jr., partner in Consultants, Inc., a San Francisco public relations firm; Mrs. Kathryn Fletcher, prominent civic leader in the city of Berkeley; and Stanley E. McCaffrey, executive manager of the association, as the committee's secretary.

Bechtel wrote identical letters to Regents Dickson, Neylan, Warren, and Hale and to President Sproul and Professor Hicks, advising each of the committee's interest and hope to be of help when circumstances warranted its involvement.[91]

In response, Regent Neylan, who was personally acquainted with Bechtel, called from Phoenix, reviewed the dispute, and suggested that a strong affirmative vote by the Senate on the Davis–Hicks–Stanley resolution might pave the way for an agreement between the various parties.[92] Hicks replied on March 20, offered the cooperation of the Committee of Seven, and urged the Bechtel committee to help bring about a solution to the controversy consistent with the Davisson–Grant resolution then being voted on by the Senate. The committee, however, chose not to become involved in the dispute at that point, and, indeed, refused to participate in any way prior to the March 31 meeting of the Board — even when importuned on the eve of that meeting by Hicks, who pled for its support. Neither, however, did the committee intercede in behalf of the Neylan faction of the Board. Rather, it preferred to remain aloof until after the Santa Barbara meeting.

Professor Hicks wrote Bechtel in early April and again invited alumni involvement. Thus, following instructions of his committee, a meeting of which had been called for April 7, Bechtel met with Professors Hicks and Kidner and then with Regent Neylan. After reporting these conversations to the committee on April 12, Bechtel urged his committee members to take an active role in seeking to reconcile the differences threatening the University with disaster. The President proved receptive to the proposal, and by letter April 13 to Bechtel confirmed his hope that the committee would be helpful in bringing about a solution.[93] Hale confirmed the plan by telegram from New York.

During the next week, the Bechtel committee flew, by private plane, from one end of the state to the other, meeting with representatives of the several faculty committees, with non-signers, with individual Regents, with individual members of the faculty, with alumni, and with the President. The course and direction their recommendation was to take and the reasons for it were noted in a letter of April 19 from Professor Roger Revelle of the Scripps Institute of Oceanography to Professor Carl Epling, a member of the Steering Committee at Los Angeles, vice-chairman of the southern section of the Academic Senate, and a non-signer. Revelle summarized the conversation he and Professors Elkus and Tussman, both associated with the non-signers' group on the Berkeley campus, had had with the Bechtel committee earlier that day:

> The Committee repeatedly asked us whether a statement on the appointment forms that the signer is not a member of the Communist Party would be an acceptable compromise. It seemed evident that, in spite of our protestations to the contrary, they would recommend that this be done. One of their reasons seemed to be that it was undesirable to retain two separate requirements — an oath for some and an acceptance of appointment, subject to the non-Communist policy for others. Because they feel that the oath should not be too obviously rescinded, they believe that a non-Communist statement on the appointment form is the best way out.[94]

The Bechtel committee, Revelle continued, argued in support of retaining the substantive wording of the oath in the belief that the Regents would lose public confidence if they simply rescinded the special oath requirement.[95] "I am naturally much distressed about the probable effect on Faculty morale," Revelle concluded, "if the appointment forms contain a statement of denial. But I feel that preservation of the principle of tenure is even more basic, and I urge you to take no action which will jeopardize this."[96]

The Bechtel committee reported its recommendation to the Alumni Council the evening of April 19, and then forwarded it to the President for presentation to the Board on April 21.

The Steering and Policy committees met with the President at International House on the Berkeley campus on March 20 to discuss the alumni proposal. Although discouraged with and critical of the Bechtel committee's recommendation, the faculty representatives were of the view "that nothing better was likely and there was nothing to do but get behind it."[97] In the north as well as in the south despair among faculty leadership was apparent. What energies remained would be devoted to salvaging tenure.

Efforts to change the votes of individual Regents, however, continued unabated. Regents in the minority brought pressures to bear on the majority members of the Board from wherever influence could be drawn, such as personal friends, business associates, nationally prominent educators, scholars, newsmen, and public officials. The President worked with those who might go either way. The faculty, working principally through the Committee of Seven and the non-signers, succeeded in bringing to the University upwards of seven hundred individual communications supporting the faculty cause from colleagues in better than a score of colleges and universities across the country. A group of prominent alumni of the University, including such well-known personalities as Monroe E. Deutsch, Vice-President and Provost Emeritus of the University; James K. Moffitt, Regent Emeritus, former chairman of the Board of Regents and prominent San Francisco businessman; Robert Sibley, former executive-manager of the California Alumni Association; Walter A. Haas and Daniel Koshland, both prominent San Francisco businessmen and benefactors of the University; and Msgr. Charles A. Ramm, former Regent of the University, working mostly under the guidance of Harley C. Stevens, well-known San Francisco attorney, combined their influence to bring members of the Board over to the Warren side.

The Regents met April 21 on the Davis campus. The President introduced a resolution prepared by him the previous day substantively identical to the alumni recommendation, which because of its great significance is quoted in full (emphasis added):

The Regents of the University of California confirm and emphasize their policy designed to bar members of the Communist

Party from employment by the University as members of the faculty or otherwise, as embodied in various statements and resolutions including those of October 11, 1940 and June 24, 1949, which policy is hereby reaffirmed. The Regents are gratified that the Academic Senate, both Northern and Southern sections, has concurred in this policy by an overwhelming vote, reported on March 22, 1950.

The Regents have given further consideration to the most effective methods for the implementation of this established policy, and it is their view that the objectives previously defined and announced can best be achieved in the following manner:

After July 1, 1950, which will mark the beginning of a new academic year, conditions precedent to employment or renewal of employment of American citizens in the University shall be (1) *execution of the constitutional oath of office required of public officials of the State of California and (2) acceptance of appointment by a letter which shall include the following provision:*

> Having taken the constitutional oath of office required of public officials of the State of California, I hereby formally acknowledge my acceptance of the position and salary named, and *also state that I am not a member of the Communist Party* or any other organization which advocates the overthrow of the Government by force or violence, and that I have no commitments in conflict with my responsibilities with respect to impartial scholarship and free pursuit of truth. I understand that the foregoing statement is a condition of my employment and a consideration of payment of my salary.

Inasmuch as aliens are not lawfully subject to an oath of allegiance to the United States or the State of California, their letters of acceptance shall be drawn without reference to such oath but shall otherwise in all respects be identical with those of American citizens.

In any case of failure to sign the constitutional oath and the prescribed form of letter of acceptance the right of petition and review (referred to below) will be fully observed.

The foregoing is intended to govern employment and re-employment after June 30, 1950. *For the balance of the current academic year, to wit, until July 1, 1950, account must be taken both of the large majority of faculty and employees who have subscribed to the loyalty oath of June 24, 1949, and of the minority who have not.* The Regents have on various occasions indicated that an alternative affirmation would be accepted from the latter group if in form approved by the Regents. *It is hereby provided that execution of the constitutional oath of office required of public officials of the State of California, and acceptance of appointment in the form herein stated, will be acceptable affirmation in lieu of the oath of June 24, 1949.*

The Secretary of the Regents shall promptly mail to all faculty members and employees of the University new letters of acceptance of appointment for the academic year 1949–50, containing the text of the provision set forth above, and accompanied by the text of the constitutional oath of office of the State of California. Acceptance in the form prescribed shall be obligatory for all who have not filed with the Secretary the loyalty oath previously required by the Regents. Those who have already taken the latter oath need not follow the described procedure for the current academic year but may do so if they wish. In such case the oaths to which they have subscribed may be withdrawn.

In the event that a member of the faculty fails to comply with any foregoing requirement applicable to him he shall have the right to petition the President of the University for a review of his case by the Committee on Privilege and Tenure of the Academic Senate, including an investigation of and full hearing on the reasons for his failure to do so. Final action shall not be taken by the Board of Regents until the Committee on Privilege and Tenure, after such investigation and hearing, shall have had an opportunity to submit to the Board, through the President of the University, its findings and recommendations. It is recognized that final determination in each case is the prerogative of the Regents.

In order to provide a reasonable time for completion of the foregoing procedures, the Regents hereby fix May 15, 1950 as the date on or before which the constitutional oath and contract form shall be signed, and June 15, 1950 as the date on or before which all proceedings before the President and the Committee on Privilege and Tenure shall be completed and their findings and recommendations submitted to the Regents.

The regulations and procedures herein enacted, as applied and enforced by the administrative authorities of the University, will henceforth govern and control over all previous actions of the Regents to the extent they may be inconsistent with such previous actions to the end that the policy of the Regents and the Academic Senate barring members of the Communist Party from employment in the University may be fairly and effectively implemented.[98]

The resolution represented:

(1) Conclusive defeat for those who had contended against the Regents' policy automatically barring Communists from employment in the University.

(2) No relief for those who had considered the oath a political test, an invasion of privacy, and an affront to the academic community.

(3) Little satisfaction for those who had sought greater faculty authority in the appointment, promotion, and dismissal of colleagues.

(4) Hope that the integrity of the Senate's Committee on Privilege and Tenure would remain unimpaired.

(5) Immediate relief for the non-signers from the April 30 deadline and, seemingly, an alternative method of satisfying the conditions of employment for those who refused to sign either the oath as adopted June 24, 1949, or the oath of allegiance and the letter of appointment as specified in the resolution; the alternative being, namely, "the right to petition the President of the University for a review of his case by the Committee on Privilege and Tenure of the Academic Senate, including an investigation of and full hearing on the reasons for his failure to do so."

On the motion of the President that the resolutions be adopted, Regents Hale and Neylan seconded. Then followed expressions of appreciation and commendation of the Bechtel committee's work, that is, until Regent Giannini advised the Board of his intention to vote against the resolution and to resign from the Board. For Giannini, a vote in favor of the motion was a vote for communism and "if the original loyalty oath were rescinded the flag would fly in the Kremlin."[99] The remainder of the session was devoted to an attempt to dissuade Giannini from his announced intentions. The relative strengths of the alumni plan in comparison with the February 24 resolution of the Board were emphasized for Giannini's benefit by Neylan, Jordan, Dickson, Sproul, Warren, and others. Interestingly, the point most frequently made was that the Communist denial provision in the contract was significantly more enforceable than it had been in the old oath. Others argued that the real issue had been the University's policy on communism, not the method of its implementation, and with the Senate on record in favor of the policy, the victory had been won. Ehrman made the point (emphasis added):

> Speaking to Regent Giannini, Regent Ehrman stated that the *real contest from the beginning was brought about by the fact that the Academic Senate Committees* [Davisson–Grant] *with whom the Regents met evidently did not represent the real voice of the faculty in claiming that it would be impossible to pass a resolution in the Senate endorsing the Regents' policy against Communism.* When that was put to the test, however, the overwhelming majority of the faculty voted to adopt the policy. This, he felt, was the victory. It was not a victory for the Regents nor for the faculty, but it was a victory for the University of California. . . . *The matter of implementation was a secondary* matter to his mind, but he thought that the proposal submitted by the Alumni was equally as good as, if not better and more effectual method of implementing the policy than the oath.[100]

Giannini remained unconvinced and was the only Regent recorded as voting no on the resolution.

The resolution was termed a compromise by the alumni and the Regents, and this understanding of what it represented was shared generally by the news media, where it was noticed nationally. Whether it was a compromise or not, the faculty had salvaged only a hope that the non-signers would be given a hearing by the Senate's Committee on Privilege and Tenure and that the Regents would regard the recommendations of the committee as *conclusive*. Should that supposition prove false, the non-signers, along with the University generally, would only have postponed the final question: Would the Regents dismiss a member of the faculty against whom no charge could be brought other than refusal to sign the oath or what amounted to its equivalent on the contract of employment? The decision was six months in coming.

The period January to April, 1950, represented the bitterest part of the loyalty oath controversy for the greatest number of persons. It was a time of general involvement by all participants and was noticed more widely by the press than at any other time — even when the dismissals came later in the year. The issue in principal dispute had shifted in late fall from the oath to the policy it implemented, and in late winter and early spring from the policy, once it was approved by the Senate, to the locus of governing authority in the University. As the controversy continued through the spring and into the summer of 1950, the adversary forces gathered their strength for a last encounter. The authority of the Board of Regents and the Academic Senate in the appointment, promotion, and dismissal of members of the faculty would be tested, and those on the faculty and on the Board who held unyieldingly to their principles were in the final confrontation nearly isolated, resented by many of their colleagues, and condemned for an intransigence that their associates regarded only as harmful to the general welfare of the University.

Chapter Six

A Test of Will

I

The Senate leadership moved quickly to mobilize the faculty behind the alumni "compromise." Their purposes were several: to reduce to a minimum the number of non-signers and, consequently, the number asking for hearings before the Committee on Privilege and Tenure; to establish sympathetic relations with the Board; and to make clear to the Regents the basis upon which the faculty was willing to cooperate in the implementation of the "compromise." The latter two of these objectives were sought in part by Hicks upon his return to Berkeley from the Regents' meeting on the evening of April 21 when he released a statement to the press, a portion of which read as follows:

At the hearing [of non-signers by the Committee on Privilege and Tenure] the objection of the faculty member [to signing] may be clearly stated and there is a guarantee that no man or woman shall be dismissed provided the Committee, the President, and the Regents can find assurance that his inability to sign the contract required arises solely out of good conscience. *Unless such individuals are proved to be members of the Communist Party, a condition we believe cannot be shown in any instance to exist, they will not be dismissed from the University, in spite of their unwillingness to sign the suggested contract* [emphasis addd].[1]

The release marked the end of the effective responsibility of the Committee of Seven.[2] The statement appeared over

Hicks's signature to capitalize on the regard in which he was held by the more conservative members of the Board and to establish publicly certain procedural understandings important to the non-signers. The third purpose — to reduce to a minimum the number of non-signers — was the most sensitive, difficult, and significant task confronting the leadership. The faculty meeting the next morning in Berkeley was crucial.

The morning's first speaker was Professor Morrough P. O'Brien, a member of the Committee of Seven and the representative of that committee in its discussions with the Alumni Committee. O'Brien reported to the faculty the negotiations which had occurred between the Committee of Seven, its counterpart in the southern section, and the Bechtel committee. While attesting to the sincerity of the alumni committee, he made it clear that its recommendations were by no means wholly consistent with the views of the faculty committee.[3] Once admitted, however, the differences were not seen by O'Brien as sufficient to cause further antagonism and he urged the faculty to cooperate in implementing the "compromise."

Professor Stephen C. Pepper then spoke in behalf of the Committee of Seven. (It had been decided the evening before that because of Pepper's closeness to the non-signers and owing to their suspicion of Hicks, the Committee of Seven's report would be more hospitably received if presented by Pepper.) He reported that the committee would shortly disband, read portions of the alumni plan, and expressed his disappointment with the "compromise." Nevertheless, he continued, it was by no means a total defeat. Pepper stressed the importance of the gains made on the faculty side, that is, recognition of the responsibilities of the Senate's Committee on Privilege and Tenure, and good relations with a number of loyal and sympathetic Regents. Therefore, Pepper concluded, "all who can conscientiously do so among the non-signers should sign."[4] Professor S. S. Surrey of the law school spoke next and, in reference to the

Regents' policy on communism, emphasized that the new contract plan did not change in any legal way the conditions of employment that had been in effect since 1940; rather, "You are simply stating expressly in the contract what the law implies and what you represented when you signed the contract before [before April 21, 1950, that is]. . . . Consequently, in short, legally we are being asked to do what in effect we have been doing ever since 1940." [5]

With the "moderate" and "conservative" members of the Senate urged by O'Brien to support the "compromise," and with the non-signers and their sympathizers encouraged to the same end by Pepper, and with the policy of the Regents cast in a somewhat ameliorating perspective by Surrey, the Senate was ready to hear proposals on how it should proceed.

The evening before, at the Durant Hotel, Hicks and members of his committee had been persuaded to relinquish to a Committee of Five whatever responsibilities the Committee of Seven sensed toward the implementation of the "compromise." [6] Endorsement of this new committee and acceptance of its recommendations by the Committee of Seven were required by the non-signers in return for their cooperation. Professor Clark Kerr, a member of the Committee of Five, negotiated the acquiescence of Hicks and his associates in the authority of the new committee. [7] The five members were Professors Edward Strong of philosophy, chairman (later Berkeley's third chancellor), Harry Wellman of agriculture (later vice-president of the University), R. A. Gordon of economics, H. B. Gotaas of engineering, and Clark Kerr (later Berkeley's first chancellor and then successor to Sproul as president of the University). Strong spoke, following Surrey's remarks, and advised the Senate that earlier in the week the Committee of Seven had authorized him to form a committee of five members and to prepare resolutions for Senate consideration in response to whatever action the Regents took on April 21. [8] Strong then read the committee's Recommendation I, which asserted the right of the individual faculty member to decide for himself on the basis of conscience to sign or not to sign and in relation to that right proposed that the Senate *"consider that the principles of tenure have been violated* [emphasis added] if any member of the Senate not signing the new contract is dismissed by the Board of Regents after a finding by the Committee on Privilege and Tenure that such person is 'not a member of the Communist Party or any organization which advocates the overthrow of the Government by force or violence' and that he had 'no commitments in conflict with my responsibilities in respect to impartial scholarship and for pursuit of truth.' "[9]

Recommendation I also instructed the Committee on Privilege and Tenure to assume that a faculty member met the Regents' and faculty's requirements for University service unless specific charges were brought against him or unless the committee were to have evidence to the contrary.[10] Strong concluded by urging that special committees be appointed to review the cases of non-signers among the non-Senate academic employees and nonacademic employees. On motion of Professor Strong, Recommendation I was approved. Strong gave notice that parts of Recommendation I would be submitted to the Senate when it next met in regular and formal session.

Professor Wellman then offered the second of the committee's two recommendations. This proposal asked authorization to submit to the Senate at its next regular and formal meeting legislation to create a Senate Committee on Academic Freedom. He asked also that the Senate appoint an interim committee of six members to investigate the possibility of forming a permanent organization "to educate the public, alumni, and students concerning the role which the University plays in the life of the state and nation and concerning the conditions necessary to maintain a free and great University."[11] Recommendation II was adopted.

Professor Edward C. Tolman, titular head of the non-signers, then announced that he would not sign the new contract of employment but would ask for a hearing before the Committee on Privilege and Tenure.[12] Tolman asked if the Regents intended "*to regain control over the mechanisms of appointment and dismissal at this University* [emphasis added]" and predicted that if the Board were successful in its purpose it would at the same time "have achieved a group of timorous and cowed men and women on the faculty and among other employees." Tolman proposed that the Regents' objective could be thwarted if the faculty refused to sign the new contract. He argued that if large numbers of the faculty were to refuse to sign, the Regents would be hard pressed to act: "The safety of the conscientious non-signers of the contract from abuse and contumely, lies in numbers."[13] The second important advantage of not signing, Tolman pointed out, was that it would demonstrate "to the public that we are a courageous and united faculty which as a group of highly selected and competent professional men and women demand autonomy, as far as that is legally possible, in the selection and dismissal of our own members." Tolman offered no resolutions for Senate action and none was urged by others because of Tolman's remarks.

Two resolutions were then passed by the Senate, one expressing confidence in the President and the other appreciation to those who had worked to bring about understanding and support of the faculty position. The morning's final speaker was Vice-President and Provost Emeritus Monroe E. Deutsch. Deutsch talked briefly, and in supporting the position taken earlier by O'Brien and Pepper indicated that if he were yet in active service he would sign the oath.[14] In closing, he pleaded for loyalty to the University and to its cause.

As the meeting adjourned, it was clear that some of the non-signers would make an effort to render ineffectual the procedural provisions of the "compromise" by seeking to encourage large numbers of the faculty not to sign. The hope was that the Committee on Privilege and Tenure would find it virtually impossible to conduct meaningful hearings, thus forcing the Regents to discard the plan as unworkable. Meanwhile, efforts were to be made to make the public more aware of the issues in dispute (the interim Committee of Six) so that if the matter were later reopened, the faculty would enjoy some greater measure of comfort from the outside community than had been evident previously. It was equally clear, however, that the Senate leadership was of no mind to cooperate in this purpose. The division in the faculty was to grow greater rather than less during the next four months as faculty support for the non-signers waned. The alumni "compromise" had apparently meant the end of the controversy for the great majority of the faculty. For a dedicated few, however, both among the regents and among the faculty, the "compromise" was but a battle in the war.

The southern section of the Academic Senate met in special session on the Los Angeles campus three days later to consider resolutions relating to the Regents' action of April 21, 1950. Following more than two hours of discussion, the resolutions were laid on the table to be considered at the next meeting of the Senate on May 2, 1950.[15]

II

Regent Farnham Griffiths called Sproul on April 25 and reported a recent conversation with Neylan on the meaning of the alumni "compromise." Neylan, said Griffiths, vigorously stated the view that "the hearing [Committee on Privilege and Tenure] is intended *only to give people like Quakers, and religious or conscientious objectors, a way out* [emphasis added]."[16] Griffiths, in response, asked Neylan that if this were so, why was this purpose not plainly stated in preference to the words used in the Regents' resolution of April 21? Griffiths reported that Neylan was shaken somewhat by this argument and finally said, "Maybe you're right, but we are in a hell of a fix if you are."[17] Griffiths also advised the President of a talk he had with a business associate of Bechtel's, John Simpson, who had participated in the work of the Bechtel committee though not a member of it, and who, Griffiths said, was certain that it was the intention

of the Bechtel committee to permit non-signers to petition
for a hearing for any reason whatsoever, and to have their
petitions considered by both the Committee on Privilege
and Tenure and the Regents.[18] Sproul told Griffiths that
Simpson's interpretation was at variance with Bechtel's, for
when Sproul had talked to Bechtel two days before, Bechtel
had taken the view that the burden of proof was on the non-
signer, not on the faculty or the Regents.[19]

III

The following day the secretary of the Regents mailed
to members of the faculty and staff a copy of the April 21,
1950, resolution of the Board, a copy of the constitutional
oath of office required of public officials of the State of
California, an appointment letter for the 1949–50 academic
year, and a form letter addressed to the secretary of the
Regents for signature by the appointee acknowledging acceptance of the terms of employment as specified in the letter
of appointment. The communication aggravated the already
delicate rapprochement being sought with the Regents by
the Senate leadership, as the wording of the appointment
letters and the letters of acceptance implied an abrogation of
tenure. Previously, letters of appointment to tenured members of the faculty had read in their critical part:

At the annual meeting of the Regents of the University of California your salary for the year ending June 30, 19___, as Professor of _____, was fixed at $_____.

The appointment letter mailed in late April and early May
of 1950 read in its relevant portion as follows:

This is to notify you that you have been appointed Professor
of _____, for the period July 1, 1949 to June 30, 1950 with a
salary at the rate of $_____ per annum.

The letter of acceptance to be signed by the appointee was
also changed to reflect the difference in wording, namely,

from notification of salary assuming continuous employment to *appointment* to position. Criticism of the change in the appointment and acceptance letters, strangely, was slow in rising and limited in scope. The objection was best expressed in a personal letter to Sproul from Berkeley Professors Joel Hildebrand, George S. Louderback, and Robert J. Kerner:

> It is assumed that the resolution [April 21] did not abolish the tenure of associate professors and professors who signified their willingness to sign letters of acceptance which include the provisions of the resolution. . . . It has . . . seemed obvious to us that the resolution, which in its wording does not assert that tenure has been abolished or imply in effect that it has been abolished does not require implementation [letters of appointment and acceptance] which expressly abolishes tenure *by reducing associate professors and professors to one-year appointees* [emphasis added].[20]

Although no general criticism of the letters in question developed for better than a year, the implicit threat they carried was sufficient to cause among an already sensitive and distrustful faculty a heightened suspicion of the Regents at the very time strenuous efforts were being made to recover some measure of civility and respect between the faculty and the Board.

IV

The Senate's northern section met in formal session on May 1 in Berkeley — the first official meeting of that body since the previous March. Some four hundred fifty members were present. Professor Strong, in behalf of the Committee of Five, moved adoption of that portion of Recommendation I which on April 22 had passed the Senate in informal session instructing the Committee on Privilege and Tenure on procedure and declaring that the principles of tenure would be regarded by the Senate to have been violated should the Regents dismiss any non-signer not found by the

Committee on Privilege and Tenure to be a Communist or one whose commitments prevented the free pursuit of truth. The Senate minutes report that this motion was followed by extended debate and parliamentary maneuvering.[21] Strong finally withdrew the motion. Professor Wellman, for the Committee of Five, then moved adoption of that part of Recommendation II which on April 22 had been presented by him to the Senate and which the Senate had authorized him to introduce at its next regular meeting, namely, legislation proposing to establish a Special Committee on Academic Freedom. The motion carried. The Special Committee on Academic Freedom was instructed to consult with the President and with the Committee on Privilege and Tenure on procedures to be followed in the hearings and to assess the implications of the "compromise" as it related to tenure and academic freedom, to the University's reputation in the academic world, and to the effect of it on faculty coming to and leaving the University. The committee was asked to report its findings to the Senate in June and again in September of 1950. Strong's resolution, with one minor amendment, was then referred to the newly created Special Committee on Academic Freedom.

Although the northern section had refused officially to instruct its Committee on Privilege and Tenure in its duties, its action of April 22 and its lengthy discussion of the question on May 1 led some members of the Board of Regents to believe that the hearings were to be conducted in violation of the spirit if not also the letter of the "compromise." Where the new letters of appointment and acceptance had created among the faculty doubt and suspicion of the Regents' ultimate intentions regarding tenure rights, the Senate discussions in Berkeley on April 22 and May 1 had stirred among the Regents a similar sense of hostility and estrangement. How significant in the final analysis these factors were is uncertain. It is probable, however, that the incidents strengthened the resolve of those on the Board and those on the faculty already determined to force the issue to a final test. And when the Senate's southern section in Los Angeles the next day instructed its Committee on Privilege and Tenure to regard those who refused to sign for reasons of conscience and principle as fully protected in their tenure, some members of the Board grew even firmer in their conviction that the Committees on Privilege and Tenure were under obligation to render instructed verdicts.

Antagonism, however, was in many ways less severe between the Board and the Senate than among members of the faculty holding positions of leadership and their non-signing colleagues. The more visible and generally perceived resentment between these two groups may be shown in a letter written by Hildebrand to members of the northern section May 4, 1950, reading in part:

The resolution offered near the end of the meeting of the section on May 1 [Strong resolution] seemed intended to encourage persons not to sign the contract, under promise of protection by the Committee on Privilege and Tenure, which was to be instructed in advance regarding the findings to be expected of it. You should know that this committee can provide no such protection. . . .

A tactic has been advocated of presenting to the Committee on Privilege and Tenure so many cases of non-signers that it could not handle them individually and so the procedure would be broken down, with the expectation that all non-signers would be saved. The result would be quite contrary to any such expectation. . . .

I venture to interpret the position of a large majority of the Senate as believing that the contract form is not unreasonable, and as devoutly desiring to have an end to the turmoil, division and ill-will under which we have so long suffered.

The Senate cannot dictate to the individual conscience, but in a democratic organization, policies adopted by a majority, following proper procedures, must not be obstructed by a minority.[22]

In the south, too, members of the Senate were tugging and pulling and maneuvering for advantage and influence. A letter from Professor J. A. C. Grant (of the Davisson–Grant committee) to Professor Charles Mowat, a non-signer and president of the UCLA chapter of the American Association of University Professors, best suggests the character of the struggle in the southern campuses, particularly in Los Angeles. The AAUP chapter at UCLA met on May 8 and by voice vote without dissent affirmed the national AAUP position that members of the Communist party should not for that reason alone be barred from faculty positions; and the chapter authorized a poll of the UCLA faculty to determine the extent of faculty sympathy for that view.[23] Grant objected to the proposed poll and pointed out that, as a member of the Senate committee commissioned to negotiate with the Board, he had worked to convince the Regents that they should reconsider their policy barring members of the Communist party and restate it in terms of the individual's freedom from commitments that impair objective teaching and the free pursuit of truth. Grant emphasized that it was he who had asserted that the Regents' policy would fail of Senate approval if put to a vote, and "largely as a result of this uncompromising stand taken by the faculty and its appeal to the public press, we were maneuvered into a position making it necessary to vote on this very issue." Grant concluded, "The faculty's record over the past year for inconsistency is already an unenviable one. . . . The previous mail vote in which the great majority of our members cast their ballots in the affirmative either means that we concurred in the Regents' policy, or it meant less than nothing."[24]

V

With members of the Senate pulling in opposite directions regarding the procedures to be following by the Committees on Privilege and Tenure in hearing the petitions of non-signers, faculty interest centered on the composition of committee membership. In the south, no concerted effort was made to alter the 1949–50 membership of the committee as no member had been so personally involved in the controversy as to render his participation in the hearings ex parte, and none was a non-signer. Members of the southern committee included Professors Joseph W. Ellis of physics, chairman, Gordon H. Ball of zoology, Winston W. Crouch of political science, Kenneth Morganson of theater arts, and Homer Stone of chemistry. As the Santa Barbara campus was not a part of the Senate, it had its own Committee on Privilege and Tenure, chaired by Professor A. Russell Buchanan of history. The northern section, however, faced a tactical and substantive problem. Among the membership of its Committee on Privilege and Tenure were included non-signers and men who had been and remained strong adversaries (Chaney and ten Broek, for example). The President and the chairman of the committee, Professor Victor Lenzen of physics, a senior and conservative member of the faculty, believed that the members of the committee should be replaced.[25] Privilege and Tenure, however, was a standing committee of the Senate whose members had been appointed by the Senate's Committee on Committees for the term July 1, 1949, to June 30, 1950. New members, therefore, could be appointed only if the incumbents were persuaded to resign. Most of the incumbents agreed without qualification. The adversaries on the committee agreed, however, only if their successors proved acceptable to them. Prior approval was regarded by some members of the Senate's Committee on Committees to be a constraint insulting to the integrity of the Senate and its committee system, and they refused to cooperate. One member of the Committee on Committees, however, privately "cleared" the new appointees with those on the Privilege and Tenure committee who would otherwise have refused to resign. When word of this "leak" came to the other members of the Committee on Committees it engendered considerable resentment. The decision to appoint the new Committee on Privilege and Tenure, however, was finally affirmed. On May 8 Professor Lenzen reported to Sproul the resignation of the members of the Committee on

Privilege and Tenure effective May 6, and asked that the decision by the Senate to elect a new committee be reported to the Regents as "an act of good faith on the part of the Faculty."[26] The resignations, it was reported to the press, were tendered to allow the committee the advantage of continuing authority beyond June 30, 1950. The appointment of the 1950–51 Committee on Privilege and Tenure to take office early was made public on May 11. Chairman of the new committee was Professor Stuart Daggett of economics. Other members were Francis A. Jenkins, professor of physics; Clark Kerr, professor of industrial relations; Harry B. Walker, professor of agricultural engineering; Percy M. Barr, professor of forestry; and Griffith Evans, professor of mathematics. (Each member of the committee had signed the oath required by the Regents on June 24, 1949, each was in sympathy with the Regents' policy of excluding Communists from the University, and each had voted to support the Regents' policy in the mail ballot of the Senate.)[27] The same day, the appointment of the Special Committee on Academic Freedom was made public. Chairman of the group was Baldwin Woods, Vice-President of the University in charge of University Extension. Serving with Woods were Robert Nisbet, associate professor of sociology; William R. Dennes, professor of philosophy and dean of the Graduate Division; Wendell M. Stanley, director of the Virus Laboratory; and, Dixon Wecter, professor of history.

The northern and southern sections' Committees on Privilege and Tenure met jointly in Berkeley with Sproul on May 13. The committees decided against permitting petitioners to be represented by counsel at hearings, against allowing a court reporter to record the proceedings, and against preparing a formal transcript of the sessions.[28] The committees agreed to seek from each petitioner his reasons for not signing the contract, to determine if such reasons arose from a conscientious objection to the requirement or from disloyalty, and to ascertain whatever affiliation or relationship the petitioner may have had or continued to have with the Communist party. (The whole issue of academic due process was at issue here and California's experience with it anticipated the difficulties that later were to afflict other universities and colleges dealing with members of their staffs refusing to sign oaths, refusing to testify before legislative committees investigating subversion, and so on.) May 15 was the deadline for signing either the oath as specified by the Regents' action of June 24, 1949, or the new contract of employment as worded in the Regents' resolution of April 21. The southern committees had already heard one case (Professor John Caughey) and the northern committee was scheduled to begin hearings May 16. Later, in conference with the President, the chairman of the Special Committee on Academic Freedom agreed with Sproul that a committee of three should be appointed to hear non-Senate academic petitioners, to consist of the vice-chairman of the Senate (1950–51), the dean of the college involved, and the chairman of the department concerned (or in the case of non-academic employees, the director of personnel as substitute for the vice-chairman of the Senate).[29]

VI

As the days passed, concern mounted for the success of the alumni "compromise." As Neylan and some of his associates on the Board thought of it, the hearing procedure was to accommodate conscientious objectors, Quakers, and others whose religious loyalties conflicted with the oath or disclaimer. The non-signers, however, regarded the hearings as a means to avoid signing for whatever reason seemed legitimate to them — except, of course, for membership in the Communist party. It was the non-signers' expectation that a favorable finding by the Senate Committee on Privilege and Tenure would secure the petitioner in his post. The Regents, of course, would be expected to review the findings but not to reverse them. The disagreement over the meaning of the procedural provisions of the "compromise" was merely the more visible evidence of the final point in contention, namely, the *authority* of the faculty and the Regents in the appointment, promotion, and dismissal of faculty members.

Neylan made public his interpretation of the hearing provisions of the "compromise" on May 26, when he advised the Board in open session that as he saw it the plan did not provide that a non-signer of the anti-Communist statement would be retained by the University simply by petitioning the Committee on Privilege and Tenure and it being reported by the committee that the appellant was not a Communist.[30]

As the hearings drew to a close in early June, President Sproul, the northern section's Committee on Privilege and Tenure, the chairman of the southern section's Committee on Privilege and Tenure, and members of the Bechtel committee met to review the tentative results. The conference clearly indicated that the individual members of the Alumni Committee would take a much sterner position toward the non-signers than had the members of the Committee on Privilege and Tenure. The hearing procedures were not criticized severely, but Bechtel and Davies of the Alumni Committee expressed their preference that the proportion of petitioners cleared be much reduced, that is, instead of ninety percent of the non-signers recommended favorably and ten percent not, the percentages should be reversed. The following morning, in a call to Sproul, Bechtel predicted that if the percentage of non-signers recommended favorably remained as high as seemed probable, there would be difficulty with the Regents, the alumni and the public.

VII

The Committees on Privilege and Tenure forwarded their recommendations to the President on June 13. The southern section reported on hearings for twenty-seven petitioners — eighteen regular members of the Senate, three visiting professors, one assistant supervisor in physical education, and five lecturers. The Santa Barbara campus reported hearings on two Senate members, both assistant professors. All petitioners, with the exception of Mrs. Eleanor B. Pasternak, assistant supervisor in physical education on the Los Angeles campus, were considered by the two southern committees as having fulfilled all conditions of employment at the University except the signing of the new contract form. The recommendation was that, because the petitioners' reasons for not signing were based on reasons of conscience and principle, they should be accepted in lieu of signing.[31] The reasons given by Mrs. Pasternak for not signing, however, were not regarded by the committee as fulfilling the requirements of the Regents' policy on communism, and, therefore, were not sufficient to allow the committee to accept them in lieu of signature. The conclusion was tantamount to an unfavorable finding. Every other petitioner, either by reference to previous or current clearance for secret government work, or by promising that he would sign a non-Communist oath if requested by the government as a prior condition of employment, or by stating that he was not a Communist or in sympathy with Communist doctrine, had personally "cleared" himself of suspicion. Mrs. Pasternak, however, had refused to comment in any way on whatever association or sympathy she may or may not have had with communism. Apart from this single consideration, Mrs. Pasternak's reasons for not signing were as legitimate and based on principle and conscience as were those of other petitioners heard, for example, political test, attack on academic freedom, invasion of privacy, guilt by association, thought control, and so forth. The committee, however, regarded her refusal to disavow communism as an overriding disqualification.[32]

Fifty-two persons had appeared before the northern Committee on Privilege and Tenure, of whom three were lecturers and forty-nine were members of the Academic Senate. The committee reported favorably in forty-seven cases because no individual heard was considered to be a member of the Communist party or of any other allegedly subversive organization.[33] The conclusion was reached, the committee said, on the basis of several types of evidence, including security clearances granted a petitioner by military or federal authority, statements to the committee by a petitioner that he was not a Communist or sympathetic to communism, and assurance by a petitioner that his refusal to sign stemmed not from disloyalty but from principle and conscience. The petitioners had refused to sign, the committee reported, for one or more of the following reasons: a resentment that their personal loyalty was being challenged and that the requirement singled the faculty out from other parts of the educational system; a disagreement with the University's policy on communism; a conviction that the requirement constituted a political test for membership in the faculty; an assertion that the oath was ineffectual and intruded on prerogatives traditionally reserved to the academic profession (selection of colleagues); and a fear that the University would be hampered in its efforts to attract young scholars.

In the cases of five petitioners, however, the committee recommended unfavorably, for in each of these instances the individual had "refused to discuss with the Committee either the question as to whether or not he had any connection with the Communist party or his views with respect to this organization."[34] The petitioner had seen no more reason to divulge his beliefs to the committee than to the Regents, and, therefore, the report continued, although no evidence of disloyalty may be asserted in any one of these cases, the committee "cannot recommend continuation of employment" because "the individual has not complied with the conditions of employment established by the Regents on April 21, 1950. . . ."[35] As with Mrs. Pasternak, none of the five (one full professor, two associate professors, and two assistant professors) had stated orally what he had refused to repudiate by signing; and as in the south, the north deemed such refusal or "lack of cooperation" as ground to recommend the petitioner unfavorably to the President.

The Committee on Privilege and Tenure, while not presuming disloyalty on the part of the appellant toward the nation, did require of the petitioner a statement of disloyalty toward communism. This took the form either of a specific statement of fact by the petitioner or of a hypothetical situation, for example, "He said that if the Government, as distinguished from the University, presented him with the oath, or an equivalent contract he would sign it." [36] The committees relied for their appraisal almost wholly on the personal statement of the petitioners, their University records, and the personal and scholarly background of each already known to the University. The committees did not consult extramural sources of information.

Overall, the Committees on Privilege and Tenure found favorably in seventy-five out of a total of eighty-one cases (sixty-four out of sixty-nine cases for regular members of the Academic Senate). The recommendations irritated the majority faction of the Board and some members of the faculty. In the former instance, the nearly 93 percent affirmative findings appeared inordinately excessive and served to qualify the regard in which the Board viewed the hearing reports. In the latter case, the six unfavorable recommendations provoked resentment toward the committees, as it was felt that the individuals not recommended for continuation of employment were as intellectually free and untainted by disloyalty as those recommended favorably.

VIII

Hearings began on June 2 for non-signing non-Senate academic employees and nonacademic employees. Of the eighty-one cases, the hearing committees recommended favorably in fifty-eight instances, unfavorably in seven, made no recommendation in fifteen where the petitioner was in any event not to be reappointed, and reported unfavorably in one case regardless of the fact that the non-signer was not expected to be reappointed. (Approximately half of the non-signing non-Senate academic employees and nonacademic employees never petitioned for a hearing.) The petitioners uniformly had argued that the oath constituted a political test for membership in the faculty. The contention was consistent with the unswerving stance assumed early in the controversy and held continuously throughout by the Non-Senate Academic Employees (NSAE). Those associated with this group, most of whom were graduate students on part-time teaching or research appointments, objected to the oath primarily because they were in unqualified opposition to the policy it implemented. The NSAE looked upon the Senate's Committee on Privilege and Tenure as being little more than a "loyalty review board" and was pointedly contemptuous of the Senate's acquiescence in the alumni "compromise": "The faculty have accepted these controls [terms of employment as specified by the Regents April 21, 1950] as a condition of their own employment. In so doing they have agreed to restrict their effort to seek and to teach truth, in direct contradiction to their social obligations." [37] Interestingly, in spite of their consistency, their intensity of opinion, and their numbers, the Non-Senate Academic Employees counted for little influence in the controversy with either the Senate, the President, or the Regents; and their more recalcitrant members were rather summarily dispatched when the Regents met to consider the reports of the Committees on Privilege and Tenure and the President's recommendations on all non-signers.

IX

The Regents met on June 23 to hear Sproul's recommendations on the non-signers. The President predicted, in a lengthy prefatory statement, that should the recommendations of the Committee on Privilege and Tenure be "flouted" by the Board the result would be tragic and perhaps irreparable. Much of the heart would go out of the enterprise, Sproul declared, and the better men would no longer be attracted and held at the University. "As to the chief administrative officer of the University under such conditions,"

Sproul continued, "I can only say 'God help him.'"[38] The President then recommended:

(1) That 157 nonacademic and non-Senate academic employees be terminated as of June 30, 1950.[39] Named were those who had given notice of their intention to resign and those who had not petitioned for a hearing. Also included were eight who had been recommended unfavorably by the hearing committees, eighteen who had been recommended favorably by the hearing committees to the President but unfavorably by him to the Board, and thirteen whom the hearing committees had referred to the President with no recommendation as the non-signer was not expected to be reappointed in any event.[40]

(2) That six members of the Senate "in the absence of favorable recommendations from the Committees on Privilege and Tenure be regarded after June 30, 1950, as no longer in the employ of the University." (One of the six was Mrs. Pasternak who, although not regarded by the southern Committee on Privilege and Tenure as a regular member of the Senate, was, nevertheless, apparently considered by Sproul to be properly included with the five northern Senate members not favorably recommended.)

(3) That sixty-two members of the Senate reported favorably by the Committees on Privilege and Tenure be confirmed in their appointments.[41]

(4) That eleven non-Senate academic employees and nonacademic employees recommended favorably by the hearing committees be appointed. "*These are all clear cases of membership in religious organizations* [emphasis added]. There are no uncertain ones in my [Sproul's] opinion."[42]

(5) That appointees covered by recommendations (3) and (4), be sent an appointment letter to include the following paragraph:

Consistent with the policy of the Board of Regents of the University, the *conditions of your employment and the consideration of payment of your salary are* [emphasis added] that you are not a member of the Communist Party or any other organization which advocates the overthrow of the government by force or violence and that you have no commitments in conflict with your responsibilities with respect to impartial scholarship and free pursuit of truth.[43]

(6) That the contracts of eighteen non-Senate academic employees and nonacademic employees be allowed to expire June 30, 1950, without action by the Board because of inadequate reports from hearing committees.[44]

(7) That no action be taken on two members of the Senate on leave from whom no replies had been received.

Only the reports of the Committee on Privilege and Tenure had been forwarded to members of the Board in advance of the meeting. The President's recommendations on all non-signers and the reports of the hearings for non-Senate academic and nonacademic employees, however, had not been made known to the Regents until distributed by the secretary of the Regents at the meeting.[45] Consequently, some Regents felt that the Board could "not act intelligently and with wisdom on the recommendation presented to us this afternoon,"[46] and urged a delay to allow further study. No motion to postpone was made, however, and so discussion began. "The main question that does bother us all are the people in category 3 [non-signing members of the Senate favorably recommended by the Committees on Privilege and Tenure and by the President]," said Regent Ehrman. "I know a number of those persons," he continued, and "I am just as convinced as the Academic Senate seems to be . . . that they are not Communists." The difficulty, Ehrman said, is "that there are 62 of them." Suppose, he continued, there are 620 next year who do not wish to sign? *"You let 62 through who are not Communists and you have in a way, in effect, nullified everything that has gone before* [emphasis added]. . . . I am very much troubled by this thing and have been, *but still we cannot forget that we are nothing more or less than representatives of the people of the State of California* [emphasis added] and their voice has been heard in no uncertain

terms on this whole subject. I don't know how much further
we can go than we did at the meeting of April 21." [47]

Regent Neylan then reviewed the history of the controversy and concluded his lengthy remarks by commenting
on the position of the American Association of University
Professors, which, said Neylan, "holds you cannot discriminate against a man because he is a Communist. That is the
policy of the Association and *that is the issue we are facing*
here today and that has been the issue right along — by indi-
rection to overcome the action of the Board [emphasis
added]." Regent Jesse Steinhart answered by observing that
he, Steinhart, was not concerned with all the history of the
controversy, for the purpose of the April 21 resolution was
to remove the past and start anew; and in assessing the meaning and implication of the April 21 resolution, he said that
it was his intention to support the President's recommendation, for it followed the traditional method of handling such
matters. Regent Griffiths agreed. Siding with Neylan was
Regent Jordan, whose support of the April 21 resolution
never "contemplated the President's bringing in the names
of sixty-two non-signers [Senate rank] and recommending
that they be employed." What was contemplated, said Jordan, was "that any man could be heard. That was all we
agreed to and that has been done"; and "that it [alumni
"compromise"] *was for a protection of people with religious
scruples* [emphasis added]." [48] The discussion grew increasingly bitter. Finally, on motion of Regent Edwin Pauley, a
powerful force in the Democratic party nationally and a
prominent Los Angeles oilman and land developer, action
on recommendations 3 (to appoint sixty-two Senate non-
signers) and 4 (to appoint eleven non-signing non-Senate
academic and nonacademic employees) was postponed until
the July meeting of the Board. [49] Next, on motion of Regent
Neylan, recommendation 1 (to dismiss 157 nonacademic
and non-Senate academic employees) *passed unanimously*.
Neylan then moved that recommendation 2 (to dismiss six
Senate non-signers) be considered in July with recommen-

dations 3 and 4. The motion carried. Recommendations 6 (to allow contracts to expire in the cases of eighteen non-Senate academic and nonacademic employees) and 7 (no action on two Senate members on leave) were then approved by the Board, and the meeting adjourned.

X

During the Board meeting, contradictory reference had been made to what Bechtel regarded as a proper interpretation of the "compromise." Whatever in fact was Bechtel's opinion, if consistently held, was consistently misinterpreted by members of the Board on both sides of the issue. As Bechtel's attitude was proving to be increasingly of significant import to the principals striving for influence, some clearer notion of his position was sought. On June 26, Professor Curt Stern, a zoologist and a geneticist of national repute, and a non-signer on the Berkeley campus, wrote Bechtel to urge his intervention. The "compromise," Stern said, surely was not a "desire to trap loyal men who happen to hold a view of their obligation to their students and to the people which diverges from the view held by some others."[50] Rather, as he thought of it, it offered an alternative method of assuring conformity to the University's policy instead of a mere affirmation of the February 24 ultimatum.[51] Bechtel answered Stern two days later. The hearings, Bechtel said, were not meant to be an alternative to signing, but were specified in order to investigate "the reasons for the failure of the individual to sign the contract. These are not the same things."[52] It was clear, at least to the non-signers, that there would be no support from the alumni committee. It was equally clear that the vote on the President's recommendations would be very close and not predictable when the Board met in July. It was also certain that with summer settled on the University, during which no meetings of the Senate could be scheduled, the non-signers were without a forum. To complicate matters further, North

Korea had invaded South Korea on June 25, 1950, and the subsequent involvement of the United States in that conflict was reason enough for some non-signers to sign, thus weakening whatever residual protection remained in numbers.[53] The faculty by this time had generally wearied of the controversy, and as the number of non-signers dwindled so also did the support of the faculty for those remaining who refused to sign. By the end of June conditions were unhappy in the extreme for the non-signers.

At a meeting of non-signers on June 29, Professor Tolman painted a remarkably accurate picture of what those who continued to resist could expect, namely, dismissal, "smears" in the press, difficulty in finding good jobs, and criticism from signing colleagues, some of whom would consider non-signers to be "stiff-necked malcontents."[54] As to his own position, Tolman reported that by not signing he was neither jeopardizing an academic future nor his own security (he was near retirement) and he was able, therefore, to "indulge in the sin of self-righteousness and in the luxury of an untrammeled conscience."[55] For a great many of his non-signing colleagues, however, the personal situation proved more compelling, and in the next few days several chose to sign, including many of the leaders.

Those choosing to see the matter to a close organized the Group for Academic Freedom on July 6, 1950. Thirty-one non-signers affiliated.[56] An executive committee was elected with membership composed of Professors Edward C. Tolman, chairman, Walter D. Fisher, secretary-treasurer, and Professors Emily Huntington, Charles Muscatine, Gian Wick, and Harold Winkler members-at-large. The group formed to provide employment or financial assistance to those dismissed for failure to sign; to assist financially non-Senate academic employees similarly dismissed; to promote understanding of the issues among persons outside the University; to maintain liaison with other groups in the University with similar objectives; and to formulate plans and provide finances for the legal defense of any member of the group whose rights were adversely affected.[57] The group authorized Tolman's son-in-law, Professor T. J. Kent, to seek legal assistance for any member of the group who should be dismissed for not signing.[58] Kent contacted several law firms in the San Francisco Bay area and found the response to be generally negative. On July 13, however, he was able to report to the group that Stanley A. Weigel, San Francisco attorney, of the firm of Landels and Weigel, was willing to take the case or cases and that the executive committee had entered into a tentative agreement with the firm.[59]

XI

As the non-signers organized expecting the worst, members of the Board of Regents were maneuvering for position. Ehrman, on July 5, wrote to Neylan his impression that it would be in the best interests of the Board and the University if the Regents were to accept the President's recommendations. His reasons were fundamentally pragmatic. His argument was that the non-signers were "bitterenders" and anticipated the "martyr's role." The Regents, therefore, ought not to accommodate the non-signers by dismissing and creating for them "public sympathy . . . most of which has now evaporated." To dismiss them, Ehrman continued, would be to place the Regents in the role of "Simon Legrees," while at the same time administering a snub to the faculty as a whole for failing to give any consideration to their committee's recommendations. The Senate appeared to be under the control of the moderates, Ehrman continued, and the Committee on Privilege and Tenure had done a credible job; and in view of these several factors and because "we have won the principle for which we have been contending [non-employment of Communists policy] . . . it may be more important to the welfare of the University to end the strife now."[60] Neylan was unmoved. Like the members of the Group for Academic Freedom, he would press his postion to the end.

The Committee on Academic Freedom, it will be recalled, had been charged by the Senate with responsibility to oversee the hearings and to review the decisions of the Board. By mid-July, it was clear to nearly all concerned that further negotiation was no longer a practical possibility. The battle would be waged on the set of conditions already existing. The committee, therefore, took steps to directly influence pivotal votes on the Board.[61] Colleagues in other universities and colleges across the country friendly to the non-signers or sympathetic to their cause did what they could to bring persuasion and pressure to bear on "unfriendly" Regents.[62] The non-signers also took steps to support the President in his highly precarious position and urged him not to resign if the Regents should vote not to accept his recommendations.[63]

On July 18, Tolman and Professors Donald A. Piatt and Abraham Kaplan (UCLA non-signers) met in Berkeley with Sproul. The President informed the three that the Regents were evenly split except for four doubtful cases of whom three would probably be allied with the Neylan faction of the Board.[64] The unanswerable objection of the Neylan groups, Sproul continued, "was that if the non-signers are not fired, more will refuse to sign the following year, and after that no one will sign." Sproul added that the Korean situation made matters very difficult and that the reduction in numbers of non-signers made less effective his argument that the faculty strongly supported the non-signers. With Sproul's observation that "it's a tough life," the meeting ended.

XII

The July 21 meeting of the Board of Regents was a long and tense affair. The President first reported that because of resignations, signatures, late hearing reports, changes in earlier recommendations, and administrative errors, the 157 non-Senate academic and nonacademic employees had been reduced to 84,[65] and that of the 62 Senate non-signers recommended favorably on June 23, 22 had signed and one had resigned. Sproul pleaded for the Board's support in the recommendations he was about to make and stressed the importance of the fact that the petitioners were not Communists but non-signers and that the objective of the oath had been not to protect the University against loyal men who happened to refuse to sign but rather to protect it against Communists.[66] Sproul asked the Board to: (1) strike 73 names from the list of 157 (non-Senate academic and nonacademic employees) dismissed by the Regents June 23, 1950; (2) dismiss 6 Senate non-signers as of June 30, 1950, "in the absence of favorable recommendation from the Committee on Privilege and Tenure"; and (3) confirm in their positions the remaining 39 non-signing members of the Senate recommended favorably by the Committees on Privilege and Tenure.

Regent Neylan's reaction was immediate. He argued that the times called for aggressive recognition of the Communist threat (Korea), that the April 21 resolution had been construed by Sproul so as to render the Board's intentions wholly ineffective, and that the non-signers not only were mistaken but were also in an adversary relation with their colleagues who had signed. Neylan indicated his intention to support the President's recommendation on the list of 157 persons; to back the President's recommendation to dismiss the 6 Senate members unfavorably reported, although "*I confess in studying those records I can see little difference between those records and the records where the Committee found favorable to the individuals* [emphasis added]"; and to vote against Sproul's proposal to confirm in their posts the 39 Senate members enjoying favorable recommendations.

Five members of the Senate, who had been asked to the meeting to represent their views, were invited to speak by Governor Warren. Professor John Caughey, a non-signing member of the UCLA faculty, spoke first. Caughey asserted that the oath imposed a political test on the faculty and, as administered, infringed on tenure. He stressed the relation between a political test and totalitarianism, and the implications nesessarily inherent in that relationship for minority rights and particularly for a University dedicated to the free pursuit of truth and its full exposition. He affirmed his good faith and that of his fellow non-signers in pursuing what was to them a wholly acceptable alternative to signing (hearings). Finally, he said, to sign now would compromise his initial stand, would appear to be an act of fear, would indicate a loss of confidence in the hearing committee, would abandon the President, and would impugn the good faith of the Board.

Professor Stuart Daggett, chairman of the Committee on Privilege and Tenure, northern section, followed Caughey and stressed the sincere and conscientious effort of his committee to meet fairly and equitably the conditions specified by the Regents' resolution of April 21. He argued that a personal encounter of one to two hours with an individual was in every regard as adequate a means of determining one's fitness as was one's signature to an oath; and that he shared the opinion of his colleagues that if the non-signers presented evidence before the Privilege and Tenure committee which would demonstrate that they were not Communists, then the Board should accept this evidence of loyalty as conclusive. Six of the petitioners, Daggett continued, *"did not cooperate as we thought they should have, and we advised the Regents, through the President, that we could see no reason why their employment should be continued. We did not make the positive assertion that they were Communists, however. That is a difficult thing to say. We said that we did not think we could advise the continuation of their employment because they had not met the terms of the resolution of April 21* [emphasis added]."

Professor Clark Kerr, a member of the northern Committee on Privilege and Tenure, followed Daggett. He asked two questions and made one suggestion. First he asked, "Can the Regents, in good faith, close a channel which they themselves opened [hearing proviso in April 21 resolution for non-signers]?" And secondly, in observing that the non-signers were among the most independent spirits in the University, he asked the Regents if they would, in an attempt to proscribe Communists, be willing to dismiss the non-signers only for their sense of independence. In recognition of the disagreement over the meaning of the Board's April 21 decision and in consideration of the history of the dispute, Kerr suggested that there was a fresh opportunity to explore other methods of ridding the University of any Communists who might be on the faculty. Neylan interjected (emphasis added):

REGENT NEYLAN: Regarding the action of February 24 [Board's vote to require of appointees signature to the June 24 oath and to dismiss those not complying], did you know that was predicated on a notice served on the Regents on January 4th, that not only would the faculty not implement the policy of excluding Communists, but that the majority of the faculty did not approve the policy?

PROFESSOR KERR: I did know. I did not say that I was justifying action taken by the faculty in the past. I think mistakes were made by the faculty and committees of the faculty in the past.

REGENT NEYLAN: *The action on February 24 was predicated on an ultimatum that the majority of the faculty was opposed to the policy.* On March 22 the faculty took it into its own hands and out of the hands of the Academic Senate and voted.

PROFESSOR KERR: That vote created an opportunity for new discussions and new situations which should be explored.

REGENT EHRMAN: I have no intention of speaking at length . . . I want to clarify Professor Kerr's mind on this point. He claims there were two interpretations possible in the contracts. *Now I think the interpretation that has been taken that a man could clear himself through the faculty's channel alone without signing the contract is a very far-fetched interpretation and is not a clear intent of what followed the recommendation of the Alumni Committee.* The Committee never had that in mind. Because inherently the thing is so inconsistent that it destroys the entire plan of the Regents and the faculty that implementation should be by contract and no other method. . . .

PROFESSOR KERR: There may have been a misunderstanding. It is held almost universally by the faculty. As the result of this year and all the great difficulty, we have learned a lot. Our thoughts are clear on the faculty side. *It seems to me that rather than getting rid of 39 people who no one wanted to get rid of a year ago, there must be a new device on which we could agree upon.*

The Governor agreed with Kerr and stressed the importance of recognizing that the substance of the issue was the proscription of Communists, not the form the proscription took. Lieutenant Governor Goodwin Knight urged the very opposite, asserting that the Regents were under no obligation to prove the non-signers Communists. Rather, "they are under an obligation to satisfy the Regents and the President." (Knight, later governor of California for five years, was a Republican but more identified with the conservative element of the party than was Warren. Both were up for reelection in the fall and were rivals for party influence although running for different offices. While Warren was consistently opposed to the oath, Knight was unwaveringly for it and in the late spring, summer, and fall showed no reluctance to make his disagreement with Warren public.) Further discussion added little of substance, and following some rather elaborate parliamentary maneuvering the President's recommendation proposing to confirm the 39 Senate non-signers in their positions carried by a vote of ten to nine.[67] The remaining recommendations on the list of 157 and on the six Senate members unfavorably reported were moved by the President, were seconded, and carried unanimously. Regent Emeritus James K. Moffitt, an observer at the meeting, commented at the close of the voting:

"May I say a word. I am the oldest man in this room, a member of the Class of 1886. I had hoped to have with me today Monseigneur Ramm of the Class of '84 [also a former Regent]. We think alike. I congratulate the Board on the vote which has just been taken. I feel that 90% of the

Alumni, young and old, 90% of them are with the majority of the Board today, and would uphold the decision of the Committee on Privilege and Tenure. Thank you." [68]

As Moffitt sat down, Neylan gave notice that he was changing his vote from no to aye and that at the next meeting of the Board (August 25) he would move for reconsideration of the vote confirming the thirty-nine Senate non-signers in their appointments. (The move for reconsideration had the effect of suspending the Board's action to appoint the non-signers.) The meeting adjourned.

XIII

The chairmen of the several key committees of the Academic Senate, northern section, met the evening of July 21 with members of the committees on Privilege and Tenure and Academic Freedom. The Senate leadership, in view of the closeness of the Regents vote, requested the Committee on Academic Freedom to urge the group of non-signers to avoid any public action or speech that would aggravate the situation. [69] The following morning the Group for Academic Freedom met at its offices in the Shattuck Hotel in downtown Berkeley. There was little reason for jubilation. Their appointments had been confirmed by only a one-vote margin and then suspended pending reconsideration on August 25. No program of aggressive action to improve their margin of support was decided upon. The group felt, however, that an injustice had been done to the six Senate non-signers recommended unfavorably by the Committees on Privilege and Tenure and the President, and dismissed by the Regents. The group determined "to seek remedies for injustices found, but not to attack the committee [Privilege and Tenure] publicly or before the Regents at this time." [70]

Weigel, who had been engaged by the group to serve as counsel for any non-signer dismissed by the Regents on August 25, in collaboration with several prominent and

influential alumni, decided on a series of moves calculated
to ensure the defeat of any motion to reconsider that would
qualify or reverse the July 21 action of the Board. He met
on August 2 with Regent Emeritus James K. Moffitt, Provost
and Vice-President Emeritus Monroe E. Deutsch, Harley C.
Stevens, San Francisco attorney, and Professor Edward Tolman. Professor Malcolm M. Davisson was invited but was
unable to attend. The men agreed to bring the facts of the
case to the attention of individual Regents and to the officers
of the California Alumni Association; to enlist the support of
colleagues who had signed; to investigate the validity of the
move for reconsideration announced by Neylan; to seek
the support of scholars throughout the United States; to
ascertain the attitude of the AAUP chapter at Berkeley; and
to urge the non-signers to make no public statements.[71]

Weigel reported these plans to the members of the Group
for Academic Freedom. He advised the members of the
group to agree, which they did, "that no member will, without first giving notice three days before to the Chairman, take
any independent action along the lines of resigning, signing,
making statements or anything of a character which might
separate him from the Group."[72] Weigel also said that the
chances of winning a legal case were less than one in three,
that to fail would lose the case for academic freedom, that
the issues were not legal but moral, and that the chances
of securing a writ of mandate were very slim.[73]

While the non-signers and those sympathetic to their
cause prepared to persuade and influence, some members
of the Board, whose votes were and would be negative on
the recommendation to retain non-signers, more precisely
and meticulously delineated their stance. Their rationale
was essentially as follows (emphasis added):

Under the procedure set forth, it is within the province of the
Regents, after considering the recommendations of the Committee on Privilege and Tenure, to determine, in the case of a member of the faculty who has refused to sign, whether "the reason

for his failure to do so" is sufficient. Doubtless, inability to sign, as a result of physical incapacity, would be a good reason for allowing the substitution of an oral contract. Doubtless also the absence of the non-signer from the state preventing his signature before May 15, 1950 would be accepted as sufficient reason for deferring the date of his signature. Whether other reasons are sufficient is a matter for the determination of the Regents after considering the findings and recommendations of the Faculty Committee. It has been suggested that, by analogy to the Selective Service Act, a sufficient reason for not signing might exist in the case of a non-signer (to quote the language of the Selective Service Act) "who, by reason of religious training and belief, is conscientiously opposed to" the signature of the statement. This question, however, does not arise in the case of the non-signers who have appeared before the Committee on Privilege and Tenure, because none of them have based their refusal on "religious training and belief." *It would be contrary to the intention of the resolution, which contemplates the signature to the acceptance letter as a condition precedent to employment, to admit as a sufficient reason the mere caprice or preference of the non-signer, on such grounds as that (1) the non-signer disagrees with the Board of Regents as to the most effective method of implementing the policy against Communism, or (2) that the non-signer considers that a condition of hysteria prevails on the subject of Communism and that his signature would add to this hysteria, or (3) that the non-signer would disclose his attitude towards Communism to "the government" (meaning thereby an agency of the federal government) but not to the agency of the state government charged with the administration of the University.* These particular reasons are mentioned because they appear in the reports submitted by the Committees on Privilege and Tenure and are examples of reasons which clearly conflict with the purpose and spirit of the resolution of April 21. . . .

There is not the slightest indication in the resolution of any intention to exonerate an employee from signing merely because he satisfied the Faculty Committee or the Regents that he is not in fact a member of the Communist Party. If he were known to be such a member, the contract would not have been tendered him, he would have had no opportunity to sign and his case would never have come before the Faculty Committee. The apparent intent of the resolution is that *all* employees of the University shall sign the statement, so that the University may be in a position to terminate their employment in the event that the statement proves to be untrue. There is no warrant in terms of the resolution for the assumption that any good employee may refuse to sign for any reason, whether good, bad or indifferent, merely because the Committee on Privilege and Tenure or the Board of Regents finds that he is not a member of the Communist Party.

Furthermore, the resolution recites that the Regents have given consideration to the most effective methods for the implementation of the policy against employment of Communists, and it is apparent that the rule adopted requiring the signature of the statement as a condition precedent to employment is adopted as "the most effective method" for implementation. *It is apparent that if a member of the faculty may refuse to sign for any reason whatever, provided only that he satisfy the Faculty Committee that he is not a member of the Communist Party, it may be expected that in future years fewer and fewer faculty members will sign the statement. Thus the whole scheme of the resolution is likely to be defeated if the interpretation advocated by the Committee is adopted.*[74]

As the adversaries labored, so also did those members of the faculty hoping to prevent a final encounter. Strenuous efforts were made by members of the faculty in the north and in the south to induce the non-signers to sign — quite the opposite of what Weigel and members of the Group for Academic Freedom had hoped for. The principal points of persuasion rested on the nation's involvement in the Korean conflict and on the damage a continued recalcitrance would inflict on the University. Personal calls, letters, and even a general circular titled *A Final Appeal to Non-Signers*[75] were methods employed. The results were meager. The non-signers were committed, as may be demonstrably established in quoting but a sample from the non-signers' responses. Tolman answered Hicks's plea that he sign by saying: "Personally I feel that nobody would have any respect for me if I should sign now, and I certainly would have no respect for myself, and I think the great majority of our Group feels the same way with respect to themselves";[76] and again in a letter to Hicks from Tolman: "I cannot see that for us all to sign now or to resign is in any way going to help the University or foil the Regents. In fact, it seems to me, it would be a complete victory for the Regents and it would mean complete acceptance of the principle that the Regents, not only legally, but also in actual practice, need pay no attention to the recommendations of the President, and the Committee on Privilege and Tenure. Maybe the public doesn't understand what it is all about, but the Regents do."[77]

Similar correspondence was exchanged at Los Angeles. Perhaps the most poignant response to the pressure being exerted on the non-signers was made by an unidentified non-signer in a letter to Hicks, August 10:

. . . the fact that some of us have stood up and have been fired for our principles here may perhaps help prevent similar things from happening at other Universities and it may even in the long run help to recall this University to its own principles at a later date.

Further, I don't worry too much about any of the predicated dire and immediate short-term effects. We non-signers are not kidding ourselves that our loss to the University will injure it in any appreciable degree. If the rest of the University is what I think it is, the rest of you will carry on quite successfully without us.

Professors come and go; Presidents come and go; Regents come and go; but a University of this size and eminence continues on. If times are favorable, this University will continue to be great. If the times are unfavorable, this University like all others in the country will suffer, but not because a few of us sticking to our principles are being fired, but because the world climate and the national climate will no longer make intellectual freedom and university greatness possible.[78]

A final effort to interest the Bechtel committee in preventing reconsideration and in supporting the faculty's interpretation of the "compromise" was made by Hicks on August 3.

In his letter to Bechtel, Hicks argued the same essential points as had repeatedly been made in behalf of the faculty view. Hicks ended his letter with the hope that the Bechtel committee would help.[79] Bechtel's answer was unqualifiedly negative and ended with his personal wish that the non-signers would "make the direct statement 'I am not a member of the Communist Party.'" The statement, Bechtel went on, "would put an end to this time and energy absorbing controversy which is so unessential and unwarranted." To argue over words, he concluded, "when the very existence of our nation is involved, seems untenable to me."[80] Bechtel was joined in his opinion by Milton H. Esberg, Jr., a member of the Bechtel committee.[81] The opposite view, however, was taken by two other members of the Bechtel committee, Mrs. Kathryn Fletcher[82] and Dr. Donald H. McLaughlin (later a Regent appointed by Warren to succeed Giannini).[83] The views of the fifth and final member of the committee, Paul Davies, are not documented, although it may reasonably be supposed from his earlier participation in discussions with the Committee on Privilege and Tenure that he would have shared Bechtel's persuasion. There would be no formal intercession of the Bechtel committee to prevent reconsideration or to corroborate the faculty's interpretation of the "compromise."

Regent Canaday, newest ex officio member of the Board (July 1, 1950, president of the UCLA Alumni Association) sought the opinions of the members of the Alumni Council (Berkeley) who in April of 1950 had endorsed the Bechtel committee's report and forwarded it to the President. Of the fifteen written responses received, opinion was evenly divided, seven to support the President's recommendations, seven to reject the recommendations, and one so qualified that it fit neither category clearly.[84] Canaday's vote was critical. Assuming full attendance on August 25 and voting consistency on the part of the Regents, the predictable action of the Board would be to reconsider and reverse its July 21 decision by a vote of thirteen to eleven.[85] If Canaday, whose vote on July 21 was to dismiss, but who was believed to be flexible, could be persuaded to the faculty's view, the motion on August 25 to reconsider would fail because under the Board's rules of procedure an even vote — it would be twelve to twelve if Canaday voted no on the motion to reconsider — would prove insufficient to reconsider, and the July 21 action of the Board would, as a result, be confirmed. Moreover, Canaday's alternate on the Board (non-voting member 1950–51), Maynard Toll, president of the California Alumni Association (Berkeley) would have voted on July 21 to accept Sproul's recommendations and on August 25 would have voted not to reconsider.[86] The uncertainty of Canaday's personal commitment, the divided opinion of the Alumni Council, and the attitude expressed by Toll, were all considered to be mitigating factors in the Canaday vote, and strenuous efforts were made to influence him to vote against the motion to reconsider.[87]

The Committee on Academic Freedom met for a lengthy discussion of the controversy on August 17. The consensus was that faculty sentiment since the Korean situation developed had shifted strongly to support of the Regents' position (O'Brien, vice-chairman of the Senate's northern section, believed that three-fourths of the faculty were definitely opposed to the stand of the non-signers), and that the faculty campaign was lost and the support of the public and alumni as well.[88] Professor Woods, chairman of the Academic Freedom committee, further elaborated on the points discussed by his committee in a memorandum to Sproul on August 21:

a. The great majority of the faculty are weary of the discussion. They are unwilling to continue it and believe only harm can result from a continuance. Apathy, fear, insecurity — all play a part.

b. The faculty is generally critical of the Regents and their procedure in this matter, but I believe they will do nothing about it. It does not appear that a sufficient number of signatures [faculty] can be had to the letter discussed in the conference with you to make the return significant. [The letter in question was prepared for general circulation among the faculty August 9, 1950. It was addressed to the President and urged strong regental support for the President's recommendations.] O'Brien questions greatly the wisdom of the effort to get signatures. Some people have signed and then asked that their names be taken off. [The letter continued to circulate, however, and was released to the press August 22 over the signatures of 165 faculty members.]

c. I believe that anxiety concerning the possibility of disaster to you is the most general feeling which motivates faculty members at present. On the other hand, there is no spontaneous movement to give you general support. This is also, I believe, attributed to weariness and confusion.[89]

The evening of August 21, 1950, nineteen members of the Group for Academic Freedom heard Weigel give a rather discouraging report of what was most likely to occur when the Regents met four days later. He advised the group that there was little chance that the non-signers would have an opportunity to sign if dismissed, and that the decision to sign or not to sign should be made that evening. On a ballot of those present, twelve indicated that they would not sign, two said they would sign, and five remained undecided, of whom two were not expected to sign.[90] The group was divided into those who admitted defeat and would sign, those who would resign, and those who would see the issue to its conclusion.[91] Tolman estimated that somewhere between twenty and twenty-five of the thirty-nine non-signers remaining would neither sign or resign.[92] Professor Charles Muscatine, then acting secretary-treasurer of the group, was asked to gather from each member of the group information relative to his personal finances, to his interest in seeking employment elsewhere, and to his teaching responsibilities for the fall. The non-signers were preparing for dismissal.

XIV

The Regents met in Berkeley on August 25. Only Regents Giannini and Nimitz were absent. California's newspapers had paid relatively slight attention to the controversy during August. The three days immediately preceding the Regents' meeting, however, saw considerable space devoted to the dispute in the expectation that the August meeting of the Board would finally conclude the battle. The Hearst press, in editorials colorfully written but off the point, urged the Regents to dismiss the non-signers. Under the headline "No Room For Compromise," for example, the *Los Angeles Examiner* asserted editorially the day before the Board meeting that "The real question is whether educators, under the cloak of academic freedom, shall be free to poison the minds of American youth with the fallacious doctrines of a foreign despotism."[93]

While editorials of this ilk added more heat than light to a fast darkening scene, the Korean War promised to extinguish whatever hope the non-signers continued to glimpse. The war was going badly for the United States in August of 1950. The Pusan perimeter in Korea's far south was in no wise secure and there remained a very real possibility that the nation stood to suffer a stunning defeat should the United States Army continue to be pushed out of position by the Communist armies from the north. While the country's undermanned and ill-equipped forces were fighting for their lives with their backs literally to the sea, there would be at home little allowance for suspected disloyalty, little sympathy for unpopular views or dissent. And it was against this foreboding background that the governing board of the University of California met.

The motion to reconsider was made by Neylan and challenged on a point of order by Regent Hansen. The attorney for the Regents, Jno. U. Calkins, Jr., was asked by Warren for his opinion on the admissibility of the motion. Calkins advised the Board that the motion divided into two parts: procedure and legality. On procedure, Calkins considered the motion to be in order, as prompt notice of reconsideration had been given by one voting with the prevailing side (Neylan had changed his vote from no to aye July 21 prior

to giving notice) and written notices had been filed with
the secretary in accordance with the by-laws and standing
orders of the Board. On the second point, legality, Calkins
apprised the Board that its authority was both executive and
legislative. Because the July 21 action of the Board to appoint was executive, his opinion was that it was not subject
to reconsideration. Extended discussion ensued during which
Neylan and his associates sought to esablish that the executive action in question was subject to reconsideration, while
the Governor and his allies argued that reconsideration of an
executive act was illegal. The disagreement in part bore on
the public character of the appointments in question, and
the legal cases cited by the Governor, the attorney for the
Regents, and Regent Steinhart drew heavily on this distinction, as the following example will suggest (emphasis added):

REGENT EHRMAN: *I still maintain that the Baker case* [McAllis-
ter vs. Baker, 139 CAL. app.] *and every case it cites refers to
people entitled to public office and makes no reference to people
who are employed. If this doctrine of the Baker case applied to
the University, does it mean that a man who was employed as a
gardener — would have a vested right to the office? I cannot see
where a man employed in one capacity, such as we have illus-
trated, or is employed as a professor or an instructor, has any
distinction* [legal] *between them.* There is no legal authority and
I deduce after hearing the case that warrants a ruling that there
is any vested right to the appointment by reason of the resolution
that was adopted at the last meeting of the Board.
GOVERNOR WARREN: *Regent Ehrman, as far as I am concerned,
I am of the opinion that whether these people are public officers
or whether they are executing a public trust is a distinction without a difference.* We recognize that these people are performing
an important function. That is the reason we are having this discussion here today. The importance of appointment of a president of the University, or a vice-president, or a dean or the head
of a department, or a professor, or an instructor, seems to me is of
equal importance to the public as the appointment or election
of any other public officer and I don't believe we have the right
to consider here that these people don't rise to the dignity of a

city councilman or a constable, or to public officers coming under this rule. *They are performing a public function as much as I am as Governor of this State. I believe their rights and their preroga- tives before this Board should be treated with equal solemnity and consideration.*[94]

The Governor, as president of the Board of Regents and as its presiding officer, concluded that as to procedure Ney- lan had taken the necessary steps to bring his motion before the Board, but that the substance of the motion was not subject to reconsideration as it contemplated the review of an executive action. Warren ruled the motion to reconsider out of order. Neylan appealed the ruling of the chair, and on a second from Regent Jordan the Board voted twelve to ten to overrule Warren. The motion to reconsider was put to a vote and by the same majority passed. The way had been cleared to vote again on the President's recommendation that Senate non-signers who were reported favorably by the Com- mittee on Privilege and Tenure be confirmed in their posi- tions. (The President reported that of the thirty-nine non- signers in question five had signed and three had resigned since July 21. The motion to be reconsidered, therefore, excluded these eight.)

As the antagonists continued to argue the implications of the question before them, the fundamental issue underly- ing the dispute emerged, namely, the locus of governing authority in the University. Regent Arthur McFadden, presi- dent of the State Board of Agriculture, was the first to pay it explicit attention: "The question has become, should any discipline whatever be enforced in the University, on its employees, or shall each be allowed to settle his own stand- ard of employment. . . . I don't want to lose scholars from the Academic ranks, but much greater harm would result [to the University] from giving in to discipline rather than individual losses."[95] Regent Haggerty, in expressing total dismay, commented on McFadden's assessment:

Now I learn we aren't discussing Communism. The issue now, as I see it, we are talking about a matter of discipline of the professors who refused to sign the oath and employment contract as submitted. There is no longer an impugning of those individuals as Communists. *It is now a matter of demanding obedience to the law of the Regents* [emphasis added]. . . . My position is still the same as in the past [for retention].

REGENT HELLER: Is it understood by all the Regents that no accusation of Communism is made against any member of the faculty on the list of 32 [meant 31]?

GOVERNOR WARREN: Regent Heller wants to know if there was any accusation that any of these people were Communists or committed to its principle. He says that if that was not an issue here, he would not pursue the reading of the Committee's reports [Heller had read earlier from one of the reports of hearings of the Northern Committee on Privilege and Tenure].

REGENT MCFADDEN: No Regent has ever accused a member of the faculty of being a Communist.

Regent Canaday then apprised the Board of conversations he had had with members of the Bechtel committee, the majority of whose members, Canaday reported, would not consider the Board to be acting in bad faith if it chose not to accept the recommendations of the Committee on Privilege and Tenure. Canaday's personal view was that the April 21 resolution in no way instructed the Committee on Privilege and Tenure to determine if the non-signers were Communists. "I don't think anybody could arrive at an intelligent decision on that score by a mere hearing." [96] He would vote to dismiss. Regent Ahlport then moved the question. On a second by Canaday, the roll was called, and by a twelve to ten majority the President's recommendation was defeated.[97] The thirty-one were dismissed. (See Appendix E for a list of non-signers dismissed and sample biographical data.) The Board adjourned upon granting all non-signers of Senate rank the right to sign without penalty within ten days and after authorizing severance pay equal to one academic year — or to whatever earlier date other academic employment were secured — to all non-signers of Senate rank who within ten days filed a resignation with the secretary.

XV

On March 25, 1949, the Board of Regents had unanimously enacted an amendment to an already existing oath of allegiance for the purpose of more precisely implementing a policy of nine years' standing that automatically barred members of the Communist party from employment in the University. Seventeen months later the Regents had acted to dismiss thirty-one members of the faculty no one of whom was accused by any member of the Board of tendencies or affiliations in contravention of that policy. The oath had given way in the fall of 1949 to the policy it implemented as the principal point in contention between the faculty and the Regents. In the spring of 1950, in like manner, the policy had given way to the final issue in dispute, namely, the authority of the faculty and the Regents in the appointment, promotion, and dismissal of members of the faculty. By August of 1950, each adversary had given but one choice to the other. On one side, the non-signers, rather than sign and violate their concepts of academic freedom, tenure, and faculty self-government (mostly as expressed in the ten Broek resolution), chose not to sign. On the other side, a majority of the Board of Regents, rather than accept the authority of the Senate Committee on Privilege and Tenure in lieu of their own in the selection and retention of faculty members, voted to dismiss. The courts were to act as final arbiter and judge.

Chapter Seven

The Final Irony

I

Members of the Group for Academic Freedom still in Berkeley met briefly on the evening of August 25. Each had ten days either to sign, resign, or be terminated. Members of the group that night, as an expression of the respect and high regard in which he was held, awarded to Professor Tolman the degree "Doctor of Academic Freedom."[1] As a degree at graduation marks both a conclusion and a commencement, so too did this symbolic gesture signify an end and a beginning. The controversy was to move, and soon, from the campus to the courts.

II

The executive committee of the Group for Academic Freedom met Sunday morning, August 28, with Stanley Weigel, San Francisco attorney, who earlier had agreed to represent any non-signer wishing to seek reinstatement by legal action. Weigel said that the Regents' action on August 25 had measurably improved the non-signers' chances for legal redress, as the Board had admitted that communism was not an issue, the attorney for the Regents had held opinion contrary to the majority view of the Board, and the Governor of the State, the President of the University, and Admiral Nimitz and eight other Regents had voted to appoint the non-signers to their teaching posts. Weigel proposed, therefore, to file either in the District Court of Appeal or in the Supreme Court a writ of mandate (a proceeding in this case asking the court to compel the officers of the Board to issue appointments to the non-signers) and an alternative writ of mandate (a proceeding which would direct the secretary of the Board of Regents to take no further action against the non-signers until the final decision of the court). Failing court issuance of an alternative writ of mandate, Weigel proposed to seek an order to show cause, which would force the secretary of the Regents to show why appointments made July 21 should not be confirmed. As part of the order, the court would be asked to instruct the Regents not to terminate any non-signer until a decision was rendered. The executive committee agreed to take legal action and to engage Weigel.[2] The group approved this action two days later. On August 31, 1950, in behalf of twenty non-signers, Weigel filed a petition with the District Court of Appeal, Third Appellate District;[3] the day after, the court issued an order to show cause, the effect of which was to place on the Regents the necessity of legally substantiating its resolution of August 25, and to forbid the Regents meanwhile to implement that resolution.

III

The court's action was reported by Weigel that evening to members of the group and to fifty-six "sympathetic signers" — colleagues invited by the non-signers to learn of the group's decision to undertake legal action. Following a brief resumé by Tolman of the situation then existing, discussion turned to ways and means of aiding the non-signers financially. Several proposals were advanced but none commanded a clear consensus. Consequently, a second meeting of the group and "sympathetic signers" was scheduled for September 15.

While the northern faculty was yet formulating its plans, the southern had already moved with a program of its own to assist financially those of its number who had been adversely affected by the Board's decision of August 25. An executive committee of nine members of the faculty undertook to organize the Committee for Responsible University Government (CRUG) for the principal and immediate purpose of underwriting the salaries of those dismissed and to help defray expenses of litigation should the need later arise and appear appropriate to the majority of donors.[4] The committee's name was chosen to emphasize that the only issue was that of faculty privilege and tenure in the University — of responsible University government.[5] On September 7, CRUG's executive committee, by a general circular letter to the UCLA faculty, invited colleagues to give or pledge up to 2 percent of their academic salaries to assist the non-signers.[6] By the end of two weeks one hundred and thirteen donors had pledged $9,000.[7] The success of the southern effort (which was expected to be less than any corresponding northern undertaking) gave encouragement to those in the north who were responsible for the financial security of their non-signers.[8]

IV

The Senate Committee on Academic Freedom, meanwhile, had requested all department chairmen in the Senate's northern section to report the name of any departmental member who, since July 1, 1949, had resigned his post because of the oath controversy, and the name of any person approached by the department for appointment, who, because of the controversy, had been unwilling to accept.[9] Of the replies received, ninety-eight departments indicated no resignations and ninety-five no unwillingness of persons to accept appointment because of the controversy. (There are no data showing the number of offers made either by department or for the University as a whole.) Nine departments reported a total of eleven resignations, and eight reported a total of eleven cases of unwillingness of appointees to come because of the oath. The Committee on Academic

Freedom also received from the faculties of other universities and colleges and from the Boards and memberships
of several learned and scholarly societies a substantial number of letters and resolutions criticizing the Regents' action
and supporting the principles of academic freedom and tenure.[10] The committee continued to assess the damage and
to prepare a full report for submission to the Senate later
in the year.

V

Eight members of the Senate friendly to the non-
signers called a special meeting of the Senate's northern
section for September 19 in order to arrange financial support for the non-signers, to ensure that the non-signers remained as members of the Senate, and to denounce the Regents for violating tenure rights in the University. Nearly
all those in the Senate holding key committee positions opposed the call for the special meeting, and on September 5,
Professor O'Brien, vice-chairman of the Academic Senate,
northern section, wrote to the eight who had requested the
meeting and asked that their notice be withdrawn.[11] When
the eight refused, the Coordinating Committee of the Senate's northern section (chairmen of the Senate's key committees) met on September 11 and decided to ask the eight
to postpone the meeting for one week. The request was made
as the President was unable to attend a September 19 meeting;[12] the general character of the call was considered by
many to be inflammatory; and the matters proposed for discussion should, in any event, await the reports of the committees on Privilege and Tenure and on Academic Freedom,
neither of which would be prepared to report until September 26.[13] In subsequent conversation, and upon receiving
assurances that the resolution on financial support for non-
signers would be included in the call for a September 26
meeting, that the secretary would continue to include non-
signers in the invitations to Senate meetings, and that the

report of the Committee on Privilege and Tenure would meet substantially the same objectives sought in the resolution on tenure already proposed, the eight agreed to the postponement.[14]

Sproul lunched on September 13 with the Committee on Privilege and Tenure, representatives of the Committee on Academic Freedom, and the vice-chairman of the northern section of the Senate. The Board's action, Sproul reported, "represents the unchangeable will of the present Board. There is no hope that it will be reconsidered or reversed as long as the Board is constituted as it now is." To denounce the Regents as some now propose to do, continued Sproul, would accomplish no good purpose. Rather, he argued, it would only "further divide Regents and faculty and make infinitely more difficult the task to which the Senate should now devote itself, namely, securing a definite and satisfactory statement of the meaning of 'tenure' in the University of California."[15] The reports of the committees on Privilege and Tenure and on Academic Freedom, therefore, Sproul concluded, should be worded moderately and should seek to encourage the Board to amplify and clarify existing regental regulations and standing orders dealing with tenure. The President's suggestions were accepted.[16]

The next morning Sproul wrote to department chairmen advising them that non-signers could neither teach nor perform any other duties of the position to which they were offered appointment. The prohibition, ordered four days prior to the start of the fall semester, forced the cancellation of fifty-five courses.[17] Of the thirty-one non-signers unsuccessfully recommended for appointment by the President, and of the five remaining non-signers not recommended, three by this time had resigned, six had signed, two traveling abroad had promised to sign upon their return, and twenty-five had not signed (of the twenty-five, eighteen were petitioners in *Tolman* v. *Underhill* — two of the original twenty petitioners having signed — and seven were not involved in litigation).[18]

That evening members of the Group for Academic Freedom met in their headquarters at the Shattuck Hotel in Berkeley to draft a resolution of no confidence in the Regents, which the group wanted brought before the Senate on September 26. The group decided to invite Monroe Deutsch to move its adoption. The following evening the group and "sympathetic signers" met for the second time and unanimously endorsed a plan for financial assistance to non-signers. As at UCLA, the objective was to secure contributions equal to 2 percent of gross salary from all members of the Academic Senate's northern section. These funds in turn were to be consigned to a Faculty Committee on Financial Assistance which would have the responsibility to disburse monies to non-signers of Senate rank and to coordinate its efforts with the other campuses of the University, with alumni and friends, and with colleagues in other universities wishing to contribute.[19] As the plan included no provision for the non-signing, non-Senate academic employees, a three-member committee was appointed to consider that question. Also, a five-member committee was appointed to prepare resolutions for Senate action September 26 stressing the critical importance of the principle of tenure.

VI

The Berkeley chapter of the AAUP met on September 18 and adopted a resolution directing its secretary to request the national office to investigate the University of California "with respect to faculty tenure and status."[20] To supplement the Berkeley chapter's resolution, Tolman wrote a personal letter to Dr. Ralph Himstead, general secretary of the AAUP, and affirmed the non-signers' interest in an investigation.[21] Professor Ludwig Edelstein, a non-signer, flew to Washington, D.C., for the express purpose of emphasizing the urgency and immediate necessity of investigation. Shortly thereafter, Himstead authorized an investigation of the University's administration. The association's Committee

A, Academic Freedom and Tenure, appointed Professors Quincy Wright of the University of Chicago, and R. F. Aaragon of Reed College as investigators. Their study began in the spring of 1951 and was completed in the fall. The Report of Investigation was sent to the AAUP in December of 1951. The long-expected censure of the University's administration did not materialize, however, until more than four years later when on April 7, 1956, delegates to the annual meeting in St. Louis, on recommendation of a special committee, voted to censure the administration of the University of California: "The net effect of the action of the Administration [University of California] has been to weaken academic freedom and to deny essential rights to the faculty members who resisted." [22] The meeting at which censure was voted was angry and unpleasant. One of the delegates to the session from the University of California was George R. Stewart, professor of English, and one highly sympathetic to the nonsigners, who regarded the censure as so offensive an action at that late date that he walked out of the meeting, and was reported by the *New York Times* as saying: "I shall return to the University of California where I shall inform my colleagues that the action you [AAUP] have taken is tyrannous. I shall also tell them that they should wear their censure proudly as a badge of torture given by a tyrant." [23]

As far as the faculty of the University of California was concerned, the AAUP had not voted to censure when the action would have helped (1950–1952) but had censured when it hindered the rapprochement between the faculty and the Regents. Censure was lifted in 1958; and in 1964 the association's seventh annual Alexander Meiklejohn award was made to Clark Kerr, President of the University since 1958, and to the Board of Regents for contributions to the cause of academic freedom.

The author has been unable to determine the reasons for the AAUP's dilatory handling of the California censure. Opinion is widely held in the University that the organization's central staff in Washington at the time was unable or unwilling to move aggressively. The delay was regarded by many of the non-signers and other members of the faculty as an inexcusable affront to the University of California and a betrayal of the principles undergirding the AAUP. The incident left a residue of ill feeling in the University toward the AAUP which only in recent years seems to have waned.

VII

During the last week of September, both sections of the Senate met to consider the reports of the committees on Privilege and Tenure and on Academic Freedom. The southern committee, while regretting the impact of the Regents' action on the status of tenure in the University, did not expressly deplore or censure the Board.[24] Consequently, a resolution was introduced from the floor more harsh in its criticism and more explicit in its condemnation of the Board's vote to dismiss the non-signers.[25] The section, while accepting the report of the Committee on Privilege and Tenure without qualification, voted also to pass the resolution of censure. With that action, the southern section retired from battle. No further formal cognizance of the oath or its effects would be taken in the south except as noted from time to time in committee reports.

The meeting of the northern section of the Academic Senate the following afternoon in Berkeley was bitter and long. Some seven hundred voting members were present. Professor Stuart Daggett, chairman of the Committee on Privilege and Tenure, moved that the report of his committee be referred to all members of the northern section for approval or disapproval by letter ballot.[26] The committee's report to the Senate was temperate in tone as was the corresponding report of its counterpart in the south the previous day. The ten-page document recorded rather fully the work of the committee in hearing the cases of the non-signers and the interpretation given by the Regents to the alumni "compromise." The committee expressed regret that the Board of Regents had not accepted its findings and recommendations and had not considered individual cases.[27] On the matter of tenure, the committee reported its view that security of employment at the University had not been permanently destroyed, and that, upon the general principle, agreement with the Regents could be reached.[28]

Professor Lawrence Harper (earlier noted as friendly to the non-signers) then moved to amend Daggett's motion by proposing that the report of the Committee on Privilege and Tenure be received and filed.[29] The Harper amendment reflected the disenchantment of the non-signers both with the Committee on Privilege and Tenure and with its report. The non-signers and their sympathizers believed that the committee had been grossly unfair to the five Senate non-signers recommended unfavorably by the committee to the President, and considered the committee's report far too mild in its criticism of the Regents and timid in its defense of tenure and academic freedom. The Harper amendment sought to prevent the report from being voted on by mail ballot, presumably for fear that it might be accepted, by persuading members of the Senate attending the meeting to file the committee's report without comment. The non-signers and others friendly to them were successful when, following extended debate, the Harper amendment carried. (It should be remembered that the northern section encompassed not only the campus at Berkeley, but also the campuses at San Francisco, Mt. Hamilton, and Davis. The Senate meetings were traditionally held in the late afternoon during the regular workweek. It was difficult, therefore, for members of the Senate at the campuses some distance from Berkeley to arrange to attend regularly. Members of the faculty at these outlying campuses were not generally opposed to the oath; on the contrary, they regarded the non-signers unfavorably and their action inimical to the welfare of the University as a whole. The non-signers and those sympathetic to their cause, therefore, strove throughout the controversy to transact the Senate's business in Berkeley and not by mail ballot.)

Vice-President and Provost Emeritus Monroe E. Deutsch next moved Senate acceptance of a resolution censuring those Regents who had voted to dismiss.[30] In the course of the ensuing two and a half hours of debate, Professor Baldwin Woods, chairman of the Committee for Academic Freedom, offered a substitute motion that sections B, C, D, and E of the report of his committee (earlier circulated to the membership) be referred to members of the northern section for vote by mail ballot, the relevant portions reading as follows:

B. The Academic Senate, Northern Section, supports and approves the action and recommendations of the President with respect to non-signers of the form of contract [this included endorsement of the five unfavorable recommendations].

C. The Academic Senate, Northern Section, wishes to express its deep appreciation to those Regents who held steadfastly to a course of action which the Senate regards as just and reasonable. The Senate wishes to express its appreciation to loyal Alumni and other friends of the University.

D. The Academic Senate, Northern Section, disapproves the action of the Regents in dismissing loyal and competent members of the faculty. This action stands in marked contrast to the record of the Regents over the years, during which they, as Trustees of the University, have fostered the conditions under which the University has flourished so magnificently.

E. The Academic Senate, Northern Section, petitions the Regents to appoint a committee to confer with the President and with a similar committee to be named by the Academic Senate on basic principles of academic freedom and tenure.[31]

The Woods motion was seconded, but immediately thereafter was tabled by a vote of 271 to 205. The section then adopted Deutsch's resolution, the entire text of which read:

RESOLVED: That to each of the Regents who voted to maintain good faith in the relations of the Board of Regents to the faculty, namely, Governor Earl Warren, President Robert Gordon Sproul, Fleet Admiral Chester W. Nimitz, Victor R. Hansen, Edward H.

Heller, C. J. Haggerty, Farnham P. Griffiths, Jesse H. Steinhart, Earl J. Fenston, Superintendent [of Public Instruction] Roy Simpson and William G. Merchant, the President be requested to send the following vote of thanks:

> The Academic Senate, Northern Section, desires to express to you its heartfelt thanks for your steadfast support of honesty and integrity in the Board of Regents and your defense of those elemental principles that alone make a true university possible in a free land.

BE IT FURTHER RESOLVED: That inasmuch as the majority of the Regents has grossly violated its own resolution of April 21 and has moveover arbitrarily dismissed members of the faculty, despite the fact that not one of them is charged with being a Communist, and said majority has broken faith with the Senate and has furthermore revoked reappointments lawfully made by the Board and has above all violated the principle of tenure, an absolutely essential condition in a free university;
THEREFORE BE IT RESOLVED: That the Northern Section of the Academic Senate condemns such acts on the part of the bare majority of the Board.[32]

The day's final resolution was submitted by Professors Bronson, Fontenrose, Landauer, Morrey, and Stanier — the five-member committee appointed jointly by the Group for Academic Freedom and the "sympathetic signers" on the evening of September 15. The resolution instructed the Committee on Privilege and Tenure to reconsider its negative recommendation to the President concerning the five nonsigners, and, in the absence of membership in the Communist party, to reverse its unfavorable findings.[33] The Bronson resolution — as it came to be known — was debated at length. During the discussion a move to adjourn was put and seconded but failed by a vote of 250 to 170. Shortly thereafter, the Bronson resolution carried. Professor Richard Jennings of the law school (having given notice of his intention to do so prior to the vote on the Bronson motion) asked that the Senate reconsider the Bronson resolution at its next meeting. Under Senate rules, the reconsideration notice had the effect of nullifying the action just taken. The minutes of the meeting record: "Before the full import of the motion [Jennings] and the parliamentary procedure that it involved could be made clear to the members present, a motion to adjourn was made and duly voted."[34]

The meeting of September 26 was the longest of any held by the Senate during the oath controversy, lasting for four full hours. It had not been a happy one even for the non-signers and colleagues sympathetic to their cause, although their resolutions had carried the day. Considerable resentment was engendered because of the way reports that were moved by their authors for Senate action by mail ballot were instead considered, received, and filed by the majority of those voting at the Senate meeting; and by the introduction of the Deutsch resolution which had not been previously circulated as required by Senate rules. Evidence of this irritation was to be found in the threat of the Committee on Privilege and Tenure to resign, in the criticism by several Senate members on the Davis campus who considered the vote against a mail ballot particularly prejudicial to members of the northern section not living in Berkeley,[35] and in the preparation of a five-page document by Professor Hildebrand titled "A Criticism of Procedures in the Academic Senate, Northern Section." This latter document was widely publicized. Said Hildebrand:

1. The Senate By-Laws provide that new legislation for Senate consideration must be circulated with the call for the meeting. This rule was "not observed at the special meeting of September 26, 1950, where the Deutsch resolution, more serious in its possible effects than any recent piece of formal legislation, was presented without notice, and even without written copies to permit scrutiny of its wording."

2. The Senate should submit matters of general concern to mail ballot when a substantial number of members request it. On September 26, 1950, on a crucial vote (Woods reso-

lution), the Senate by a majority of 271 to 205 received and filed a report which had been requested by the reporting committee (Academic Freedom) to be referred to the Senate for action by mail ballot. "The Regents were roundly criticized for acting as a 'bare majority'; evidently a bare majority is all right for the faculty but not for the Regents." A similar incident occurred on November 7, 1949, when a "resolution lecturing the Regents on their duties was voted down early in the meeting [ten Broek resolution]," and reintroduced in amended form later after a large number of the Senate had gone, and "its passage [was secured] by a vote which, of course, represented but a small minority of the Section. This resolution was insulting to all Regents . . . and it hung like a millstone around the neck of the Conference Committee [Davisson–Grant] at its meeting with the corresponding committee of the Regents on January 4, 1950. The Conference in September [September 29, 1949] had left a bright ray of hope, but that resolution extinguished it. *No single item contributed more to bring about the situation we now face* [emphasis added]."

The Senate must be willing to depend upon its committees if it is to act wisely. On September 26 reports of two major committees were "brushed aside with scant consideration . . ." and the Senate voted to censure the Regents "for rejecting the recommendations of our Committee on Privilege and Tenure while itself acting contrary to the recommendations of that very committee and of the Committee on Academic Freedom." The effect of such disregard is "*to demonstrate to the Regents that no committee of the Senate is trusted by this body and hence need not be taken too seriously by the Regents* [emphasis added]."

3. The Senate cannot serve as a deliberative body "unless members strive to come to meetings with open minds, ready to be influenced by argument; this is not the case if any considerable number organize apart from the Senate to impose by the aid of parliamentary maneuver, prolonged ap-

plause, cynical laughter, and even hissing, a prepared program to which they have pledged themselves."

4. The University has suffered grievous damage because of the oath controversy. "The Board of Regents is responsible for some of this damage, but the Senate itself has done a certain share of it by furnishing the very ammunition which has been used against us." The Senate must not prove "incompetent to carry on the essential academic government of the University . . ." or some other body will be substituted.

And, among the non-signers and their associates was to be found resentment also, but it was directed against those members of the faculty who continued to seek further negotiations with the Regents. "There is still much to be feared from the moral lassitude of some members of the Senate," wrote Professor Brewster Rogerson, secretary of the Group for Academic Freedom to Professor R. H. Bainton of Yale, "who advise a meek tolerance of our situation in the hope of further negotiations. . . ."[36]

VIII

The second meeting within two weeks of the Senate's northern section took place on October 9 with some four hundred and fifty members present. Professor Bronson moved and the Senate adopted as a substitute for his resolution of September 26 (voted but nullified by the move to reconsider) one inviting the Committee on Privilege and Tenure "to make further review of the cases of the five persons whom the Committee was unable to recommend favorably in its report to the President of June 16, 1950 . . . [so that they] may be fully cleared of all imputation of disloyalty and honorably restored to the enjoyment of their respective positions."[37]

Acting on these instructions the northern Committee on Privilege and Tenure reviewed its earlier five unfavorable recommendations and wrote Sproul asking that the five be reinstated.[38] The report did not make clear why the earlier unfavorable recommendations were being reversed other than to mention the Bronson resolution. Presumably, the committee felt that if the Regents did not regard the hearing procedure for non-signers to be a legitimate and honorable alternative to signing, then failure on the part of the five to cooperate in an essentially futile and meaningless procedure could hardly remain a sufficient cause to disbarment, particularly as no distinction between the five and the forty-seven favorably recommended was either made or asserted to exist with regard to individual loyalty and scholarly competence.

Although the letter was important substantively to the parties affected and to the long-range reestablishment of harmony among the faculty, the depth of disagreement and animosity extant among the members of the faculty of the University of California was perhaps greater in the fall of 1950 than at any other time during the previous eighteen months. Certainly, the sense of antagonism and aggravation among the more committed elements was manifestly as severe among the members of the faculty as among the members of the critically divided Board of Regents.

IX

On September 21, 1950 — the opening day of a special session of the California legislature — Governor Earl Warren called for that law-making body to adopt a special loyalty oath for every public employee in the State of California — state, county, and city. As to the applicability of the proposed oath to the University of California, the Governor publicly professed uncertainty because the University, he observed, "is a quasi-public institution with practically all the attributes of a private corporation organized for a public purpose."[39] Warren was able to be uncertain comfortably, as it was not his but the state controller's decision to include the University under the terms of the proposed oath. The Governor gave no public reason for his support in September of an oath for state employees similar to one he had opposed in August for University employees. Warren had consistently voted with the minority on the Board of Regents who viewed the University's oath to be a dispensable and debilitating condition of University service; yet, within a month of his vote to confirm non-signing faculty members of California's State University in their teaching posts, he had urged the California legislature to enact a similar oath to be sworn to or affirmed by all state employees as a condition of initial or continued public service. During the course of the controversy, Warren had often expressed criticism of the Regents' oath on the ground that it singled out for a special loyalty test members of the University's faculty and staff. Although this objection was but one of several he had publicly asserted, it was to him one of the more important; and it may in part have accounted for his seemingly contradictory behavior. One may wonder, however, if consistency of behavior and belief proved less compelling than public confidence. In the fall of 1950, Warren was in the middle of his campaign for a third term as governor. Lieutenant Governor Goodwin Knight had unswervingly supported the Regents' oath and had publicly and unabashedly broken with Warren on this issue — even though both were Republicans. The Governor may have viewed his earlier opposition to the Regents' oath as a luxury he could not publicly continue to afford in an election year — particularly with the nation's critical and nearly diastrous involvement in Korea threatening the country's sense of security. For whatever reasons, Warren chose to give his full support to a state-adopted oath, and with the enthusiastic support of Senator Jack Tenney and Assemblyman Harold Levering, the legislature enacted a state loyalty oath only five days later. On October 3, 1950, it was signed by the Governor. Known by the name of its principal author, Assemblyman Levering, the oath required every civil defense worker and public employee in California to swear to or affirm the following:

I, _____, do solemnly swear (or affirm) that I will support and defend the Constitution of the United States and the Constitution of the State of California against all enemies, foreign and domestic; that I will bear true faith and allegiance to the Constitution of the United States and the Constitution of the State of California; that I take this obligation freely, without any mental reservation or purpose of evasion; and that I will well and faithfully discharge the duties upon which I am about to enter.

And I do swear (or affirm) that I do not advocate, nor am I a member of any party or organization, political or otherwise, that now advocates the overthrow of the Government of the United States or the State of California by force or violence or other unlawful means; and within the five years immediately preceding the taking of this oath (or affirmation) I have not been a member of any party or organization, political or otherwise, that advocated the overthrow of the Government of the United States or the State of California by force or violence or other unlawful means except as follows:_____

_____

(if no affiliations, write in the words, "no exception")
and that during such time as I am a member or employee of the

_____

(name of public agency)
I will not advocate or become a member of any party or organization, political or otherwise, that advocates the overthrow of the Government of the United States or of the State of California by force or violence or other unlawful means.[40]

The act was passed as an "urgency measure necessary for the immediate preservation of the public peace, health or safety . . . and shall go into immediate effect."[41] The "present emergency in world affairs" (Korean War) was given in the act as cause for adoption of the oath. On the same day that Assembly Bill 61 (Levering oath) was passed, the State Senate, by a vote of twenty-seven to five, voted to commend those members of the University of California's Board of Regents who had voted to dismiss the non-signers on August 25.[42] The Levering oath and the resolution of commendation were enacted in Sacramento on the same day that in Berkeley the northern section of the Academic Senate passed the Deutsch resolution censuring the Regents. A more dramatic contrast of viewpoints between the public and faculty positions on the propriety of oaths and of the Regents' August 25 action could hardly have been arranged.

The effect of the Levering oath upon the University remained uncertain only until October 13, when State Controller Thomas H. Kuchel (later United States Senator from California) announced that the "University of California's 11,000 employees must sign the new State loyalty oath or go without pay. . . ."[43] The order was discussed at length by the Regents the following week.

For Neylan, Kuchel's decision was an immediate and direct threat to the constitutional authority of the Board of Regents. He asked if the Board intended to accept an administrative interpretation of its constitutional powers? And would the Board honor its contracts with some 10,000 University employees?[44] Regent Fenston wondered, inasmuch as the faculty and staff were obligated to sign the Levering oath, if the faculty "might be willing to withdraw their objections to a loyalty test and sign this one in lieu of the present anti-Communist declaration set forth in the employment contract."[45] Prevailing opinion regarded Fenston's proposal as unwise, however, as some feared that it would prejudice the case then pending before the district Court of Appeals (*Tolman* v. *Underhill*). Regent Harrison best stated what governed the Board in its reaction to the Levering Act when he observed that "The matter of the independence of the University from legislative control was of very vital importance and he felt that if the Regents acquiesced to the power of the Legislature at this time, it might be used against them in the future when interference would be most harmful. If any employee wants to sign the oath . . . the University should do everything to aid him, but . . . [he] did not believe it should be compulsory."[46] Then, on motion of Regent Ehrman, the Board adopted a resolution which requested, without making it a requirement, however, that all University employees sign the Levering oath.

On October 23, the University's controller, Olaf Lundberg, mailed to all University department chairmen and administrative officers the full text of the Regents' statement regarding the Levering oath and added the following clarification: "The Act [Levering], which became effective October 3, 1950, requires, and the Regents, without making it any requirement, request that all persons in service of that date, including all temporary and part-time employees, execute and file the oath within 30 days thereof but not later than November 2, 1950."[47] In a special session called on October 27 to discuss in more detail the applicability of the Levering oath to the University, the Regents heard the controller report a tally of employees who had signed the new oath.[48]

Campus	Number of Signatures	Number of Employees	Percent Signed
Berkeley	2,669	7,000	38.0
Los Angeles	984	4,700	20.9
San Francisco	1,195	1,750	68.3
Davis	1,117	1,400	79.8
Riverside	200	250	80.0
Santa Barbara	452	700	64.6
Mt. Hamilton	No report	50	No report
La Jolla	99	150	66.0
Various projects	No report	4,000	No report
	6,716	20,000	32.0

The controller, in advising the Board of the results, pointed to the fact that the procedure for signing had been in effect but three days and late reports indicated that large numbers of employees were signing. A rather lengthy discussion ensued both in regular and executive sessions as to the proper and legal University position in relation to the Levering oath. Finally, the attorney was asked to report at the next meeting of the Board his opinion on whether the act applied to the University, and if it did apply, whether it was valid under the constitution. The attorney was asked to suggest remedies open to the Regents and the advantages and disadvantages of each.

The Board's next meeting was scheduled on November 17. Thirteen Regents appeared. The attorney for the Board reported that the Levering oath placed University employees in the same category as other State employees subject to the Civil Defense Act, but that the Regents could continue to pay non-signers from the University funds derived from non-State sources, that is, endowment income, gifts, federal monies, and so forth. Regent Hansen moved to compel the University's faculty and staff to comply with the requirement and to refuse to pay salaries and wages to any non-signer of the new oath. Regent Neylan strongly opposed the motion, "first, because he did not believe it should be acted on in executive session, and second, because there are too few Regents present to act on a matter as important to the welfare of the University. He [Neylan] felt that the adoption of such a motion would concede the University's position with regard to its constitutional independence, and would place the Regents in the position of dishonoring employment contracts." [49] Hansen's motion was laid on the table by a vote of ten to three, Regents Hansen, Steinhart, and Dickson voting no. [50] A special meeting of the Board was called November 24 to discuss the Hansen motion. On that day only ten members of the Board appeared and the business for which the meeting had been especially called was put over a month.

Seventeen members of the Board were present on December 15, 1950. When the Levering oath was discussed, Regent Griffiths moved that the business be reviewed in executive session. Neylan opposed the motion, arguing that "since the subject previously had been discussed in open session and in view of the unfortunate experiences which followed the disposition in executive session of the Regents' anti-communist declaration, it would be a grave mistake to debate the issue now before the Board in closed session." [51] On a roll call, Griffiths' motion was defeated by a vote of ten to seven.[52] Regent Steinhart offered a substitute motion for Hansen's, which required University employees to sign the Levering oath by December 31, 1950, on the penalty of the Regents refusing to pay salaries to non-signers after that date. Neylan was the most outspoken member of the Board in opposition to this proposal. His view was that salaries could be paid to non-signers from University funds, that the Regents were obligated to honor "their contracts with men of good faith who have signed the anti-communist declaration [Regents'] and who thereby have complied with the lawful government of the University of California"; and that to concede authority to the State would be to give notice to the academic world that conditions of employment were subject to revocation at the next session of the legislature. Neylan was little encouraged by his fellow Regents, and with the majority of the Board rather firmly of the opinion that to take issue with the State would be not only unwise but legally untenable, the Steinhart motion was carried with only Neylan voting no.

As the year ended, members of the faculty and staff of the University of California were obligated to swear not only to the oath of allegiance and anti-Communist declaration as specified on their employment contracts, but also to a State oath which in spirit if not in wording very nearly duplicated the Regents' requirements. *By January 11, 1951, however, every University employee except one research assistant and eleven teaching assistants, all at Berkeley, had signed.*[53]

X

While the Regents had spent most of the fall coming to their decision to accept the Levering oath as binding on the University, the arguments in *Tolman* v. *Underhill* had been made in full to the Third District Court of Appeal.

The brief filed by the petitioners (Tolman *et al.*) on

August 31 and November 10, 1950, argued the non-signers' case on four principal grounds:

(1) The State Constitution expressly forbade any oath, declaration, or test of loyalty as a condition of appointment to any public office or trust beyond the oath of allegiance specified therein (Article XX, Section 3).

(2) The stipulation in the State Constitution required that "The University shall be entirely independent of all political or sectarian influence and kept free therefrom in the appointment of its regents and in the administration of its affairs . . ." (Article IX, Section 9).

(3) The constitutional guarantees designed to maintain the University free of all political and sectarian influence were essential to academic freedom, to the integrity of the University, and to the public character of the work of its faculty.

(4) The Board's action of July 21, 1950, to appoint the non-signers was irrevocable as an executive act and not subject, therefore, to reconsideration on substantive grounds. Furthermore, tenure as a necessary condition of academic freedom implied the right of members of the faculty to participate in the appointment, promotion, and dismissal of colleagues; and tenure was meant generally in the academic world to mean the right of a member of the faculty to his position during good behavior and efficient service, with discharge permitted only on grounds of moral turpitude or incompetency. The petitioners, therefore, enjoyed even greater security and rights to their positions than might normally be considered to apply in the case of other officers of a public trust.[54]

The respondents (Regents), in briefs filed on October 11 and December 14, 1950, argued chiefly that the petitioners were not public officers within the meaning of the constitution and exercised no legal sovereignty in the governance of the University. Rather, the constitution gave the Board of Regents full powers of organization and government (Article IX, Section 9). In the exercise of these powers, it was contended, the Regents rightfully reserved to themselves final authority in the appointment, promotion, and dismissal of members of the faculty. The Regents, it was argued, made their own rules and set the conditions of employment in the University of California. Moreover, the requirement in dispute was a reasonable and valid condition of employment regarded by the Regents to be in the best interests of the University and in no way improperly intruding on the rights of citizens. On the contrary, an individual's freedom could be quite rightfully limited for the performance of work of a particular sort. Moreover, since the Communist party was not in fact a political party, but rather a conspiracy, the contention of the petitioners that the requirement constituted a political test was invalid. Finally, it was argued, tenure, "whatever it may mean," assumed as a condition of good behavior and efficient service adherence to regulations legally required of them by the Board of Regents acting as the legally constituted governing agency for the University of California; and the "enactment and enforcement of a lawful and reasonable regulation by the governing body of a University is not an infringement of academic freedom."[55]

Counsel for the litigants appeared December 22, 1950, in Sacramento for the final hearing of the case. Stanley Weigel, representing the petitioners, spoke for more than an hour without interruption. Eugene Prince, counsel for the Regents, had only begun his statement before the justices started to question him. Two exchanges between the presiding justice, Annette Adams, and Prince suggest that the respondents had little reason to be pleased with the hearing. Justice Adams asked Prince "whether faculty members with tenure rights could be discharged without formal charges or a hearing by the Board." The response was that the non-signers had refused to compy with the legal regulations of the University. Justice Adams's retort was that if this were so, "tenure doesn't mean anything if the Regents can destroy it."[56] In answer to Weigel's assertion that his clients were anxious to submit themselves to examination to prove their loyalty, Prince countered by asserting that individual loyalty was not the issue, to which Justice Adams replied, "The issue, then, is that they were naughty boys and girls because they didn't obey the teacher and sign."[57] The court was to deliberate for three and a half months before rendering its decision.

XI

In October of 1950, James K. Moffitt, Monroe E. Deutsch, Robert Sibley, and Harley Stevens — well-known alumni of the University, and all influential earlier in supporting the non-signers — moved to strengthen their power by inviting fourteen other prominent alumni to join them. A meeting of the group was called for October 26 at the Palace Hotel in downtown San Francisco.[58] Both at this meeting and at its second session on November 28 the committee discussed means of strengthening tenure at the University and of rescinding the Regents' anti-Communist declaration. Stevens and Deutsch were authorized to write Maynard Toll, president of the California Alumni Association (Berkeley), to invite his cooperation in calling a special meeting of the Alumni Council. The Stevens committee, with eleven of its eighteen members present, met with the council the evening of January 12 on the Berkeley campus. The committee distributed a four-page document titled "A Recommendation to the Alumni Council of the California Alumni Association." The document asserted that the basic issue was the preservation of tenure.[59] The repercussions of the Regents' vote of August 25, it was said, had removed the controversy from local hands and had placed it with the national community of scholars. Next mentioned was the damage done to the University, such as courses dropped, resignations, resolutions of condemnation adopted by colleagues at other universities and colleges and by scholarly societies, academies, and associations.

Finally, the Council was urged: to ask the Regents to rescind their action of August 25 and to reinstate all non-signers; to confer with Regents, faculty, and students for the purpose of gaining a formal reaffirmation by the Regents of the continuance of tenure at the University; and to initiate an educational program designed to acquaint the public with the nature and functions of a university in a free society.[60] After a brief recess and the departure of the Stevens committee, the council authorized the president to appoint a committee to study the recommendations and report its findings to the council at its next meeting.[61]

At its first and final meeting, the council's committee decided (1) Not to recommend that the Regents rescind their August 25 resolution. (The committee believed that the Board could not be expected to take any action on the matter until the court had decided the case of *Tolman* v. *Underhill*.) (2) Not to appoint a committee of the Alumni Council to consider the matter of tenure as the Senate had already appointed a committee and as the association would be out of place in making such a recommendation to the Regents. (3) Not to recommend that a new educational program be undertaken along the lines suggested by the Stevens committee, as the existing effort (alumni magazine) was regarded as adequate.[62]

The conclusions reached, although more tactfully worded, were recommended to the Alumni Council February 12, 1951, and were adopted unanimously. The council's action was reported two days later by Toll to Stevens with this comment: "Where we differ, I think, is in our conceptions of the course best calculated to achieve this objective. As you know, there are situations in which silence, rather than activity is best calculated to achieve the desired end."[63]

The Alumni Association's governing board could not be induced to participate even by the earnest entreaties of several of the University's most prominent and influential alumni. Nevertheless, what for the past two months had been urgently pressed upon the consciousness of the Alumni Council was in early February comprehensively and authoritatively treated by the Senate's Committee on Academic Freedom.

XII

On February 1, 1951, the Committee on Academic Freedom, northern section, published a report titled, *The Consequences of the Abrogation of Tenure.*[64] The document was widely circulated both within the University and outside through the cooperation of the Stevens committee. The report was concerned primarily with the Berkeley campus.[65] The indices of harm done the University because of the August 25 resolution of the Board were reported:

Loss of Staff. Twenty-six members of the teaching staff of Senate rank were reported as having been "ejected." Additionally, thirty-seven protest resignations were reported received from Senate and non-Senate members of the teaching staff. Excerpts from the letters of resignation were liberally quoted in the text and the committee concluded the section with this comment: "Without raising the question of whether the assumption that there were Communists in the University was not in the first place as false as it was damaging, we believe these letters [resignations] indicated that the men who have been forced out under the present policies of the Regents are precisely those to whom all forms of totalitarianism are equally loathsome."[66] Reference was also made to the 157 other academic employees of non-Senate rank recommended for dismissal by the President, but no further detail was included for lack of information on the ultimate disposition of those included.[67]

Disruption of Program. This section reported the particulars regarding the fifty-five courses dropped from the curriculum owing to the dismissal of non-signers:

In the Department of Physics, for example, where three out of four of the department's theoretical physicists have been lost, only three graduate courses have been actually dropped from the curriculum; nevertheless, rearrangements have been necessitated in fourteen courses. Extra loads in graduate research instruction have been assumed. In certain sections the enrollment limit, already high, has been perforce raised. Three additional staff members were urgently needed and authorized in the budget to take care of increased graduate enrollment, but as the result of the present crises, the staff has actually been reduced.[68]

Reactions in the Profession. Signed protests from over twelve hundred colleagues in more than forty American colleges and universities were reported received. The protests took the form of resolutions adopted by departments from such institutions as Harvard, Columbia, Princeton and its Institute for Advanced Study, Yale, Johns Hopkins, Dartmouth, Bryn Mawr, Vassar, Sarah Lawrence, and Union Theological Seminary, and communications from individuals among whom were included Frank Aydelotte, Albert Einstein, Archibald MacLeish, John von Neumann, Reinhold Niebuhr, J. Robert Oppenheimer, I. I. Rabi, and Arthur M. Schlesinger.

Refusals of Offers of Appointment. This section reported the refusals of forty-seven persons to accept appointment at the University because of the oath, including such personalities as Howard Mumford Jones, Rudolf Carnap, Robert Penn Warren, Joseph Strayer, and Henry Scheffe.

Resolutions of Learned Societies. This section reported condemnatory resolutions passed by twenty professional societies and groups including the American Historical Association, the American Mathematical Society, and the American Anthropological Association; and the AAUP chapters of Ohio State University, Oberlin College, Brooklyn College, Northwestern University, and New York State College for Teachers at Albany. The report concluded:

More than a hundred scholars have been lost by ejection, resignation, or refusal of appointment, among them some of the illustrious minds of our generation. A great university, famous for its sacrifice in war, for its scientific and humane accomplishments, for its devoted service to the State, and for the prideful regard in which it was held by the citizens has in the space of about six months been reduced to a point where it is condemned by leading scholars and learned societies as a place unfit for scholars to inhabit. . . . Until the 26 are fully restored there can be in this faculty no peaceful progress and in the profession at large no removal of the interdict. . . . Meanwhile, and in the lack of these measures, there is every indication that the University is fated to continue a tragic course toward bankruptcy in those resources of repute, intellectual power, and integrity which are its essential treasure.[69]

On March 6, 1951, the Senate's northern section received and placed on file the interim report of the Committee on Academic Freedom. During the next three months the committee continued to receive communications from colleagues and other Universities and colleges of the sort included in its interim report. The final report for the year was accepted by the Senate on June 5, 1951.

XIII

The District Court of Appeal handed down its decision in the case of *Tolman* v. *Underhill* on April 6, 1951. The unanimous decision of the court in favor of the petitioners was grounded in the constitutional mandate that the University was to be independent of all political or sectarian influence (Article IX, Section 9) and that members of the faculty, regarded by the court to be included within the term of office of public trust as used in Article XX, Section 3, could not, therefore, be subjected to any narrower test of loyalty than the constitutional oath prescribed.[70]

The application of a loyalty oath more narrow than that prescribed by the constitution violated the State's highest law and was judged by the court to be an abuse of regental discretion. The writ of mandate sought by the petitioners was granted and the Regents were ordered to issue to the non-signing members of the faculty whose rights of tenure were otherwise unquestioned letters of appointment for the academic year. The court offered no opinion on the irrevocability of the Regents' action of July 21 nor on the petitioners' contention that the August 25 resolution constituted a violation of tenure rights. The decision was front-page news in all the major California newspapers, was reported prominently in the leading newspapers across the nation, and was carried on news broadcasts throughout the country that evening. Chairman of the Board, Edward A. Dickson, predicted that the case would be appealed by the Regents to a higher court, while Governor Warren, who was by then serving his third term as governor, expressed his pleasure with the decision and stated that it "satisfies my sense of justice." [71]

On March 14, 1951, the Regents' Committee on Finance and Business Management had instructed Prince to file a petition for rehearing with the court in the event of an adverse decision. Following the decision, the Committee on Finance and Business Management met and authorized Prince to prepare a brief asking for a rehearing but not to file it before April 20 (the next scheduled meeting of the Regents), unless by not filing, the Regents' position would be jeopardized. [72] Prince decided that to delay beyond April 20 would in fact jeopardize the Regents' case. Accordingly, at 9:00 A.M. on April 20, 1951, the respondents petition for a rehearing was filed with the District Court of Appeal, Third Appellate District. The Regents met that afternoon. It was a lively session. Following some preliminaries, in which the authority of the Committee on Finance and Business Management to instruct Prince was questioned, Regent Steinhart moved that the petition for a rehearing be withdrawn. Heller seconded. The attorneys on the Board engaged in a spirited dispute over the merits of the court's decision in *Tolman* v. *Underhill* and over the need for the Supreme Court of the State of California to consider the question. The motion to withdraw the Regents' petition carried eleven to ten. [73] Neylan then switched his vote from "no" to "aye" and gave notice that at the next meeting of the Board he would move for reconsideration. Regent Hansen moved that, should the case not be reheard, the Board not take it to the Supreme Court. By a vote of eleven to ten the motion carried.[74] Neylan, as before, changed his vote from "no" to "aye" and gave notice that he would move for reconsideration of the Hansen resolution when the Regents next met. The net effect of the voting and notices of reconsideration was to prevent the two motions passed from becoming final and to leave the respondents' petition for rehearing with the court as filed. Individual Regents, however, gave notice of their intention to see the matter through to the Supreme Court even if the Board decided not to do so.[75]

Prince believed his obligation was "to see that no rights are lost by inaction or default while we are awaiting receipt of further authoritative instructions";[76] thus, when the appellate court denied the Regents a rehearing, Prince filed an appeal with the Supreme Court of the State of California. The Regents met on May 25 and by a vote of twelve to ten (Neylan was absent because of illness) refused to reconsider the motions passed April 20, thus validating those motions and confirming the withdrawal of the Regents appeal from the Supreme Court. Six members of the Board reaffirmed their intention to seek, with Regent Ehrman as counsel, a hearing as individuals before the Supreme Court. Consequently, Weigel filed with the Supreme Court, in behalf of the non-signers, answers to respondents' petition for hearing by the Supreme Court. On May 31, 1951, the Supreme Court on its own motion took the case of *Tolman* v. *Underhill* under advisement as it did several other loyalty oath cases then pending in various courts of the state (mostly Levering oath cases). By choosing to hear the case, the court suspended the decision of the District Court of Appeals. The Regents, therefore, were no longer obligated to reappoint the non-signers. And they did not reappoint them.

XIV

The northern section's last meeting of the academic year was held at Berkeley on June 5, 1951. The final report of the Committee on Academic Freedom was received and filed. Professor Wendell Stanley, committee chairman, then proposed, and the three hundred and fifty members of the Senate present adopted without dissent, a memorial to the Regents asking the Board to reinstate the non-signers and to rescind the oath.[77] The memorial was transmitted to the President by the Academic Council (representing both sections of the Senate) for Board consideration at its August meeting.

XV

By the August meeting of the Regents, the composition of the Board had shifted favorably to the Warren faction and away from the Neylan group. The Governor had appointed three new Regents to the Board in the early months of 1951: Gerald Hagar, Oakland attorney, to replace Regent Farnham P. Griffiths who had resigned because of ill health; Donald McLaughlin, former member of the Harvard University and University of California faculties and president of Homestake Mining, Inc., to replace Regent Giannini, resigned; and Gus Olson, agriculturist, to replace Regent Maurice Harrison, who had died the previous February. Additionally, Maynard Toll, president of the California Alumni Association, had succeeded Regent John Canaday on July 1 as the voting member of the Board representing the alumni association. Toll was more in sympathy with the Warren view of the oath than had been Canaday. The net result of these changes was to increase by three the number of men on the Board who could be counted on to rescind the anti-Communist declaration.[78] Clear evidence of the shift was apparent on August 24, when the memorial passed on June 5 by the Senate's northern section was reported. A heated discussion ensured during which Neylan moved that the Regents vote to reject the memorial. Following some sharp exchanges among the members of the Board, particularly between Neylan and Steinhart, the Regents on a roll call voted ten to six not to permit discussion of the Neylan motion (as Neylan had not earlier given notice of his motion, an affirmative vote of thirteen was required to consider it).[79] The memorial was then filed by the chairman. Those who had controlled the votes of the Board since the inception of the oath had been tested and found to be a minority. Little time was spent in consolidating the strength of the newly prevailing bloc of Regents.

Twenty members of the Board were in attendance on October 19 when the move was made to rescind the oath. The President reported that forty-eight members of the academic staff (twelve of whom were of Senate rank) had refused to accept 1951–52 appointments because of the anti-Communist declaration.[80] Each of the forty-eight had signed the Levering oath and had continued to teach or otherwise perform his respective responsibilities. None, however, had been paid since August 30, 1951. Following this report, Regent McLaughlin moved adoption of a resolution reading (emphasis added):

WHEREAS the current methods of implementing the Regents' policy with regard to membership in the Communist Party have given rise to serious controversy between groups whose devotion to the University cannot be questioned and should be modified not only to restore harmony but to increase the effectiveness of the accepted policy;

THEREFORE BE IT RESOLVED:
(1) That the special declaration in the contract of employment with regard to membership in the Communist Party or other organization that advocates the overthrow of the Government by force or violence, as provided by the vote of April 21, 1950, be *discontinued* as applied to appointments for the current academic year and in the future [had no reference to 1950–51 and therefore no bearing on the status of non-signers dismissed in the case

of *Tolman* v. *Underhill* still pending in the State's Supreme Court], and that letters of notification and acceptance as in 1949 [included to remove objections that the documents alluded to implicitly disavowed tenure] be followed with the *additional requirement* that the State "Oath of Allegiance for Civil Defense Workers and Public Employees," generally referred to as the "Levering Oath," if not already executed, be taken and subscribed to.

(2) *That the Regents' policy to bar members of the Communist Party from employment by the University is again emphatically asserted.*

(3) That the Academic Senate, as part of its recognized responsibility for maintenance of a competent and distinguished faculty, be advised that it will be expected to conform to this policy in its recommendations for appointments at all levels and to *implement* the accepted policy in an effective manner; and

(4) That approval of specific appointments recommended by the President with the advice of the Academic Senate will not be granted by the Regents where it has been established to the satisfaction of the Board that the appointment of the individual in question would violate the policy stated by the Regents and overwhelmingly endorsed by the Academic Senate with regard to membership in the Communist Party or other organizations that impose restrictions upon impartial scholarship and freedom to seek the truth.[81]

The resulting clash proved to be the most personally bitter of the entire controversy. Principal criticisms of the resolution bore on the yet to be decided cases then pending in the Supreme Court, on the constitutionality of the Levering oath, and on the legality of the Regents' anti-Communist declaration. Those opposed to the McLaughlin proposal were also highly critical of the facts that the resolution had not been circulated with the call for the meeting and that in a matter as important as the one in question only a notice of intent to offer a resolution in relation to the subject had been mentioned in the call. The proponents argued with equal vigor the inapplicability of the resolution to *Tolman* v. *Underhill*, as the petitioners in that case were in no way

affected. Rather, they contended, the need was to remove
the oath requirement as a first step toward recovering some
measure of harmony in the University and to recover the
University's stature, prestige, and repute in the academic
world. The question was finally called, and on a roll-call
vote the McLaughlin resolution carried by a majority of
twelve to eight. (Of the twelve voting to rescind, six had
come on the Board during the previous eighteen months.
All six voting not to rescind had been on the Board since
the inception of the controversy.)[82] Regent Ahlport changed
his vote from "no" to "aye" and gave notice that he would
move to reconsider the motion at the Board's next meeting.
The attorney ruled the reconsideration in order. The Mc-
Laughlin resolution, therefore, was without effect. As the
meeting drew to its conclusion, Neylan expressed the hope
that the Board would soon return to its customary means of
governing "when questions were solved on their merits, and
we didn't have blocs of votes on this Board." The Governor
answered:

WARREN: You know Jack [Neylan], your statement reminds me
of the Swede who was in the Irish Society and there were a hundred Irishmen and 28 Swedes, and the Swede decided he would
run for President. He ran and got 28 votes and the Irishman got
a hundred, and they asked him why he didn't win. He said "Irishmen are too clannish."
MR. NEYLAN: That's right——
THE CHAIRMAN [Warren]: It may be the same thing here.[83]

The probability was high that the anti-Communist declaration that was made a part of the contract of employment by
the Regents on April 21, 1950, would be withdrawn. Curi-
ously, no member of the Board of Regents had argued against
the propriety of an oath, per se, but rather all seemed agreed
that the Levering oath was a more than adequate substitute
for the University's anti-Communist declaration and sufficient to implement the University's policy on communism.
No question was raised or intimated that the policy itself

should be reconsidered or reviewed or that there should be any realignment of authority among the faculty, President, and Regents in the appointment, promotion, and dismissal of members of the faculty. Professor Edward Tolman commented on the meeting in a letter to Benjamin Fine of the *New York Times* (emphasis added):

Even if they [Board of Regents] do withdraw their special declaration, we are still saddled with the so-called Levering Act which, as to content, *seems even worse than the Regents' declaration*. Its only virtue is that it is required of all public officials — and hence does not discriminate against the teaching profession as such.

From my personal view one of the most discouraging features of the last Regents' meeting [October 19, 1951] was that even the Regents who are on our side were all arguing as if some special oath was desirable (in addition to the standard oath). That is they backed their arguments for withdrawing the special declaration largely in terms of saying that the Levering Act oath was stronger and had more teeth in it.[84]

The Regents' November meeting was held the sixteenth day of that month, and with extraordinary dispatch Regent Ahlport's motion to reconsider the October 19 vote on the McLaughlin resolution lost by a vote of twelve to five. The net effect was to confirm the McLaughlin resolution as University policy. For the University it meant:

(1) A return to the conditions of employment existing prior to March 25, 1949, except for the express requirement that the Levering oath be taken. As all members of the faculty and staff of the University had already signed the Levering oath, the qualification had relevance only to new appointees, and for the same reason no provision was made for non-signers of it to petition the President for a hearing by the Committee on Privilege and Tenure.

(2) An acceptance of a legislatively imposed oath as a condition of employment in the University.

(3) A reaffirmation of the University's policy to bar members of the Communist party from employment, *ipso facto*.

(4) An expectation that the Senate would in its competence and responsibility ensure adherence to the policy in making its recommendations on appointments and promotions of faculty members.

(5) A reaffirmation of the Board's right to refuse the recommendations of the President and the advice of the Senate.

(6) An implicit assumption that the case of *Tolman* v. *Underhill* would remain in the Supreme Court for decision without the Board acting to reinstate the petitioners — a circumstance quite acceptable to the non-signers.[85]

For the Group for Academic Freedom, the McLaughlin resolution meant "little net gain . . . except, perhaps, a psychological one and a rebuff to the one-time majority of the Regents, who arbitrarily imposed the Regents' own special loyalty declaration."[86] The Senate Committee on Academic Freedom, on the other hand, issued a statement expressing its profound gratification with the Regents' action to rescind the oath. The great majority of the faculty probably agreed.

XVI

The single hearing held before the Supreme Court in the case of *Tolman* v. *Underhill* was witnessed by the largest crowd ever to assemble in the chambers of the Supreme Court of the State of California.[87] Chief Justice Phil S. Gibson, sitting with six associate justices, heard Weigel's and Prince's pleas in behalf of their respective clients and then recessed without setting the date for a second hearing. Toward the end of 1951, when it was thought a decision was imminent, the litigants were requested by the court to respond to seven questions:[88]

QUESTION I: "What persons in public service, state, or local, come within the scope of the provision of Section 3, Article XX, of the State Constitution: 'And no other oath, declaration or test shall be required as a qualification for any office or public trust'? Does the quoted provision apply to any persons who are not required by Section 3 to take the constitutional oath?"

ANSWER: Attorney for the non-signers contended that his clients fell within the meaning of Section 3, Article XX, of the State Constitution, while attorney for the Regents urged on the court the reverse conclusion. The petitioners claimed that they would fall within the intent and spirit of the section even if it were not inclusive of all public employees, whereas the respondents argued that only members of the legislature, judges, and executive officers as designated in Article V of the constitution itself were meant to be affected.

QUESTION II: "In what respect is there any substantial difference between the oath prescribed by Section 3 of Article XX and the statement required by the Regents of the University?"

ANSWER: Weigel claimed for the non-signers that a substantive distinction existed between the constitutional oath and the statement required of the faculty by the Regents, for to swear to the constitutional oath was to swear affirmatively to be loyal. The Regents' statement, on the other hand, insisted that one disavow membership in a subversive organization, which was not at all the same as pledging one's loyalty to the constitution. The opposite view was held by Prince, who denied that any difference existed in any respect material to the case. The loyalty statement required by the Regents, he asserted, would be valid even if the section in question were applicable to the non-signers, as there existed no inconsistency between an oath to sustain the constitution and a disavowal of membership in the Communist party.

QUESTION III: "Are the recent decisions in the United States Supreme Court, in particular Garner v. Board of Public Works, 341 U.S. 716 and Dennis v. U.S., 341 U.S. 494, decisive upon the questions raised with respect to the Federal Constitution, including free speech, equal protection, and due process?"

ANSWER: The petitioners urged that no applicability existed, while the respondents argued the applicability of *Tolman* v. *Underhill* to the cases cited. The Garner case (1951), heard by the United States Supreme Court, declared constitutional a loyalty oath required of all employees of the city of Los Angeles which included a statement that the affiant had not within five years of taking the oath been a member of any organization advising, advocating, or teaching the overthrow of the government by force or violence. The Court considered the requirement to be neither an ex post facto law, nor a bill of attainder, nor violative of the due process clause of the Fourteenth Amendment. The Dennis case (1951), also heard by the United States Supreme Court, had affirmed a lower court's conviction of Communist party leaders under the Smith Act for conspiracy to organize the Communist party of the United States with knowledge of its purposes and for knowingly advocating the overthrow of the Government by force.

QUESTION IV: "What is the meaning of the statement required by the Regents that 'I have no commitments in conflict with my responsibilities with respect to impartial scholarship and free pursuit of truth?' Is this provision subject to an interpretation which would cause it to operate as a political or sectarian test?"

ANSWER: The non-signers contended that only so long as the interpretation of the statement in question remained subjective on the basis of individual conscience was it prevented from being a political or sectarian test. As the controlling interpretation rested with the governing board, however, the element of abuse existed, and therefore it constituted a political or sectarian test. (To regard the statement in point as a political or sectarian test was at the same time to regard several resolutions of the Academic Senate and recommendations of its committees to be equally at fault, for the wording was not only first offered by the faculty but urged on the Regents by it as the basis upon which fitness for appointment, promotion, and dismissal should be determined.) The Regents claimed simply that the language of the statement was drafted following considerable consultation with alumni, faculty, administration, and Regents and should be regarded by the court to mean literally what it said: simply, intellectual freedom of the scholar to determine his own conclusions free of externally imposed restrictions.

QUESTION V: "Does the required statement 'I am not a member of the Communist Party' constitute a political test? If so, may the Regents properly require it as a condition of employment?"

ANSWER: Weigel argued that the use of the term Communist party clearly made the statement a political test. Moreover, if the statement applied to unlawful organizations — which the Communist party was not — the Regents had "arrogated" to themselves police powers exclusively the concern of other government agencies. Prince claimed that the word "political" in no way applied to the Communist party. The use of the term "political party" in the traditional American sense meant orderly government. In contrast, when applied to the Communist party, it meant revolution and violence.

QUESTION VI: "May this court take judicial knowledge that the Communist Party advocates the overthrow of Government by force and violence, or that membership in the party would otherwise render a person unfit to serve on the faculty?"

ANSWER: Petitioners argued that insufficient knowledge existed to determine conclusively that the Communist party advocated the violent or forceful overthrow of the government; and that there was even less evidence to determine one's unfitness as a teacher or a scholar on the single criterion of party membership. Respondents represented the opposite position and claimed that the court had sufficient judicial notice of the facts about the party to warrant the University's governing board in so determining.

QUESTION VII: "Did the action of the Regents in singling out the Communist Party in the required statement amount to a legislative declaration that its members advocate the overthrow of Government by force and violence, or that they are otherwise unfit to serve on the faculty?"

ANSWER: The non-signers took the view that the singling out of the Communist party by the Regents did not represent a legislative act and in fact was taken without reference to any investigation, report, testimony, or any other evidence. The Regents' action only added supposition to hearsay, they claimed. The Regents viewed their action as a legislative declaration that members of the Communist party were considered to be unfit to serve the University; and that the declaration of April 21, 1950, merely gave more precise implementation to a policy of ten years' standing that members of the Communist party would not be employed. Moreover, there was ample precedent within the federal government for the Regents' position, witness the President's federal loyalty program.

XVII

The California Supreme Court finally handed down its decision on *Tolman* v. *Underhill* on October 17, 1952. The opinion, written by Chief Justice Phil S. Gibson, read in its critical portion as follows: "We need not discuss the numerous questions raised by petitioners with regard to alleged violation of their civil rights and impairment of contract because we are satisfied that their application for *relief must be granted on the ground that state legislation has fully occupied the field* [emphasis added: has reference to the Levering oath] and that university personnel cannot properly be required to execute any other oath or declaration relating to loyalty other than that prescribed for all state employees."[89]

On the point of the University's constitutional rights, the decision continued: "Laws passed by the Legislature under its general police powers [as had been true in the Levering Act] will prevail over regulations made by the regents with regard to matters which are not exclusively university affairs." Further: "We are satisfied that the Legislature intended to occupy this particular field of legislation . . . and that there is no room left for supplementary local regulation."

Finally: "No question is raised as to petitioners' loyalty or as to their qualifications to teach, and they are entitled to a writ directing respondents to issue to each of petitioners a letter of appointment to his post on the faculty of the University upon his taking the oath now required of all public employees by the Levering Act. Let a writ of mandate issue for the limited purpose above indicated."[90] Justice Carter dissented and would have issued a writ as prayed for in the petition. The non-signers were reinstated.

The court decided *Tolman* v. *Underhill* the same day it handed down decisions on several other loyalty cases, the principal one of which was *Pockman* v. *Leonard*, in which the validity of the Levering oath had been challenged by a member of the San Francisco State College faculty. The court judged the Levering oath to be valid and in so doing overruled in that case the same constitutional objections as had been argued by the Tolman group, that is, political test, conflict with Article XX, Section 3, of the State Constitution (no oath other than that specified), and so forth. The court also overruled in the Pockman case arguments based on tenure and academic freedom. In the case of *Fraser* v. *Regents of the University of California* — Fraser, an instructor at the University, had been terminated for his refusal to sign the Levering oath — also decided that day, the Levering oath was found by the court to apply to the University and it held the act valid for the reasons given in the Pockman case.

Ironically, *Tolman* v. *Underhill* had been decided on a ground raised by the court, not by the petitioners. Moreover, rulings contrary to the petitioners' basic arguments had been made in the Pockman case. Finally, reinstatement was conditional on acceptance by the non-signers of an oath more burdensome than the one they had opposed. Nevertheless, the State Supreme Court had struck down the Regents' anti-Communist declaration and ordered the Board to issue letters of appointment to the non-signers upon acceptance by them of the Levering oath.

The Regents met on October 31, 1952, and unanimously voted not to petition the Supreme Court for a rehearing. Among those voting not to petition was Regent Neylan.

The protracted, hostile, and futile struggle had run its course at last.[91]

Chapter Eight

Epilogue

The California controversy was constituted of three dominant issues: a disclaimer affidavit disavowing current membership in the Communist party required of the University's faculty and staff as a condition of initial appointment or continued service; a regental policy unconditionally prohibiting appointment of members of the Communist party; and the locus of governing authority in the University with special reference to the selection and retention of faculty members. The conflict over these issues arose within the University itself and made adversaries primarily of faculty and Regents. Whatever weight one may assign to the prevailing political climate in the country and the state, the fact is that University factions and groups used the issues in dispute more as weapons against each other than as instruments of orderly progress. The history of the conflict is a story of the failure of educated, competent, and allegedly rational human beings bound together in a good cause — the service of truth and knowledge — to resolve their differences without injury to the University as a whole. It is also the story of lofty principles, ideas, and ideals glimpsed and then forfeited as tribute to personal hostility, stubbornness, pride of opinion, ill manners, and bad faith. The controversy abetted more than it constrained public suspicion of free inquiry and independent thought and in the end won no victory for intellectual and academic freedom.

The conflict has long been popularly but erroneously remembered as the "loyalty oath controversy." Although the
oath was a bone of contention between the Board of Regents
and the faculty, it was not alone the reason for the dispute.
Indeed, Regent John Francis Neylan, who was to become
the Board's chief advocate for the oath, not only favored
its abolition in the early months of controversy, but never
seriously regarded it as the fundamental point of difference
with the faculty. Rather, he and those members of the Board
allied with him used the oath to gain dearer objectives: to
secure from the members of the Academic Senate formal
approval of the University's policy barring Communists from
University service, and to assert the governing authority of
the Board. While Neylan thought the oath to be "not worth
the paper it is printed on," members of the faculty generally,
although regarding the oath as ineffectual, did not see it as
sufficiently offensive to persuade them to engage the Regents
in major controversy.

Neylan and those Regents in consort with him — most of
whom lived in southern California, traditionally the more
conservative area of the state — proved able to match their
intransigence with an effective and unhesitating use of power,
designed more to carry their position than to effect a reconciliation with their protagonists. The non-signing members
of the faculty, on the other hand, while proving their capacity
for intransigence, were never able to match it with the ma-
neuverability or the sophisticated application of power ex-
hibited by the Regents. Confronted in the early stages of
controversy by a massive indifference on the part of the
faculty — a condition that enabled the non-signers and their
sympathizers to gain control over the principal mechanisms
of faculty influence — those most opposed to the oath never
proved able to bring to bear on the Board the full force of
faculty power. True, the non-signers and their supporters
were able, through tactics that sometimes brought them into
dispute with their fellows and further estranged the Board,
to secure Senate action favorable to their cause. The end

result of this caucusing, however, was to provide Neylan with the very ammunition he required to wrest from the faculty an endorsement of the University's policy on communism, which along with the oath most non-signers and those allied with them had hoped to overturn. Even when the Regents enacted their "sign or get out" ultimatum in February of 1950, it was not the non-signers and their supporters who rode the crest of opposition rising from the hostility of a faculty finally aroused, but their more moderate and conservative colleagues concerned with tenure. When at last the non-signers faced dismissal, rather than being able in that extreme situation to generate massive support from their colleagues, they discovered themselves to be, for their irreconcilability, the object of resentment and criticism. While the controversy exacted a fearful toll from them, it was, admittedly in varying degree, a call to conscience, or perhaps more correctly, a conflict of conscience; and their decision to heed the ideal and not the pragmatic inevitably brought them into a confrontation with the opposing and similarly committed force. It brought them also into a tactical conflict with some of their signing colleagues who, although opposed to the oath, chose to temper a personal adherence to principle with a higher regard for the welfare of the University. By their signing, these persons believed, the University would be less injured, and the fight to win the principles at issue could be more effectively waged. And, finally, the non-signers' stance brought them into disagreement with colleagues who not only were willing to sign but who were opposed as well to the principles for which the non-signers contended. The very independence of spirit so cherished in the scholar privately engaged in inquiry and learning proved in crisis to work severely to his disadvantage when he refused to modify his judgment sufficiently to enable those representing him and his equally independent colleagues to speak with full and unqualified authority. A last factor in the faculty's lost fight was the renown of the non-signers themselves. Although several of the University's most distinguished men were allied with or were among the non-signers, there were many others of the institution's famous personages who remained nearly or wholly aloof throughout the controversy, for example, Professors Ernest O. Lawrence, Edwin M. McMillan, Glenn T. Seaborg, Emelio G. Segre, William F. Giauque, John H. Northrop, Luis W. Alvarez, and others; and one can only speculate if the Regents would have dismissed, for not signing, men such as these on whose reputations the University's scientific fame in substantial part lay.

The controversy also took its toll of the President of the University. Although Robert Gordon Sproul survived the conflict to remain as President until 1958, he never fully re-gained among the faculty the prestige he had earlier and almost universally enjoyed. Sproul had supported the oath at its inception and during the spring and summer of 1949 as well. His estimates of faculty opposition to the oath during that time proved to be critically in error, and mistaken at the very time the Board was disposed to rescind the oath and could have done so without a significant sacrifice of prestige. Later faculty opposition persuaded Sproul in the fall of 1949 to reverse his stance and to urge abolition of the oath in exchange for faculty endorsement of the University's policy barring Communists. The strategy promised some hope of success until the Academic Senate challenged unqualifiedly not only the oath but the policy it implemented and the governing authority of the Board as well. To rescind the oath, thereafter, without loss of regental prestige, remained in the end an insuperable difficulty. And as the oath gave way to other issues more deeply felt, and as it became the weapon used by the contending parties to gain other objectives, the President lost the initiative irretrievably. As he believed that to have sided with either party would end his usefulness to the other, Sproul strove from neutral ground to effect a reconciliation of competing principles. His singular lack of success was predictable, as the role he selected to play was contrary to the nature of the dispute itself. The adversaries were tenaciously and unremittingly committed. There was to be no compromise — it would be victory or defeat. The mood was one of hostility to mediation and — as the President discovered — incompatible with his role.

The Regents too suffered from abandoned confidence and deteriorated personal relationships. Repair of these required several years as did the reestablishment of rapport between the faculty and the Board, and for that matter, among members of the faculty as well. There is lingering enmity even today, and one can only speculate about what part this played in the Berkeley Free Speech Movement of 1964, as well as in the more recent disturbances. The Regents had agreed consistently on but one issue throughout the controversy, to wit, that Communists were unfit to teach. Membership in the Communist party, the Regents were convinced, constituted a commitment so inimical to the integrity of the scholar that the association was in itself adequate and reasonable ground on which to refuse appointment. The opposing view, taken by some members of the faculty and shared by the AAUP, argued that fitness must be individually ascertained by one's colleagues without regard to one's formal affiliations or associations. And the only applicable criteria to be considered in determining fitness were impartial scholarship and objective teaching. While the faculty and the Regents unqualifiedly shared a belief in impartial scholarship and objective teaching as worthy goals, they disagreed over the means to attain them. And it was over the means that not only the Board and the faculty split but the Regents themselves. The resulting schism was perhaps more hostile than the break between the Regents and the faculty, but the division little served the purpose of those on the faculty who hoped to overturn the University's policy on communism and to strengthen the faculty's part in the selection and retention of colleagues. The Board had divided only over whether to dismiss, for refusing to sign, members of the faculty against whom no charge of disloyalty or professional unfitness was laid. In the end, a majority of the Regents regarded dismissal to be a prospect less injurious to the University than the loss of public confidence in the Board and a dilution of their governing authority.

The Supreme Court of the State of California in October of 1952 ordered the Regents to issue letters of appointment to the non-signers on condition that they sign a state loyalty oath. The decision dashed the hopes of the non-signers that the court would pass judgment on tenure rights, academic freedom, faculty self-government, and political tests for appointment to positions of academic responsibility. Instead, the court said only that the State of California, under its emergency powers, had preempted the field of loyalty, and no further requirement, therefore, could be demanded by the Regents. (In April of 1951, the California legislature voted to place on the November, 1952, ballot Assembly Constitutional Amendment 9 [ACA 9] which proposed to add the Levering oath to the State Constitution. The people of California voted affirmatively on the amendment by a majority of 2,700,000 to 1,200,000. The oath continues to be for the faculty and the staff of the University of California a necessary requisite for employment.)[1] The decision in *Tolman* v. *Underhill* confirming the non-signers in their post was a hollow victory. Not only was their reinstatement conditional on their swearing to an oath more offensive than the one they had fought earlier (and, not incidentally, almost all the non-signers were willing to swear to this new oath) but the principles for which they had been willing to be professionally injured, financially harmed, and personally hurt had been utterly disregarded by the court. Theirs had been a futile struggle, and mostly a lonely one, to gain what they had regarded as essential intellectual and academic freedoms. The tragedy of their personal lives and their frustrations mirrored a University torn and tried by three and a half years of self-imposed conflict.

The University lost, in some of the non-signers, men of great distinction, many of whom never returned to the institution. It lost stature as well from protest resignations submitted by other eminent members of its faculties. And it lost potential strength from the refusal of men to come to California under conditions regarded by them to be fundamentally hostile to scholarship. Because of the dismissals, resignations, and refusals dire predictions were made at the time concerning the University's future. Contrary to these foreboding forecasts, the University of California survived and subsequently more than regained its academic reputation, with the Berkeley campus being named in 1966 by the American Council on Education the "best balanced distinguished university in the country."[2] The controversy had been mostly a futile interlude in the life of an otherwise highly productive intellectual community.

Chapter Nine

Postscript

I

When the California Supreme Court ordered a writ of mandate to issue requiring the Regents to appoint the petitioners on acceptance by them of the Levering oath, the non-signers were scattered throughout the country, in and out of academic life, as a representative sample will show: [1]

Arthur H. Brayfield	Asst. Prof. of Education	Teaching at Kansas State College, Manhattan, Kansas
John W. Caughey	Professor of History	On Fellowship, American Council of Learned Societies
Hubert S. Coffey	Asst. Prof. of Psychology	Employed by Veterans Administration
Ludwig Edelstein	Professor of Greek	Teaching at Johns Hopkins University
Ernst H. Kantorowicz	Professor of History	Member, Institute for Advanced Studies, Princeton
Hans Lewy	Professor of Mathematics	Teaching at Harvard

Charles S. Muscatine	Asst. Prof. of English	Teaching at Wesleyan University
John M. O'Gorman	Asst. Prof. of Chemistry	National Bureau of Standards, Washington, D.C.
Pauline Sperry	Assoc. Prof. of Mathematics	Emeritus
Gian C. Wick	Professor of Physics	Teaching at Carnegie Institute of Technology

The Regents on November 11, 1952, in compliance with the order, instructed the secretary of the Board to issue letters of appointment to the remaining non-signers. Of the twenty-four tendered appointment, seven resigned immediately;[2] two accepted appointment for the spring semester, 1953, remained on leave without pay during that semester, and then resigned on July 1, 1953;[3] two, having reached retirement age on June 30, 1952, were appointed to emeritus status;[4] seven accepted appointment but remained on leave without pay or on sabbatical for varying periods of time;[5] and six accepted appointments and returned to the University for the spring term 1953.[6]

II

Although the non-signers were reinstated, the question of back pay and privileges remained uncertain. The non-signers contended that the decision of the court implicitly required the Regents to grant back pay and privileges for the period July 1, 1950, to December 31, 1952. The Regents were divided in their opinion on the legality of the claim and petitioned the court for clarification. The court's response was no more directly to the point in question than was its earlier order.

On October 8, 1953, as attorney for the non-signers, Stanley Weigel wrote the Board, laying formal claim to back pay and privileges. In response, the Regents appointed a special committee of six.[7] The committee recommended that the Board reject the claims and the Board agreed. Consequently, on February 24, 1954, sixteen of the non-signers went to court to seek a judgment against the Regents, and as the case lay pending in the Superior Court of Sacramento in March of 1956, the litigants settled. The Regents granted the non-signers the salaries they would have been paid had each remained in active and uninterrupted service on the faculty during the period July 1, 1950, to December 31, 1952, less other income received during that period[8] and gave them full credit both toward sabbatical leave and pension rights as though their service had been continuous. In turn, the non-signers waived any claim to payment of interest on back salaries, to back salaries not reduced by other income, and to expenses incurred in gaining other income.

III

In the fall of 1950 the Academic Senate had taken responsibility to assist financially the non-signers dismissed by the Board. In the south, the Committee for Responsible University Government carried the burden, while in the north, the Faculty Committee on Financial Assistance, known also and more commonly as the Faculty Fund,[9] took responsibility for organizing and administering a financial aid program. The principal objective, north and south, was to make certain that no non-signer of Senate rank (in the south, non-Senate as well) suffered out-of-pocket losses as a direct result of his dismissal.[10] The faculty committees were highly successful not only in meeting the financial requirements of the non-signers but in sharing the costs of litigation with the Group for Academic Freedom.[11] Professors Milton Chernin and Neil Jacoby (later succeeded by Edgar Warren) were chairmen respectively of the faculty committees north and south.

The northern committee supported fifteen members of that section in the fall and early winter of 1950. The number dwindled until by the fall of 1951 only two remained in financial need, the others by then having secured employment adequate to their financial requirements. The southern committee supported five colleagues at first, and, as in the north, the number dwindled as the controversy continued. Contributions to the southern group totaled $18,179, which allowed the committee not only to meet its immediate obligations but also to assist the northern committee as well. Contributions were received from two hundred and sixty individuals, almost all of whom were members of the faculty.[12] The Faculty Fund, operating for the benefit of northern non-signers, received contributions totalling $70,419 from seven hundred members of the faculty,[13] sixty friends, seventy-two colleagues from twenty-one universities and colleges, fourteen chapters of the American Association of University Professors, the Society for the Psychological Study of Social Issues, and the Associated Students of the University of California. Gifts from members of the faculty approximated 70 percent of the total dollars received.[14]

APPENDIXES

Appendix A

University of California
Regents' Resolution, October 11, 1940

The Regents have voted that the services of Mr. Kenneth May as Teaching Assistant in Mathematics, to which he was appointed for the current year, be dispensed with immediately.

The Regents believe that the Communist Party, of which Mr. May has announced that he is a member, gives its first loyalty to a foreign political movement and, perhaps, to a foreign government; that by taking advantage of the idealism and inexperience of youth, and by exploiting the distress of underprivileged groups, it breeds suspicion and discord, and thus divides the democratic forces upon which the welfare of our country depends. They believe, therefore, that membership in the Communist Party is incompatible with membership in the faculty of a State University. Tolerance must not mean indifference to practices which contradict the spirit and the purposes of the way of life to which the University of California as an instrument of democracy is committed.

Appendix B

Advisory Committee Resolutions
Northern Section, Academic Senate
November 7, 1949

(1) The Senate, Northern Section, ratifies the agreement described in the 6th paragraph of the statement issued September 30, namely, "Complete agreement upon the objectives (these objectives are defined by the Regents in their statement of June 24, 1949, in paragraphs 1, 2 and 3, and the connection with communism and the Communist Party is implicit in paragraph 4 of the same statement in Resolution 1, approved by the Senate on September 19, 1949) of the University policy excluding members of the Communist Party from employment and Communist teaching and influence from the campuses of the University. . . ." [The amendment here served only to relate the *objectives* agreed upon with specific Senate and regental acts.]

(2) The Senate, Northern Section, directs the Committee on Committees to appoint a combined Special Committee on Conference with the Regents, and the Senate now directs the Committee so appointed to explore with the Regents better and more satisfactory means of attaining the agreed-on objectives and of implementing University policy with due regard for the Senate's position as stated in Resolution 1 and Resolution 2, approved at the meeting of September 19, 1949.

Appendix C

Memorandum on the Procedure Whereby Faculty Members Are Selected and Appraised

1. Recommendation of appointment in any department is on the basis of careful investigation by that department as to the candidate's qualifications in terms of proven ability in impartial scholarship, effective teaching, and general good conduct.

2. Every such recommendation is checked by the Committee on Budget and Interdepartmental Relations and by appropriate administrative officers — deans, provost, president.

3. If the nomination is for academic rank above that of instructor, the qualifications of the nominee are also carefully scrutinized by a special appointment committee, again with particular reference to impartial scholarship, objective teaching, and general good conduct.

4. The Committee on Budget and Interdepartmental Relations each year goes over the entire membership list of the faculty and, again with these same three criteria in mind, enters a recommendation in each instance for retention or nonretention.

5. In initiating recommendations for advancement the administrative officers, the Budget Committee, or, more frequently, the department again applies these three criteria.

6. If a change in rank is involved, the Budget Committee nominates a special committee to investigate the candidate's worthiness for promotion. This committee makes an independent study of the candidate's qualifications as a scholar, teacher, and citizen.

7. The recommendations of such a committee are reviewed by the Budget Committee and by deans, provost, and president, before the Regents are asked to give final approval.

8. For instructors at or before the end of the second year in the rank, and for assistant professors at or before the end of the sixth year in the rank, there is mandatory review of fitness for continued service in the faculty by a special committee which appraises the individual's scholarship, teaching, and conduct.

9. If, at any stage in this elaborate and repetitive screening process, adequate evidence of unfitness for membership in the faculty is discovered, department chairmen, deans and other administrative officers, and the Budget Committee are charged with responsibility to recommend dismissal. If this recommendation is sustained, due notice is given of termination of appoinment.

10. Upon receipt of such notice, appeal may be made to the Committee on Privilege and Tenure, which will conduct an investigation, taking note of the evidence for dismissal and giving the appellant full opportunity to present evidence in his behalf. The findings of this committee are couched as recommendations, but without exception they have been followed by the administration and the Regents.

The procedures with regard to dismissal, as described in paragraphs 9 and 10, are in accordance with the practices endorsed by the American Association of University Professors.

This ten-fold procedure is a far more rigorous testing of personal qualities and professional qualifications than is applied in other professions and even in most other educational institutions. The University's record of integrity and its place of leadership among scholars demonstrate the adequacy of this method of selecting and sifting for membership in the faculty.

Appendix D

University of California
Regents' Resolution, February 24, 1950

On October 11, 1940, the Regents of the University of California concluded that adherence to the Communist Party disqualified a person as an objective teacher and announced the policy of excluding Communists from membership in the faculty of the University. For more than eight years there was no suggestion that the adoption of this explicit policy had invaded academic freedom.

On June 24, 1949, a form of oath implementing this policy, which had been agreed upon in substance by the President of the University, the Academic Senate Committees advisory to him, and the southern section of the Academic Senate, was adopted by the Regents. 86.5 per cent of the faculty and other employees of the University have subscribed to this oath.

On September 29 and 30, 1949, a special committee of the Academic Senate met with the Regents. After exhaustive but cordial discussions, the Regents and the members of the faculty agreed unanimously upon a joint statement reaffirming "the objectives of the policy excluding members of the Communist Party from employment, and Communist teaching and influence from the campuses of the University." Also, there was agreement that, pending further discussions, "members of the faculty and employees should make oath or affirmation of their loyalty either by signing the oath approved by the Regents on June 24, 1949, or by other equivalent affirmation acceptable to the Regents."

Further discussions have now been held, and the Regents have decided that, as trustees for the people of California, they must continue to safeguard the freedom of the University against ruthless, fanatical and subversive minorities in the body politic, such as the Communist Party; that any member of the faculty who is or shall become a member of the Communist Party has violated the terms on which he is employed, and is not entitled to tenure, which involves responsibilities as well as privileges, and shall be dismissed, after the facts have been established by the University administration, which shall consult with the Committee on Privilege and Tenure of the Academic Senate, but only as to the adequacy of the evidence of membership in the Communist Party.

In relation to all other questions regarding tenure, the Regents reaffirm that the responsibility for judging members of the faculty is a common concern of the faculty, of the President and of the Regents, in accord with the terms of University Regulation No. 5, promulgated in revised form June 5, 1944. The Regents will, therefore, adhere to their traditional practice of taking no action against any member of the faculty on grounds other than membership in the Communist Party without referring the case through the President to the Committee on Privilege and Tenure of the Academic Senate for full findings and recommendations as in the past.

The Regents, in the light of the facts herein stated, give notice that a condition precedent to employment or renewal of employment in the University shall be the execution of an oath in the form prescribed on June 24, 1949, or the equivalent affirmation that the appointee is not a member of the Communist Party, or under any oath or commitment, or a party to any agreement that is in conflict with the policy of the Regents excluding Communists from membership in the faculty of the University. Such oath or affirmation shall accompany the letter of acceptance of appointment and shall be a part thereof.

Each appointee will be notified that if an acceptance of appointment on the terms stated is not received by the Secretary of the Regents on or before April 30, 1950, he will be deemed to have severed his connection with the University as of June 30, 1950.

Appendix E

List of Non-Signers
Dismissed by the Board of Regents
August 25, 1950

ARTHUR H. BRAYFIELD, assistant professor of education, Berkeley campus

ARTHUR G. BRODEUR, professor of psychology, Berkeley campus

WARNER BROWN, professor of psychology, Berkeley campus

JOHN W. CAUGHEY, professor of history, Los Angeles campus

HUBERT S. COFFEY, assistant professor of psychology, Berkeley campus

LEONARD A. DOYLE, associate professor of accounting, Berkeley campus

LUDWIG EDELSTEIN, professor of Greek, Berkeley campus

STEPHEN ENKE, lecturer in business administration, Los Angeles campus

WALTER D. FISHER, assistant professor of agricultural economics, Berkeley campus

EDWIN S. FUSSELL, instructor in English, Berkeley campus

ROBERT E. HARRIS, lecturer in psychology, Berkeley campus

MARGARET T. HODGEN, associate professor of sociology, Berkeley campus

JAMES HOPPER, JR., assistant professor of medicine, San Francisco campus

EMILY H. HUNTINGTON, professor of economics, Berkeley campus

ERNST H. KANTOROWICZ, professor of history, Berkeley campus

HAROLD W. LEWIS, assistant professor of physics, Berkeley campus

HANS LEWY, professor of mathematics, Berkeley campus

JACOB LOEWENBERG, professor of philosophy, Berkeley campus

ANTHONY P. MORSE, professor of mathematics, Berkeley campus

CHARLES L. MOWAT, associate professor of history, Los Angeles campus

CHARLES S. MUSCATINE, assistant professor of English, Berkeley campus

JOHN M. O'GORMAN, assistant professor of chemistry, Santa Barbara campus

LEONARD OLSCHKI, lecturer in Oriental languages, Berkeley campus

STEFAN PETERS, associate professor of insurance, Berkeley campus

BREWSTER ROGERSON, assistant professor of English, Berkeley campus

DAVID SAXON, assistant professor of physics, Los Angeles campus

EDWARD H. SCHAFER, assistant professor of Oriental languages, Berkeley campus

PAULINE SPERRY, associate professor of mathematics, Berkeley campus

EDWARD C. TOLMAN, professor of psychology, Berkeley campus

HANS WELTIN, assistant professor of physics, Santa Barbara campus

GIAN C. WICK, professor of physics, Berkeley campus

SOURCE: Minutes of the Regents of the University of California, Regular Session, August 25, 1950. Office of the Secretary of the Regents, Berkeley.

Biographical Data on a Representative Sample of Non-Signers Dismissed by the Board of Regents August 25, 1950

HUBERT S. COFFEY, PH.D.

Age 40. Assistant Professor of Psychology; Chief of Training, Office of Administrator, Federal Security Agency, 1946.

War Service: Lieutenant Commander, U.S.N.R., Bureau of Medicine and Surgery, Aviation Psychology Section. Author of six monographs on Methods of Training in Aerial Free Gunnery.

Publications: "Community Service and Social Research," *Journal of Social Issues* (June, 1950), and various articles on psychological research and service.

Member of Sigma Xi; Clinical Fellow, American Psychological Association; Group Leader, National Training Laboratory; Principal Investigator, Project in Group Therapy, U.S. Public Health Service.

LUDWIG EDELSTEIN, PH.D.

Age 48. Professor of Greek; awarded Capps Fellowship of the American Archeological Institute, School of Athens, 1947; Lecturer in History of Ancient Science, Berlin University, 1932–33; Associate Professor of the History of Medicine, The Johns Hopkins University, 1934–1947; Professor of Classical Languages and Literature, University of Washington, Seattle, 1947–48.

War Service: Taught A.S.T.P. courses in German, Johns Hopkins University.

Publications: *Peri Aeron und die Sammlung der hippokratischen Schriften*, Berlin, 1931; *Asclepius: A Collection and Interpretation of the Testimonies*, 2 vols., Baltimore, 1945; *The Hippocratic Oath*, Translation and Interpretation, Baltimore, 1943; *Poseidonius*, (forthcoming, Johns Hopkins Press); and over 30 articles on Greek Philosophy and Science and related subjects. Also, Ed., *Hindu Medicine*, 1949.

EDWIN S. FUSSELL, PH.D.

Age 28. Instructor in English.

War Service: Lieutenant (j.g.), U.S.N.R., destroyer-escort duty.

Publications: Three forthcoming articles on American literature.

Phi Beta Kappa, High Honors (Pomona College).

EMILY H. HUNTINGTON, PH.D.

Age 55. Professor of Economics, 32 years' service at U.C.; 1943–1945, National War Labor Board — 10th Regional War Labor Board, Wage Stabilization Director; 1935 to present date, Chairman of Heller Committee for Research in Social Economics; Consultant, U.S. Department of Labor; Member of State Industrial Welfare Commission for three years.

Publications: *Living on a Moderate Income*, 1937; *Unemployment Relief and the Unemployed*, 1939; *Doors to Jobs*, a study of the organization of the labor market in California, 1942, and 20 articles on social economics and related fields.

Member of Phi Beta Kappa; President of the San Francisco Chapter of the American Statistical Association in 1948; Advisor to the Haynes Foundation, Los Angeles, in 1945.

ERNST H. KANTOROWICZ, PH.D.

Age 55. Professor of History, 11 years' service at U.C.; Visiting Professor of History, Oxford University, 1938; Visiting Professor, Harvard University (Dumbarton Oaks), 1950.

War Service: Instructor, A.S.T.P., University of California.

Publications: *Frederick the Second, The King's Two Bodies, Petrus de Vinea in England, The Problem of Medieval World Unity*, and over 20 articles on medieval and late antique history and art.

Member: Medieval Academy of America, American History Association, Monumenta Germaniae Historica, etc.; Symposium of the American Council of Learned Societies, 1950.

HAROLD W. LEWIS, PH.D.

Age 27. Assistant Professor of Physics.

War Service: U.S. Navy, 1944–1946.

Fellow in Physics, University of California, 1946–47; Member of Institute for Advanced Study, Princeton, 1947–48.

Publications: (All of the following published in the *Physical Review*) "Multiple Production of Mesons," 1948; "Reactive Terms in Quantum Electrodynamics," 1948; "Analysis of Extensive Cosmic-Ray Shower Data," 1948.

JACOB LOEWENBERG, PH.D.

Age 68. Professor of Philosophy, 35 years' service at U.C.

Publications: *Dialogues from Delphi*, 1949; *Knowledge and Society*, (coauthor) 1938; *Hegel Selections*, (coauthor) 1930.

Phi Beta Kappa; Visiting Lecturer at Harvard, 1947–48; Past President of American Philosophical Association.

CHARLES S. MUSCATINE, PH.D.

Age 30. Assistant Professor of English.

War Service: Lieutenant, U.S.N.R., Navigator, U.S.S.L.S.T. 355, November, 1942–April, 1945; North African Operations, Sicily Landing, Salerno Landing, Normandy Landing; Navy

Commendation ribbon from Commander in charge Atlantic Fleet for rescue work on D-day.

Honors: "Honors with Exceptional Distinction" (Yale, 1941); Willis Tew Prize (Yale Graduate School, 1942); numerous fellowships (Yale), Phi Beta Kappa.

Member of Phi Beta Kappa, Modern Language Association of America.

EDWARD C. TOLMAN, PH.D.

Age 64. Professor of Psychology, 32 years' service at U.C.

Publications: *Purposive Behavior in Animals and Men*, 1932; *Drives Toward War*, 1942; and over 80 articles in psychological periodicals.

President, Western Psychological Association, 1922; Fellow, American Association for Advancement of Science, 1922; President, American Psychological Association, 1937 (Council 1932–1934), (Board of Directors 1945–1947); Member, National Academy of Sciences, 1937 —; Vice President, American Association for Advancement of Science, 1944; Member, American Philosophical Society, 1947; Faculty Research Lecturer, University of California, Berkeley, 1947; Phi Beta Kappa; Sigma Xi; Fellow, American Academy of Arts and Sciences, 1949.

War Service: Psychologist, Office of Strategic Services, July, 1944–February, 1945.

GIAN CARLO WICK

Age 41. Professor of Physics; Professor of Physics, University of Notre Dame, 1946–1948; Consultant, Office of Naval Research, 1946–1948; Research in Atomic Energy Radiation Laboratory, Berkeley, 1948 and 1949; Fellow of American Physical Society; Fellowship, Royal Academy, Rome, 1938; Sano Fellow, University of Turin, 1931; Sella Prize, Academy of Lincei, Rome, 1935.

Publications: *Magnetic Properties of Hydrogen Molecule*; *Structure of Nuclear Matter*; *Neutron Diffusion Phenomena*; and over 40 articles on nuclear physics.

SOURCE: *To Bring You the Facts*, pamphlet privately printed and distributed by eighteen alumni of the Berkeley campus, August 17, 1950. (See chap. 6, n. 87.)

NOTES

Chapter One
Introduction

1. *San Francisco Examiner*, August 1, 1950.

2. Personal letter, Baldwin Woods, Chairman of the Committee on Academic Freedom, to Sproul, August 18, 1950.

3. Personal letter, Professor Charles Mowat to Professor Paul Dodd, August 18, 1950.

4. Of those designated "academic," 1,780 were members of the Academic Senate. This body consisted of key administrative officers, professors, associate professors, assistant professors, and instructors. All others — lecturers, teaching assistants, and research assistants — were generally known as non-Senate academic employees. Excluded from these figures were some 2,600 additional persons engaged in the various contract research projects carried on under University auspices.

5. An analysis of the positions of the forty-one appointed Regents who served between 1920 and 1949 shows:

Lawyers 12	Editors–Publishers 3
Business executives 9	Physicians 3
Bankers 7	Farmers 2
Clergymen 1	Lecturers–Authors 1
Civic workers 1	Retired naval officers 1
Clubwomen 1	

(George R. Stewart, *The Year of the Oath* [Garden City, N.Y.: Doubleday, 1950], p. 113.)

6. The University's total enrollment in 1940–41 was 29,284. During World War II it dipped to a low of 18,724 and in the middle of the first postwar year 1946 jumped to 30,000. In 1947 an additional 12,000 were added to the student body and by 1949 50,000 students were enrolled in regular session.

7. California Legislature, Senate, *Fifth Report on Un-American Activities in California*, Sacramento, June, 1949.

8. A complete and detailed history of the committee's work from 1941 to 1949 may be found in Edward L. Barrett, Jr., *The Tenney Committee* (Ithaca, N.Y.: Cornell University Press, 1951).

9. During the 1937 legislative session, for example, Tenney was among the authors of AB 311 that sought to repeal California's criminal syndicalism act and of a resolution endorsing President Roosevelt's plan for reconstituting the Supreme Court. (*Assembly Journal*, March 1, 1937, p. 653). The union he served as president in 1938 and 1939 supported the Spanish Republican Government, participated in labor's Non-Partisan League, and favored the strike against the *Hollywood Citizen's News* by the American Newspaper Guild. (Barrett, *The Tenney Committee*, p. 8.) In 1938 Tenney's political interests caused him to be named in an affidavit before the House of Representatives Special Committee on Un-American Activities (the Dies committee) as having been a member of the Communist party in 1936 and 1937. (Hearings before Special Committee on Un-American Activities, House of Representatives, 75th Congress, 3rd Session, Vol. 3, p. 2084.) In 1939 Tenney authored AB 247 that would have allowed damages to be collected by a candidate for public office from any person or group of persons falsely calling that candidate a Communist, and coauthored AB 262, which would have denied to school-board members the right to inquire into the political, religious, or economic belief of school teachers.

10. The statute may be found in California Election Code 2540.3–2540.5. In 1942 the California Supreme Court declared almost all of this legislation unconstitutional.

11. *Assembly Journal*, June 24, 1949, p. 4923.

12. Among others are included:

American Association of University Professors, "Academic Freedom and Tenure in the Quest for National Security: A Report of a Special Committee of the American Association of University Professors," *Bulletin*, Vol. 42, 1 (Spring, 1956), pp. 64 and 101.

Edward L. Barrett, *The Tenney Committee*, pp. 309–310.

Alan Barth, *The Loyalty of Free Men* (Pocket Books, New York, 1952), p. 223.

John Caughey, "A University in Jeopardy," *Harper's Magazine*, Vol. 201, No. 1206 (November, 1950), p. 70.

Lawrence A. Harper, "Shall the Professors Sign?" *Pacific Spectator*, Vol. 12, No. 1 (Winter, 1950), p. 21.

Carey McWilliams, *Witch Hunt: The Revival of Heresy* (Boston: Little, Brown, 1950), p. 102.

George R. Stewart, *The Year of the Oath* (Garden City, New York: Doubleday, 1950), p. 28.

13. For a full account of the Washington cases see *Communism and Academic Freedom: The Record of the Tenure Cases at the University of Washington* (Seattle: University of Washington Press, 1949). This booklet is a summary record of the University of Washington cases and contains the full findings of the Committee on

Tenure and Academic Freedom and the President's recommendations to the Regents.

14. American Association of University Professors, *Bulletin*, Vol. 34, No. 1 (Spring, 1948), pp. 127–128. The quote is drawn from the Report for 1947 of Committee A, Academic Freedom and Tenure, endorsed by the Association's Council on October 29, 1948. (Personal letter from Bertram H. Davis, Deputy General Secretary, AAUP, to the author, July 28, 1965). The position was reaffirmed by Committee A in its Report for 1948 submitted to the membership February 27, 1949.

15. Personal letter, Arthur Ohnimus to Robert Gordon Sproul, March 23, 1949.

16. It is not known precisely the extent of influence this resolution had on the President and the Board of Regents. It is not even clear whether the President or the Regents received Ohnimus's communication prior to March 25. Sproul's response however, hints that it played virtually no part in the oath decision. Sproul replied to Ohnimus on April 4, and said in part: "This resolution (ACR 47) reminds me, of course, of the resolution adopted by the Regents of the University of California on October 11, 1940, a copy of which is enclosed for your information." (Personal letter, Sproul to Ohnimus, April 4, 1949.)

No mention was made by Sproul of the oath adopted ten days earlier. The October 11, 1940, resolution enclosed by Sproul expressed in full the Board's policy of prohibiting the employment of members of the Communist party in the University.

17. Professor Merritt Benson was one of the minority of those of the Committee on Tenure and Academic Freedom who had recommended Phillips' dismissal because of his membership in the Communist party. Professor Benson had been recommended to Dykstra for the debate by President Allen of the University of Washington.

18. See the Sidney Hook–Alexander Meiklejohn debate in the *New York Times Magazine* Section on the question: Should Communists be Allowed to Teach? (*New York Times*, February 27 and March 27, 1949). See also, "Communism and Academic Freedom," *American Scholar*, Vol. 18, No. 3 (Summer, 1949), pp. 323–354.

19. Personal letter, Dykstra to Sproul, February 23, 1949.

20. *Ibid.*

21. *Ibid.*

22. *Ibid.*

23. The closest the incident came to prominence was on February 19, 1949, when the *Los Angeles Times* gave front-page treatment to Dykstra's restrictions on attendance.

24. Minutes of the Regents of the University of California, Executive Session, February 25, 1949. Office of the Secretary of the Regents, Berkeley.

25. The President referred here to two Board resolutions:

On October 11, 1940, the Regents of the University of California, on recommendation of the Senate Committee on Privilege and Tenure, dismissed from University employment Kenneth May, teaching assistant in mathematics on the Berkeley campus. May, an admitted Communist, had brought against him by the chairman of his department charges which asserted that he had: (a) violated the spirit of the teaching appointment by failing to devote his energies to it; (b) used the University as a platform for propaganda; and (c) joined the Communist party and thus took on commitments in conflict with the welfare of the University.

(Minutes of the Regents of the University of California, Executive Session, October 11, 1940. Office of the Secretary of the Regents, Berkeley.)

On the vote for dismissal, Regents Neylan and Patterson voted no. Regent Neylan did so because of his earlier motion (defeated) to defer action pending an investigation of the "teaching faculty of the University for the purpose of determining what members . . . are members of the Communist Party or under alien influences which believe in undermining this government by force and violence, and if these are to be the bases for dismissal, that the Board act in relationship to all cases at the same time." (*Ibid.*)

Following the vote for dismissal, the secretary was directed to release the following statement covering the Board's action on this matter:

> They believe, therefore, that membership in the Communist Party is incompatible with membership in the faculty of a State University. Tolerance must not mean indifference to practices which contradict the spirit and the purpose of the way of life to which the University of California as an instrument of democracy is committed. (*Ibid.*)

(The resolution is quoted in full in Appendix A.)

In October and November of 1945, the subcommittee on Law and Order of the Assembly Committee on Governmental Efficiency and Economy of the California State Legislature, investigated the Warner Brothers Studio strike in Hollywood (October, 1945). Some students from UCLA, self-identified as such, had marched as pickets. Consequently, they were subpoenaed as witnesses before the committe, as were Provost Dykstra and other administrative officers at UCLA and members of the faculty and student body.

In December, 1945, a special committee of the Regents was appointed to look into the matter. Also in December, the Regents, in immediate response to the question, passed a resolution to the effect that faculty and students are to be loyal to the American system of government and that prior written permission must be secured from appropriate authority before students may engage in any off-campus activity in which the impression is conveyed that they represent the University.

With the report of the special committee on the following month, the Regents on January 5, 1946, voted the following resolution:

FIRMLY BELIEVING that the purpose for which universities exist is the search for truth in all fields of knowledge and its dissemination as widely as possible,

AND BELIEVING FURTHER that this purpose is best attained under a democratic form of government which at the same time gives greater freedom and opportunity to men than any other,

THEREFORE, BE IT RESOLVED that any member of the faculty or student body seeking to alter our American government by other than constitutional means or to induce others to do so, shall, on proof of such change, be subject to dismissal.

(Minutes of the Regents of the University of California, Regular Session, January 5, 1946. Office of the Secretary of the Regents, Berkeley.)

26. Minutes of the Regents of the University of California, Executive Session, February 25, 1949. Office of the Secretary of the Regents, Berkeley.

27. Minutes of the President's Administrative Advisory Committee, February 28, 1949. Administrative Files, Office of the President, University of California, Berkeley.

28. *Ibid.*

29. Minutes of the Academic Senate, Southern Section, April 19, 1949, Vol. 8, p. 66. Office of the Academic Senate, University of California, Los Angeles.

30. Personal letter, Dykstra to the Board of Regents, March 27, 1949.

31. Minutes of the Academic Senate, Southern Section, *loc. cit.*

32. Dykstra to Regents, *loc. cit.*

33. *Ibid.*

34. *Ibid.*

35. *Ibid.*

36. Sproul later told Dykstra that he was misunderstood and that he had not intended to instruct Dykstra to withdraw the invitation. (Personal letter, Dykstra to the Board of Regents, *loc. cit.*)

37. The use of university and college facilities by alleged subversives was, as in the instance of Communist teachers, in active debate nationally. Only the previous month, for example, Professor Gerhart Eisler of the University of Leipzig had addressed an open meeting of the John Reed Club in Harvard Yard and had drawn, both to himself and to Harvard, criticism from those who regarded the event as a subversive activity. For Harvard's reply, see Howard M. Jones, *Primer of Intellectual Freedom* (Cambridge, Mass.: Harvard University Press, 1949), pp. 23–24.

38. Dykstra to Regents, *loc. cit.*

Chapter Two
Prelude to Controversy

1. Committee meetings included Southern California Schools, Colleges and Institutions at 10:30 A.M.; Finance and Business Management at 11:30 A.M.; Development and Endowments at noon; and Teacher Training Institutions at 2:00 P.M.

2. James H. Corley, who in 1949 was comptroller of the University of California and its representative in the State Capitol, recalls that on the morning of March 25, 1949, as was his custom, he reported the legislative situation in Sacramento to the Committee on Finance and Business Management. In the course of his report Corley remembers advising the committee that Senate Constitutional Amendment 13, which would take from the Regents and give to the legislature the power to ensure the loyalty of the University's employees, enjoyed considerable legislative support. Passage, in Corley's judgment, would do violence to the constitutional autonomy of the Board of Regents. As a counter, he recalls suggesting that the Regents strengthen their own already required oath of allegiance. In agreeing to this, Corley recalls, the committee instructed the attorney for the Regents, Jno. U. Calkins, Jr., to draft an amendment for submission to the Board in regular session later that day. (Interview with James H. Corley, May 6, 1965.)

The author believes that the matter of SCA 13 and the Tenney bills were discussed that morning but more likely in informal conversation than in committee, as the minutes of the Finance and Business Management committee do not report the discussion recalled by Corley.)

3. The single *written* account of these informal conversations is found in Robert Gordon Sproul's personal records, June 16, 1949, where he reports a discussion of the matter between members of the Regents' Committee on Finance and Business Management:

Regent Neylan *who was not at the Regent's Meeting when the oath was approved* [emphasis added], expressed indignation at the impression created in the press that the Regents of their own volition had required the oath. He seemed to think that they had done so only because the President made a recommendation. Regents Griffiths and Ehrman disabused him of this view, stating the truth, which is that the Regents had decided to pass the resolution in the series of informal discussions before the meeting opened, and that the drafting of the oath by the Attorney, and its presentation by the President and Regent Harrison [meant Hansen], had merely carried out the express will of the body.

4. Personal letter, Jno. U. Calkins, Jr., to the author, May 26, 1965.

5. Minutes of the Regents of the University of California, Regular

Session, March 25, 1949. Office of the Secretary of the Regents, Berkeley.

6. Minutes of the Regents of the University of California, Executive Session, verbatim transcript, March 25, 1949. Office of the Secretary of the Regents, Berkeley.

7. Minutes of the Regents of the University of California, Regular Session, verbatim transcript, March 25, 1949, Office of the Secretary of the Regents, Berkeley. (The Los Angeles oath referred to by Dickson was later declared constitutional by the U.S. Supreme Court in *Garner et al.* v. *Board of Public Works of Los Angeles et al.* [United States Reports, Volume 341, U.S. Government Printing Office, Washington, D.C., 1951, p. 716.].)

8. Memorandum, George Pettitt, assistant to the President, to Sproul, October 10, 1949.

9. The impression is gained in part from the following exchange between Neylan and Sproul during the course of the June 24, 1949, meeting of the Hutchinson committee:

NEYLAN: That morning [March 25, 1949] our Counsel telephoned north for material on which he subsequently drafted this oath at your request so that taking the factual basis of this on March 25 it was at your initiative that the Board adopted his resolution. There was no other ——

PRESIDENT: To create the impression that the Board was not with the President would be to create a false impression.

NEYLAN: That is right.

PRESIDENT: *I was told to reprimand the Provost* [Dykstra] *and I wanted a clear statement of where the Regents stood as a basis for reprimand* [emphasis added].

NEYLAN: In any event it was at your plea that the Board went overboard for this resolution. Very little consideration was given to it.

PRESIDENT: Because everyone was in complete agreement, it was not a plea.

(Minutes of the Regents Special Committee on Communist Activities, verbatim transcript, June 24, 1949. Office of the Secretary of the Regents, Berkeley.)

10. Not only does Sproul's personal record confirm this (n. 3), but it seems implicit in the dispatch with which the oath was proposed and adopted in regular session. See also n. 9.

11. Although Corley indicated that it was he who suggested it that morning (n. 2), and this may be an accurate recollection, there is some evidence to suggest that Sproul also had something of the sort in mind prior to the Santa Barbara meeting. Professor Joel Hildebrand, chairman of the Senate's northern Advisory Committee, by letter March 18, 1949, to the President, reported that among his colleagues he had found substantial agreement with the University's policy on the non-employment of Communists. There were, however, those who had disagreed, and the chairman of the AAUP chapter

at Berkeley was "being subject to pressure to call a meeting of the chapter for the discussion of the matter." Hildebrand went on to urge the President that the Regents' policies on this matter be published and sent to the faculty. (Hildebrand Papers on the Loyalty Oath. University of California Archives, Berkeley.)

Sproul responded to Hildebrand on March 24, 1949, and said that "certain additional resolutions may be adopted by the Regents in the near future, which may serve to clarify even further the situation in which you and I and the AAUP are interested. Unless, therefore, you tell me that the immediate publication of the existing resolutions is a matter of extreme urgency, I shall postpone action for a week or two." (Personal letter, Sproul to Hildebrand, March 24, 1949. Hildebrand Papers on the Loyalty Oath. University of California Archives, Berkeley.)

12. No meeting of the Advisory Committee, north or south, was called to discuss this question. The matter was not the subject of formal debate or consideration on the floor of the Academic Senate or in any of its committees. Nowhere may one find explicit written reference to the oath per se, prior to its enactment. There had been, however, informal discussion of the *policy* which the oath was later meant to implement. During the winter and early spring of 1949, Professor Hildebrand engaged in a series of communications among certain colleagues in which the AAUP policy on the employment of Communists was debated, namely, that Communists should *not* be automatically barred. Hildebrand was opposed to the AAUP position. (Personal letter, Hildebrand to George Pope Shannon, chairman of Committee A for 1947, AAUP, January 11, 1949. Hildebrand Papers on the Loyalty Oath. University of California Archives, Berkeley.)

On February 25, 1949, by personal letter to Sproul, Hildebrand indicated that he had found both support and opposition to his arguments and observed that "this question could become a hot one for us at any moment." (Personal papers of Joel Hildebrand.) Thus, it seemed important to Hildebrand that as many members of the faculty as possible be encouraged "to take a broader attitude than many have been inclined to take in the past towards the obligations of a university professor to be as intellectually respectable as he can in all matters, not merely in his own specialty." On February 28, 1949, the President's academic and administrative advisers, in their discussion of the Phillips–Benson debate, urged that the faculty be more widely informed of the "full scope of the policy [both on use of facilities and non-employment of Communists] under which the University is now operating." (Minutes of the President's Administrative Advisory Committee, February 28, 1949. Administrative Files, Office of the President, University of California, Berkeley.) Finally, there was Hildebrand's letter to the President of March 18 and Sproul's reply of March 24 (n. 11). See also n. 16.

13. On June 21, 1942, in response to passage of Assembly Bill 1510, which required an oath of allegiance to be taken by all state employees not under civil service (University of California, although not explicitly excepted, was not generally thought to be within the requirement), the Regents directed that an oath of allegiance be made a part of the appointment letter for faculty and staff, effective July 1, 1942.

14. Statement by Sproul to the Academic Senate, northern section, June 14, 1949: "The instructions of the Regents that the amended oath shall be required from each appointee under the 1949–50 budget, do not, in my opinion, alter in any way the traditional procedures of this University with reference to the dismissal of officers of instruction, including the privilege of a hearing before the Senate's Committee on Privilege and Tenure." (From handwritten statement of the President read by him at a meeting of the Academic Senate, northern section, June 14, 1949.) Sproul's later action in opposing the oath rested essentially on grounds that its interpretation by a majority of the Board violated the conditions of tenure as understood in the University. His even later support of the recommendations of the Committees on Privilege and Tenure in the face of majority opposition on the Board seems to confirm further his position in this respect.

15. During the course of the February 28, 1949, meeting of the President's Administrative Advisory Committee, Sproul pointed out that *the Regents* "see no reason why invited speakers should have the doubtful privilege of belonging to the Communist Party when members of our own staff are denied it." (Minutes of President's Administrative Advisory Committee; see n. 12.) Regardless of what the President's personal feelings may have been, this relationship was necessarily of concern to him as the questions were related in the minds of the Regents.

16. The University of Washington cases, the subject of the Phillips–Benson debate at UCLA, and the recently affirmed AAUP position, combined to cause discussion among the faculty on the merits of employing or not employing Communists (See n. 12). Sproul had been urged by his administrative and academic advisers to apprise the faculty more precisely of the University's policy in this regard. Before doing so, the President apparently preferred to strengthen the policy by making more explicit reference to the point in question. An amendment to the already required oath of allegiance seemed to Sproul a reasonable enough way of doing so.

17. Statement by Sproul to the Academic Senate, June 14, 1949 (see n. 14).

18. Pettitt to Sproul (see n. 8).

19. This was due to the fact that Pettitt was out of the room when the oath was enacted and had not learned subsequently of the Board's action.

20. Pettitt to Sproul (see n. 8).

21. University of California, *Faculty Bulletin*, Berkeley, Vol. 18, No. 11 (May, 1949), p. 2.

22. Pettitt to Sproul (see n. 8).

23. Minutes of the Regents of the University of California, Executive Session, April 22, 1949. Office of the Secretary of the Regents, Berkeley. During this session Regent Dickson reported that Laski had appeared in downtown Los Angeles and "while he did not receive much publicity from the city papers, he scored a great hit with the college students."

24. Personal letter, Hutchinson to Neylan, May 25, 1949.

25. Minutes of the Regents of the University of California, Executive Session, May 27, 1949. Office of the Secretary of the Regents, Berkeley.

26. Personal letter, Hutchinson to Neylan, June 8, 1949.

27. Personal letter, Pettitt to Sproul, June 2, 1949.

28. University of California, *Faculty Bulletin*, Berkeley, Vol. 19, No. 1 (July, 1949).

29. George R. Stewart, *The Year of the Oath* (Garden City, N.Y.: Doubleday, 1950), p. 55.

30. *New York Times*, June 12, 1949, Section 4, p. 1.

31. *New York Times*, June 13, 1949, p. 1.

32. *San Francisco Chronicle*, June 13, 1949, p. 6.

33. *Ibid.*

34. *Ibid.*

35. Membership in the northern section was 1,210. Later in the controversy attendance at Senate meetings grew to from 50 to 70 percent of the membership. On June 14, 1949, the number attending would probably have been greater were it not that the academic year had already ended.

36. Text on file in the office of the Academic Senate, University of California, Berkeley.

37. University of California, *Faculty Bulletin*, Berkeley, Vol. 19, No. 1 (July, 1949), p. 4.

38. Personal letter, Professor T. J. Kent to members of the Advisory Committee, northern section, June 20, 1949: "I believe it was appropriate for the Senate to make the formal language of the resolution indicate a willingness to meet the Regents in a reasonable frame of mind, but I don't believe that the modification [to revise] meant that you were to do anything other than to attempt to obtain the complete elimination of the proposed extension of the present oath. I realize that this is a personal interpretation." (James F. King Papers on Loyalty Oath, Bancroft Library, University of California, Berkeley.)

Professor Kent's opinion on this matter is important as he was closely identified during the controversy with those who were opposed to the oath; and even as early as June, 1949, he was close enough to those who were to form the nucleus of opposition to suppose that his opinion on this point was shared by others of his colleagues.

39. Hildebrand, an internationally distinguished chemist, a popular teacher, and a member of the American Philosophical Society and the National Academy of Sciences, had served the University since 1913 both as a member of the faculty and in administrative posts. He had been for several years chairman of the Advisory Committee and was personally close to the President.

40. The southern section of the Academic Senate did not meet until June 20, 1949. Its Advisory Committee until that date was in no way officially affected by the June 14 resolution of the northern section. Nevertheless, the southern committee did work with the northern in consulting with the President on the oath matter. On June 20, the southern section passed a resolution identical to the June 14 resolution, substituting only "Southern Section" for "Northern Section" in the first paragraph. University of California, *Faculty Bulletin*, Berkeley, Vol. 19, No. 1 (July, 1949), p. 5.

41. Personal letter, Walker to Hildebrand, June 15, 1949. Walker's assessment proved remarkably accurate. Only a small number of persons on the Davis campus were to participate in any way in the controversy.

42. Report of the Advisory Committee, northern section, to the Academic Senate, Northern Section, June 28, 1949.

43. Memorandum, Advisory Committee, northern section, to the President, June 18, 1949. This report was endorsed on June 21, 1949, by the Advisory Committee, southern section, as the previous day that section had passed the June 14 resolution and was on record with the north in objecting to the oath.

44. Charges of perjury for falsely swearing would involve the civil courts. How, then, the committee asked, would those privileges and responsibilities thought appropriate to internal review by the Committee on Privilege and Tenure be handled?

45. Personal letter, Hildebrand to Kent, July 6, 1949: "We cleared this wording with the spokesman from your group, Professor Tolman, and I don't think it is good faith for the group to repudiate the action of its leaders, nor to try to read into his motion [June 14 resolution] things that were not there." Similar evidence suggesting Tolman's approval may be found in a general circulation letter over Hildebrand's signature to members of the Senate, northern section, June 30, 1949, p. 2: "Before submitting the report to the President, we submitted the alternatives proposed in the final section to Mr. Tolman for approval." The author has no record that Tolman or any of his colleagues ever denied this assertion.

46. The single report of this conversation is found in Robert Gordon Sproul, personal records, under date of June 16, 1949 (see n. 3), Office of the President Emeritus, Sproul Hall, University of California, Berkeley.

47. Minutes of the Regents Special Committee on Communist

Activities, verbatim transcript, June 24, 1949. Office of the Secretary of Regents, Berkeley.

48. *Ibid.*

49. *Ibid.*

50. *Ibid.*

51. It will be recalled that during a meeting of the Finance and Business Management committee earlier in the month, Sproul was instructed to couple the oath with the policy statement.

52. Minutes of the Regents Special Committee on Communist Activities, *loc. cit.*

53. *Ibid.*

54. *Ibid.* Hildebrand recalls that he received a telephone call from Sproul asking about a "modification" to the oath and that not only did Hildebrand agree to it but Tolman did as well. It is not certain, however, that the "modification" was in fact the addition of the words "I am not a member of the Communist Party." It appears probable, however, that the President made the statement that the members of the faculty would not object "to declaring that they are not members of the Communist Party" with confidence that this was in fact the case but without first explicitly confirming it with Hildebrand; and that, between the morning meeting of the Hutchinson committee and the afternoon meeting of the Board, he telephoned to Hildebrand the modification of the Oath "I am not a member of the Communist Party" and received his agreement and possibly Tolman's as well.

55. Minutes of the Regents Special Committee on Communist Activities (see n. 47).

56. Minutes of the Regents of the University of California, Executive Session, verbatim transcript, June 24, 1949. Office of the Secretary of the Regents, Berkeley.

57. Edward L. Barrett, *The Tenney Committee* (Ithaca, N.Y.: Cornell University Press, 1951), p. 313.

58. *Journal* of the Assembly of the State of California, Regular Session of the California Legislature, June 24, 1949, p. 4924.

59. Hildebrand Papers on the Loyalty Oath, University of California Archives, Berkeley.

Chapter Three
The Opposition Forms

1. Handwritten note, Miss Agnes Robb, secretary to President Sproul, to the President, June 26, 1949.

2. Memorandum, Advisory Committee to members of the Academic Senate, northern section, June 28, 1949. Mimeographed.

3. Memorandum, Hildebrand to members of the Academic Senate, northern section, June 30, 1949. Mimeographed.

4. Minutes of the Regents of the University of California, Committee on Finance and Business Management, verbatim transcript, June 30, 1949. Office of the Secretary of the Regents, Berkeley.

5. *Ibid.*

6. The recommendation was made in answer to a personal letter from Hildebrand to the President, June 28, 1949, in which Hildebrand stressed that "Lehman [Professor Benjamin Lehman, a member of the Advisory Committee] and I have agreed to make a most earnest plea that the oath be separated from the contract." Hildebrand Papers on the Loyalty Oath, University of California Archives, Berkeley.

7. Minutes of the Regents' Committee on Finance and Business Management, June 30, 1949.

8. On July 1, 1949, Professor Lehman succeeded Hildebrand as chairman of the northern section's Advisory Committee. Serving with Lehman were Professors Will R. Dennes of Berkeley and H. B. Walker of Davis. Hildebrand was vice-chairman of the Academic Senate, northern section. Because of his position and former chairmanship of the Advisory Committee, Hildebrand continued as an active advisor to Sproul.

9. Robert Gordon Sproul, personal records, July 5, 1949.

10. *Ibid.*

11. Lehman to Sproul, July 7, 1949. Lehman Papers on the Loyalty Oath, Bancroft Library, University of California, Berkeley.

12. *Ibid.* Senate rules forbade meetings of the Senate during the summer months.

13. Lehman to Sproul, *loc. cit.*

14. Memorandum, Hoijer to southern section, July 15, 1949. Mimeographed. Loyalty oath files, Special Collections, University Library, University of California, Los Angeles.

15. Sproul to members of the Academic Senate, southern section, July 20, 1949.

16. George R. Stewart, *The Year of the Oath* (Garden City, N.Y.: Doubleday, 1950), p. 31.

17. Memorandum from Professors Boodberg, Camp, Edelstein, Fontenrose, Kantorowicz, and Loewenberg to members of the Academic Senate, northern section, July 25, 1949.

18. Personal letter, Lehman to Sproul, August 24, 1949. Lehman Papers on the Loyalty Oath, Bancroft Library, University of California, Berkeley.

19. *Ibid.*

20. Memorandum to the files, September 6, 1949. Hildebrand Papers on the Loyalty Oath, University Archives, University of California, Berkeley.

21. Robert Gordon Sproul, personal records, September 6, 1949.

22. *Ibid.*

23. The resolution was contained in the call for a meeting of the northern section of the Academic Senate, Monday, September 19, 1949. The proposed resolution was circulated to the members of the Senate by its secretary on September 14, 1949. Office of the Academic Senate, Berkeley.

24. Sproul said of the Advisory Committees' resolution: "They presented a resolution looking toward some kind of compromise, the spirit of which was excellent and the details such as to offer a possibility of Regents' approval. In view of the fact that nothing else could be expected, I said that I would do my best to help in getting this resolution through the Senate and the Regents." (Robert Gordon Sproul, personal records, September 13, 1949.)

25. Personal letter, Lehman to Sproul, September 13, 1949. Lehman Papers on the Loyalty Oath, Bancroft Library, University of California, Berkeley.

26. Personal letter from Lehman to Huberty and Olmstead, both members of the Advisory Committee, southern section, September 20, 1949. Lehman Papers on the Loyalty Oath, Bancroft Library, Berkeley.

27. University of California, *Faculty Bulletin*, Berkeley, Vol. 19, No. 4 (October, 1949), pp. 43–44.

28. University Regulation No. 5 was drafted in 1934, principally by Professor Hildebrand, revised in 1944, and remains in full effect today (1967). The regulation affirms the University's faith in intelligence and knowledge and its obligation to ensure the conditions for their free exercise: "To convert, or to make converts, is alien and hostile to this dispassionate duty" of seeking and transmitting truth; and in so doing, ideas are "dissected and examined — not taught, and the conclusion left with no tipping of the scales, to the logic of facts." The document declared its respect for the constitutional rights of citizens and honored belief as a private matter. In turn, the University insisted "only that its members, as individuals and as citizens, shall likewise always respect and shall not exploit, their University connections."

29. University of California, *Faculty Bulletin* (Oct., 1949), p. 46.

30. Personal letter, Lehman to Huberty, September 14, 1949. Lehman Papers on the Loyalty Oath, Bancroft Library, University of California, Berkeley. See also Sproul's answer to the first question at the Senate meeting September 19, 1949 (p. 58).

31. Personal letter, Hildebrand to Sproul, September 20, 1949.

32. Minutes of the Academic Senate, southern section, September, 1949, Vol. 8, p. 192. Office of the Academic Senate, University of California, Los Angeles.

33. Minutes of the Regents of the University of California, Executive Session, verbatim transcript, September 23, 1949. Office of the Secretary of the Regents, Berkeley.

34. Appointed as chairman was Regent Maurice Harrison. Other members included Regents Ehrman, Fenston, Jordan, and Neylan.

35. The statement was the work of Regents Hansen, Harrison, Neylan, and Sproul. Neylan felt intensely that the Regents had been put in a bad spot, owing in large part to the way in which the circumstances of the oath had been reported to the public, and he wanted it clearly stated that the Regents had not acted without faculty advice.

36. Robert Gordon Sproul, personal records, September 28, 1949.

37. Minutes of a meeting of a Special Committee of the Regents of the University of California and the Advisory Committees of the Academic Senate, September 29, 1949. Office of the Secretary of the Regents, Berkeley.

38. *Ibid.*

39. *Ibid.*

40. *Ibid.*

41. *Ibid.*

42. *Ibid.*

43. *Ibid.*

44. Minutes of the Regents of the University of California, Executive Session, September 30, 1949. Office of the Secretary of the Regents, Berkeley.

45. *Ibid.*

46. *Ibid.*

47. Although the first oath did not mention the Communist party, it did provide prohibitions against membership in any party or organization (unspecified) that "advocates or teaches the overthrow of the United States Government. . . ."

48. Minutes of the Regents, September 30, 1949.

49. *Ibid.*

50. *Ibid.*

Chapter Four

A Retreat from Civility

1. Minutes of the Academic Senate, southern section, October 7, 1949, Vol. 8, p. 204, Office of the Academic Senate, University of California, Los Angeles.

2. *Ibid.*

3. Personal letter, Lehman to Regent Harrison, October 15, 1949. Lehman Papers on the Loyalty Oath, Bancroft Library, University of California, Berkeley.

4. *Ibid.*

5. *Ibid.* The Advisory Committees had been negotiating with the Board when their function was to advise the President. If the Senate

were to appoint a special committee to negotiate with the Regents it would permit the Advisory Committees to revert to their legitimate role.

6. University of California, *Faculty Bulletin*, Berkeley, Vol. 19, No. 5 (November, 1949), p. 55.

7. Personal letter, Neylan to Regent Jordan, October 5, 1949: "I urge you to be patient while they are endeavoring to bring about a constructive result in the Academic Senate." (Neylan Papers on the Loyalty Oath, Bancroft Library, University of California, Berkeley.) At the conclusion of the Regents' meeting September 30, members of the Board had decided that no public statement other than the one then issued would be made.

8. Minutes of the Regents of the University of California, Executive Session, October 21, 1949. Office of the Secretary of the Regents, Berkeley. It was also reported at this meeting that the percentage of returned oaths had jumped from 50 to 70 since September 30.

9. Lehman to Sproul, October 28, 1949.

10. *Ibid.*

11. *Ibid.*

12. Address by Robert Gordon Sproul to American Bankers Association, San Francisco, November 1, 1949.

13. *San Francisco Chronicle*, November 2, 1949, p. 21.

14. Lehman to Sproul, October 28, 1949; and Lehman to Neylan, November 4, 1949.

15. Statement made to the Academic Senate, northern section, at its meeting of November 7, 1949, by Chairman Robert Gordon Sproul. This dual role and the duty it implied was adhered to by Sproul throughout the controversy, and later was to cause him to be subject to very harsh criticism and attack by those of the Board and Senate who felt they needed his support to win their position. Sproul apparently felt that to accede to either would be to end his usefulness generally with the opposite constituency.

16. As to the legality of the oath, Sproul only referred to the opinion of the attorney for the Regents that "the Board has the necessary legal authority."

17. See Appendix B for full text.

18. University of California, *Faculty Bulletin*, Berkeley, Vol. 19, No. 6 (December, 1949), p. 62.

19. *Ibid.*, pp. 62–63.

20. Personal letter, Neylan to Lehman, December 7, 1949. Lehman Papers on the Loyalty Oath, Bancroft Library, University of California, Berkeley.

21. Minutes of the Academic Senate, southern section, November 14, 1949, Vol. 8, p. 221. Office of the Academic Senate, University of California, Los Angeles.

22. *Ibid.*, pp. 222–223.

23. Minutes of the Regents of the University of California, Execu-

tive Session, November 18, 1949. Office of the Secretary of the Regents, Berkeley.

24. *Ibid.*

25. *Ibid.*

26. Robert Gordon Sproul, personal records, November 22, 1949.

27. Notes on a meeting at the Faculty Club, November 30, 1949, prepared by Professor Frank Newman. Members of the Steering Committee included Professors Arthur Brodeur, Phillip Griffin, Gordon Griffiths, Jack Kent, Stephen Pepper, Jacobus ten Broek, and Joseph Tussman.

28. Personal statement prepared in September, 1949, by Stanley, offering his suggestions for solution to the oath problem.

29. File Memo, Davisson–Grant Conference with John Francis Neylan, Chairman of the Regents' Special Committee, December 13, 1949. Prepared either by Davisson or Grant or both. Davisson Papers on the Loyalty Oath, Office of the Academic Senate, Berkeley.

30. Interview with Professor Malcolm Davisson, May 6, 1965.

31. Minutes of the regents of the University of California, Morning Executive Session, December 16, 1949. Office of the Secretary of the Regents, Berkeley.

32. *Ibid.*

33. *Ibid.*

34. *Ibid.*

35. Regent Farnham Griffiths did not vote on the affirmation. His son, Gordon, serving on the Berkeley faculty, had taken an active part in the Senate debates and was serving as a member of the non-signers' Steering Committee. Regent Griffiths, fearful that "action by him might be misconstrued," voluntarily disqualified himself from "any further participation" in the oath matter.

36. Verbatim transcript of the hearings may be found in *Hearings Before the Committee on Un-American Activities.* House of Representatives, Eighty-first Congress, First Session, (U.S. Government Printing Office, Washington D.C., 1950), pp. 813–831.

37. Minutes of the Regents of the University of California, Regular Session, December 16, 1949. Office of the Secretary of the Regents, Berkeley. Fox disclaimed formal membership in the party during 1942 and 1943, although he admitted participating in its activities.

38. Minutes of the Regents of the University of California, Afternoon Executive Session, verbatim, December 16, 1949. Office of the Secretary of the Regents, Berkeley. For Neylan, anyone making "pretensions of membership in a Faculty of a great university" was obligated to disclose, freely, his activities and those of his associates; and "the disclosure of a person's past history and activities is a matter of course among people aspiring to positions of honor." (Undated memo to the file written by Regent Neylan about the Fox case, Neylan Papers on the Loyalty Oath, Bancroft Library, University of California, Berkeley.)

39. *Ibid.* On November 22, 1949, Sproul, in conference with Regents Heller and Griffiths, had advised those two Regents "that a decision to dismiss Fox, with no better evidence than we now have would seriously complicate the larger problem on which we are now working and might alienate a very large part of the faculty."

40. *Ibid.*

41. *Ibid.*

42. Resolution of NSAE, sent to members of the faculty February 18, 1950. A similar organization of non-Senate academic personnel organized on the Los Angeles campus.

43. "Issues Raised by the Special Oath and Proposals for Their Solution," December 29, 1949, Confidential Copy No. 23.

44. *Ibid.*

45. The poll, authorized November 14, 1949, by action of the southern section, was taken by Professor W. A. Wenger. Question 10 asked: "Membership in the Communist Party, even though it remains a legal political party, is sufficient reason for disqualification of a faculty member? 37% agree; 54% disagree; 9% no response; or qualified response."

And, on the question of the oath: "2a. Taking into consideration all factors affecting your attitude, do you approve or disapprove of the requirement of signing the oath? 28% approve; 69% disapprove; 3% no response; or qualified response."

Also: "9. Failure to sign the oath, should, of itself, constitute dismissal from the faculty? 12% agree; 83% disagree; 5% no response; or qualified response."

46. Verbatim transcript of the joint meeting of the Regents' Committee to Confer with the Faculty and the Academic Senate Conference Committee, January 4, 1950, p. 3. Office of the Secretary of the Regents, Berkeley.

47. Although a second meeting of the two committees was suggested just prior to adjournment January 4, the record is not clear as to the disposition of that suggestion. It was later claimed by members of the Senate committee that all parties had agreed to a second meeting. A second meeting between the committees, however, was regarded by Neylan as a hope and not a promise, although most members of his own committee were otherwise persuaded.

48. *New York Times,* December 11, 1949, p. E9.

Chapter Five
The Ultimatum

1. Personal letter, Hildebrand to Neylan, January 6, 1950.
2. Robert Gordon Sproul, personal records, January 7, 1950.
3. Interview with Frank L. Kidner, May 7, 1965.

4. Minutes of the Regents of the University of California, Executive Session, verbatim transcript, January 13, 1950. Office of the Secretary of the Regents, Berkeley. It is unclear from the minutes of this meeting whether the proposals made to the Neylan committee by the Davisson–Grant committee were distributed to the full Board or not.

5. *Ibid.*

6. The 86 percent figure was for all University employees, academic and nonacademic. For the Academic Senate, north, the percentage was 81 percent and for the south, 79 percent. Neylan has claimed that his continuous reference to a "dissident minority" was a conscious and deliberate phrase used by him, at least in part, to prevent the press from attacking the entire faculty. (Personal memo to the file, John Francis Neylan. Neylan Papers on the Loyalty Oath, Bancroft Library, University of California, Berkeley.)

7. Interview with Mrs. Edward H. Heller, May 5, 1965.

8. Robert Gordon Sproul, personal records, January 20, 1950.

9. Robert Gordon Sproul, personal records, January 23, 1950.

10. Report of the Special Committee on Conference with the Regents, Northern Section, March 7, 1950, pp. 13–14.

11. Robert Gordon Sproul, personal records, February 9, 1950.

12. Comments to President Sproul by the Davisson–Grant committee, February 20, 1950. Davisson Papers on the Loyalty Oath, Office of the Academic Senate, Berkeley.

13. Minutes of the Regents of the University of California, Executive Session, February 24, 1950. Office of the Secretary of the Regents, Berkeley. The letters reported by Sproul had been received the previous week from seventy-four senior members of the faculty holding positions of administrative responsibility. Both sections of the Senate were represented among the signatories.

14. *Ibid.* Paragraphs four and five responded to the proposals made February 8, 1950, by the Davisson–Grant committee.

15. Article XX, Section 3.

16. Voting for the Neylan motion were Regents Ahlport, Dickson, Ehrman, Giannini, Hale, Jordan, McFadden, Merchant, Neylan, Pauley, Sprague, and Teague. Voting against were Regents Fenston, Griffiths, Hansen, Heller, and Sproul and Warren. The full text of the resolution may be found in Appendix D.

17. *San Francisco Chronicle*, February 25, 1950.

18. *Ibid.*

19. *Ibid.*

20. Report of the Special Committee on Conference with the Regents (see n. 10), p. 16.

21. *Ibid.*

22. *Ibid.*

23. George R. Stewart, *The Year of the Oath* (Garden City, N.Y.: Doubleday, 1950), pp. 36–37. Also, on p. 2 in an Abbreviated Chronology compiled by Professor Edward Tolman in 1951.

24. Hicks to Newman, March 2, 1950.

25. Kantorowicz to Strong, February 28, 1950. Loyalty oath materials, University Archives, University of California, Berkeley. Found also in Microfilm Reel No. 1, Bancroft Library, Loyalty Oath Series, University of California, Berkeley.

26. Statement issued by the Davisson–Grant committee, March 1, 1950.

27. *Ibid.*

28. Report of the Special Committee on Conference with the Regents (see n. 10), p. 18.

29. Information on the organization of the Committee of Seven and its subcommittees is found scattered in several randomly filed memoranda, reports, and personal notes in the Committee of Seven files (Hicks Papers), University Archives, Berkeley, in the Kidner Papers on the Loyalty Oath, Bancroft Library, Berkeley, and in certain documents to which access is restricted.

30. Information found randomly filed in the loyalty oath files of Special Collections, University Library, University of California, Los Angeles. Subcommittees of the southern committee included Press and Radio, Lectures, Alumni, Finance, Legal, and Task Force.

31. *San Francisco Chronicle*, March 1, 1950.

32. *Ibid.*

33. *Berkeley Daily Gazette*, Friday, March 3, 1950.

34. *Ibid.* But see p. 10 above.

35. *Ibid.*

36. *San Francisco Chronicle*, March 4, 1950.

37. *San Francisco Chronicle*, March 2, 1950.

38. Kidner to Kirk, March 5, 1950, p. 3. Frank Kidner Papers on the Loyalty Oath, Bancroft Library, University of California, Berkeley.

39. *San Francisco Chronicle*, March 7, 1950.

40. Sontag to Davisson, March 6, 1950. Hildebrand Papers on the Loyalty Oath, University Archives, University of California, Berkeley.

41. The northern members of the Davisson–Grant committee felt strongly that there was a great need for the Senate to vote at its meeting of March 7 on that part of the committee's report which expressed strong and unequivocal opposition to the oath. The full report, however, was to be submitted to mail ballot.

42. Robert Gordon Sproul, personal records, March 6, 1950.

43. Robert Gordon Sproul, personal records, March 7, 1950.

44. From Running Notes on Academic Senate Meeting, northern section, Wheeler Auditorium, March 7, 1950, unsigned. Frank L. Kidner Papers on the Loyalty Oath, Bancroft Library, University of California, Berkeley.

45. Minutes of the Academic Senate, northern section, March 7, 1950, Vol. 8, p. 160. Office of the Academic Senate, University of California, Berkeley.

46. Running Notes on Senate Meeting, March 7, 1950.
47. Minutes of the Academic Senate, northern section, March 7, 1950, loc. cit.
48. Running Notes on Senate Meeting, March 7, 1950.
49. Minutes of the Academic Senate, northern section, March 7, 1950, loc. cit.
50. Running Notes on the Senate Meeting, March 7, 1950.
51. Prior to the March 7 meeting, the Committee of Seven had taken rooms 328 and 329 in the Durant Hotel located just south of the Berkeley campus. The committee's office was administered by Professor Frank Kidner.
52. Daily Californian, March 9, 1950, Berkeley, California.
53. Teague to Neylan, March 8, 1950. Other Regents similarly persuaded included Ahlport, Jordan, Sprague, Knight, and Dickson. (Personal letter, Dickson to Neylan, March 16, 1950.)
54. Personal letter, Ehrman to Neylan, March 18, 1950. Neylan Papers on the Loyalty Oath, Bancroft Library, University of California, Berkeley.
55. Ibid.
56. Mimeographed circular accompanying mail ballot, Proposition No. 2, Thomas B. Steel, Secretary to members of the Academic Senate, northern section, March 13, 1950. Office of the Academic Senate, Berkeley.
57. Ibid.
58. Westwood Hills Press, March 23, 1950, Los Angeles, California. On March 21, 1950, Epling had approached Sproul urging that he join with the vice-chairman of both sections in a statement on the results and meaning of the balloting. Sproul, with Hildebrand's concurrence, declined, feeling that a commitment by him at that point would reduce his later effectiveness with the Regents. (Robert Gordon Sproul, personal records, March 21, 1950).
59. Ibid. Paraphrasing Dean Paul Dodd of UCLA.
60. Tolman Chronology (see n. 23).
61. Oakland Tribune, March 27, 1950.
62. Personal letter, Neylan to Sproul, March 21, 1950.
63. Although there is no specific proof of this assertion, one notices in all correspondence among and between Regents, faculty, and administration the assumption that the vote would be affirmative by a large majority. Nowhere was a contrary view found — even among those most opposed to its passage.
64. Draft of Resolution authored by Neylan, March 22, 1950. Neylan Papers on the Loyalty Oath, Bancroft Library, University of California, Berkeley.
65. Hicks to Sproul, March 26, 1950. Files of the Committee of Seven, University Archives, University of California, Berkeley.
66. Robert Gordon Sproul, personal records, March 28, 1950.
67. These men had been invited by Sproul with the understanding that they would be heard only on the invitation of the Board. Pro-

fessor Caughey of UCLA, a non-signer, had also traveled to Santa Barbara for the meeting, but because he was a non-signer it was agreed by his colleagues that he should not appear with them at the Regents' meeting.

68. Minutes of the Regents of the University of California, Regular Session, verbatim transcript, March 31, 1950. Office of the Secretary of the Regents, Berkeley.

69. *Ibid.*

70. *Ibid.*

71. *Ibid.*

72. *Ibid.* The piano player referred to by Warren was Mrs. Miriam Brooks Sherman, a pianist in the department of physical education on the Los Angeles campus. In a letter from Senator Jack Tenney to President Sproul, March 2, 1950, Mrs. Sherman was accused of past membership in the Communist party. The Sherman case was front-page news, particularly in the Los Angeles papers, at the time of the March 31 meeting of the Regents. Mrs. Sherman had been employed by the University since July 1, 1946. No official determination of her political persuasions or affiliations was made known by the University during its inquiry. Mrs. Sherman refused to comment either on her current political beliefs or associations except to state that both were a private matter in which the University had no legitimate interest. On April 20, 1950, Mrs. Sherman was dismissed by the University from her position, on grounds that her employment was in conflict with University Regulation 71 which prohibited employment in the same University department of members of the same family. Mrs. Eleanor Pasternak, a teacher in the women's physical education department, was Mrs. Sherman's sister. (Details of this incident were compiled from copies of the *Los Angeles Times*; from a letter of April 9, 1950, mailed by Mrs. Sherman to certain members of the Academic Senate; from an eight-page undated (probably late April or early May, 1950) personal statement prepared by Mrs. Sherman; and from a letter to Provost Dykstra from Mrs. Sherman dated March 30, 1950.)

73. *Ibid.*

74. George R. Stewart, *Year of the Oath* (see n. 23), p. 39.

75. Robert Gordon Sproul, personal records, April 3, 1950.

76. Sproul to Ehrman, April 4, 1950.

77. Neylan to Ehrman, April 5, 1950.

78. Robert Gordon Sproul, personal records, April 5, 1950.

79. Personal letter, Kidner to Sproul, April 6, 1950. Frank L. Kidner Papers on the Loyalty Oath, Bancroft Library, University of California, Berkeley.

80. Hicks to Kidner, April 6, 1950.

81. The Committee of Seven by this time had received more than $11,000 from members of the faculty, colleagues from other institutions, and friends. Of this total, $10,000 had come from 354 members of the faculty of Senate rank. From others within the

University and from colleagues and friends elsewhere came $1,600 from 117 donors. Contributions in substantial addition to these reported figures were received from persons who preferred anonymity. (Personal files of Professor Milton Chernin, School of Social Welfare, University of California, Berkeley.)

82. Robert Gordon Sproul, personal records, April 11, 1950.

83. Neylan to Collins, April 12, 1950. Neylan Papers on the Loyalty Oath, Bancroft Library, University of California, Berkeley.

84. Dickson to Ehrman, April 14, 1950.

85. Immediately following the official meeting of the Senate's northern section March 7, 1950, the faculty in informal session authorized the Committee on Committees to appoint a Committee of Four to continue the faculty fight against the February 24 action of the Board of Regents, and to enter into negotiations with the Regents if that necessity arose. The Committee of Four was composed of John Hicks as chairman and, as members, Professors Jenkins, Simpson, and Pepper, all members of the Committee of Seven. The committee never functioned, as it was considered unwise to give the impression publicly of the possible need for further negotiations. The tactical decision was to continue with the Committee of Seven, holding the Committee of Four in reserve. Meeting regularly with the Committee of Seven at this time, however, were Professors Kidner, Griffin, Jennings, and Kent. Not publicly announced, even to the Committee of Seven, was the appointment by the Committee on Committees of a four-man Committee on Conference consisting of Professors Hicks, O'Brien, Evans, and Wellman. This committee never functioned, however, as negotiations between the faculty and the Board were not resumed.

86. Personal handwritten letter, Hicks to Kidner, April 13, 1950. Kidner Papers on the Loyalty Oath, Bancroft Library, University of California, Berkeley.

87. The Steering Committee took the same form as the Committee of Seven in the north while the Policy Committee compared with the northern Committee of Four. Professor Paul Dodd chaired the Steering Committee and Professor John Caughey, a non-signer, headed the Policy Committee.

88. Frank L. Kidner Papers on the Loyalty Oath, Bancroft Library, University of California, Berkeley.

89. Jordan to Ehrman, April 5, 1950.

90. The condition of the faculty may have been rather accurately summarized by George Stewart: "The faculty, although worn down by long battle, rapidly splitting into splinter groups under the pressures of defeat, and well-nigh hopeless for themselves and for the University, rallies as best it can behind the Committee of Seven." (George R. Stewart, *Year of the Oath*, p. 39.) The Committee of Seven, on urging of the non-signers, had been quietly gathering signatures of members of the Senate who would resign should the April 21 meeting of the Board prove no more productive than had

the session in March. The committee was encouraged in this purpose both by Governor Warren and President Sproul. The occasion to use the list of men who had so committed themselves never arose, however, as the April 21, 1950, resolution of the Regents removed the immediate threat of dismissal.

91. Bechtel to Dickson, Sproul, and Hicks, March 16, 1950. Loyalty oath files, Alumni House, University of California, Berkeley.

92. Minutes of the California Alumni Council, March 27, 1950. Confidential Bulletin No. 259, p. 4, Alumni House, University of California, Berkeley.

93. Sproul to Bechtel, April 13, 1950. Loyalty oath files, Alumni House, University of California, Berkeley.

94. Personal letter, Revelle to Epling, April 19, 1950. Loyalty Oath Papers, Special Collections, University Library, University of California, Los Angeles.

95. *Ibid.*

96. *Ibid.*

97. Robert Gordon Sproul, personal records, April 20, 1950.

98. Minutes of the Regents of the University of California, Regular Session, April 21, 1950. Office of the Secretary of the Regents, Berkeley.

99. *Ibid.*

100. *Ibid.*

Chapter Six
A Test of Will

1. Personal letter, Hicks to Sproul, April 21, 1950. Most of the press releases attributed to Hicks were in fact prepared by Kidner and Griffin (publicists for the Committee of Seven), and in many instances were at variance with Hicks's own judgment. (Personal letter, Hicks to the author, May 16, 1965.)

2. The Committee of Seven moved formally to conclude its business the last of May. The committee decided to return what funds remained in its custody to those who had given them. Through the efforts of its Subcommittee on Finance, the committee in March and April had received $15,091 in contributions. Expenses had totaled $3,335. The balance of $11,656 was returned by check to each donor on June 2, 1950, in the amount of .778 percent of his original contribution. (Committee of Seven to contributors to the Committee of Seven, June 2, 1950.) The Committee of Seven was criticized by some members of the faculty who felt that the return of these monies was unpropitious, particularly in light of the possibility that the

"compromise" would fail. George R. Stewart, *The Year of the Oath.* (Garden City, N.Y.: Doubleday, 1950), p. 138. The Committee of Seven, however, regarded its action to be very much the proper course to follow as the funds in question had been collected for a specific purpose only; and if funds were needed again, they should be sought on that occasion and for that purpose.

3. Statement to the northern section of the Academic Senate, April 22, 1950, by Dean M. P. O'Brien. Office of the Academic Senate, University of California, Berkeley.

4. Statement to the northern section of the Academic Senate, April 22, 1950, by Professor Stephen C. Pepper. Office of the Academic Senate, Berkeley.

5. Statement to the northern section of the Academic Senate, April 22, 1950, by Professor S. S. Surrey. Office of the Academic Senate, Berkeley.

6. The Committee of Seven had been criticized by the non-signers for failure to devise a course of action for the Senate to follow in the event of an unfavorable regental decision April 21. Principally through the efforts of Pepper, those parties sympathetic to the non-signers brought pressure to bear on the Committee of Seven to the point where its members were willing to appoint a Committee of Five that would draw up such plans. The Committee of Five, therefore, was organized by the Committee of Seven "to explore possible actions which may be taken by the Faculty as a result of various possible actions of the Regents on April 21." (Personal letter, Pepper to Strong, April 19, 1950.)

7. Had the Committee of Seven refused its cooperation, the Committee of Five was quite prepared to move unilaterally to the Senate with its recommendations irrespective of the Committee of Seven's endorsement or approval.

8. Statement to the northern section of the Academic Senate, April 22, 1950, by Professor Edward Strong. Office of the Academic Senate, Berkeley.

9. *Recommendations of the Committee of Five — I*, mimeographed and distributed by the Committee of Five, April 22, 1950.

10. *Ibid.*

11. *Recommendations of the Committee of Five — II*, mimeographed and distributed by the Committee of Five, April 22, 1950.

12. Statement to the northern section of the Academic Senate, April 22, 1950, by Professor Edward C. Tolman. Office of the Academic Senate, Berkeley.

13. *Ibid.*

14. Statement to the northern section of the Academic Senate, April 22, 1950, by Professor Emeritus Monroe E. Deutsch. Office of the Academic Senate, Berkeley. Dr. Deutsch had been persuaded to attend the Senate meeting late the evening before by Hicks and Professor Armstrong (School of Law.) The speech he gave differed markedly from one prepared by him the morning of April 21 in that

the later speech was considerably more encouraging and optimistic. He had been urged to the later version by Pepper and Davisson.

15. Paul Dodd, chairman of the southern section's Steering Committee and representative of that committee in discussions with the alumni, wrote to Bechtel on April 27, 1950, and expressed his belief that "everything is quiet and is developing at this point on a very satisfactory basis." Dodd indicated that he had been doing "everything within my power to persuade my colleagues of the fairness and the justice of the recommendations which you have made and which have been incorporated into the Regents' action." The Senate leadership in the south as in the north was working to effect a consensus in support of the alumni plan.

16. Robert Gordon Sproul, personal records, April 25, 1950.

17. *Ibid.*

18. *Ibid.*

19. *Ibid.* As will be pointed out later, the Bechtel committee itself was divided on this question.

20. Hildebrand, Louderback, and Kerner to Sproul, May 18, 1950.

21. Minutes of the Academic Senate, northern section, May 1, 1950, Vol. 8, p. 184. Office of the Academic Senate, University of California, Berkeley.

22. Circular letter, Hildebrand to Senate, northern section, May 4, 1950.

23. The author was unable to locate the results of the chapter's poll, if in fact it was taken at all.

24. Personal letter, Grant to Mowat, May 12, 1950.

25. Robert Gordon Sproul, personal records, May 1, 1950.

26. Personal letter, Lenzen to Sproul, May 8, 1950.

27. Report of the Committee on Privilege and Tenure to the President, June 13, 1950.

28. Robert Gordon Sproul, personal records, May 13, 1950.

29. Minutes of the Special Committee on Academic Freedom, May 25, 1950.

30. Minutes of the Regents of the University of California, Regular Session, May 26, 1950. Office of the Secretary of the Regents, Berkeley. The number and proportion of signed oaths was reported to the Regents by the secretary as follows:

(1) Appointment letters mailed: 9,929.

(2) Number of acceptances received where the appointee signed the June 24, 1949, oath: 8,591. (This was 86.52% of total.)

(3) Number who did not sign the June 24, 1949, oath but who signed the new contract of employment and oath of allegiance as specified by the Board on April 21, 1950: 826 (8.32% of total).

(4) Number who had not complied with either the June 24, 1949, or April 21, 1950, resolutions: 512 (5.16%). [These non-signers were expected to petition for hearings.]

(5) Number of members of the Academic Senate (part of 512) not complying: 94.

(6) Number of regular members of the Academic Senate (part of 512) not complying (excluding visiting professors): 80.

Since May 15, 1950, the secretary reported, some additional 100 acceptances had been received in which the appointees had complied either with the June 24, 1949 resolution or with the one of April 21, 1950.

31. This wording may be found in nearly identical language in all the reports submitted to the President by the Committee on Privilege and Tenure, southern section. The Santa Barbara recommendations were substantively identical.

32. Report of the Committee on Privilege and Tenure, southern section, on Mrs. Eleanor B. Pasternak, June, 1950. Mrs. Pasternak was the sister of Mrs. Sherman who had been dismissed by the University in April of 1950. (See also chap. 5, n. 72).

33. Report of the Committee on Privilege and Tenure, northern section, to President Sproul, June 13, 1950.

34. The five, all of the Berkeley campus, included Isabel C. Hungerland, assistant professor of speech; John L. Kelley, associate professor of mathematics; Margaret P. O'Hagan, associate professor of art; Nevitt R. Sanford, professor of psychology and associate director of the Institute of Personality Assessment; and Harold Winkler, assistant professor of political science.

35. Report of the Committee on Privilege and Tenure, northern section, to President Sproul, June 13, 1950. The wording "cannot recommend continuation of employment" was used by the Committee on Privilege and Tenure rather than "no recommendation" on the urgent advice of the Bechtel committee. (Personal letter, Sproul to Baldwin Woods, chairman of the Senate's Committee on Academic Freedom, July 13, 1950.)

36. Report of the Committee on Privilege and Tenure, northern section, on Professor Edward C. Tolman, June 13, 1950.

37. Declaration of Academic Freedom, April 29, 1950, issued by NSAE, University of California, Berkeley.

38. Minutes of the Regents of the University of California, Regular Session, verbatim transcript, June 23, 1950. Office of the Secretary of the Regents, Berkeley.

39. The number of persons referred to here was not wholly accurate owing to administrative error. Corrections were made at the next meeting of the Board.

40. The Minutes of the Regents' meeting show only that the 157 included persons "who have made no response to the letter of appointment or given notice of resignation as of June 30, 1950, and that type of person." Additional information included in the text was found by analyzing the reports of the hearings and comparing the

recommendations made against the list of 157 persons recommended for dismissal by the President on June 23.

41. Non-signing members of the *Senate* whose cases were heard by the Committees on Privilege and Tenure (69) were included either in Sproul's recommendation 2 or in 3. The difference between this combined number (67) and the number of Senate cases reported to the President by the committee (69) is accounted for by resignations occuring between the hearing dates and the Regents meeting on June 23.

42. The hearing committee had recommended favorably fifty-eight non-Senate academic and nonacademic employees to the President. Of those, eighteen were included in Sproul's recommendation 1, eleven in his recommendation 4, and eighteen in recommendation 6. The records are unclear as to the situation existing for the remaining eleven, and it is presumed that these either had resigned or had signed between the hearing date and the June 23 Board meeting. Of the fifteen sent to Sproul by the hearing committees with no recommendation, because the individuals were in any event not to be reappointed, thirteen were included in Sproul's recommendation 1. The records are unclear about the remaining two, but it is presumed that they either signed or resigned before the June 23 Regents' meeting.

43. This was a separate contract to be used by the University in employing non-signers of either the June 24, 1949, oath or the anti-Communist declaration on the contract of employment.

44. Regardless of the recommendation of the hearing committees in these cases, Sproul considered the reports "not adequate for making a decision in my mind." (Minutes of the Regents of the University of California, Regular Session, verbatim transcript, June 23, 1950.)

45. Hearings for the non-signing non-Senate academic and non-academic employees continued until June 22, 1950, and in a few cases into July. The President was unable, therefore, to circulate the reports in advance of the June 23 meeting as he had been able to do with the reports of the Committees on Privilege and Tenure.

46. Text quotes Regent Nimitz.

47. Minutes of the Regents of the University of California, Regular Session, verbatim transcript, June 23, 1950. Office of the Secretary of the Regents, Berkeley.

48. *Ibid.*

49. As recommendation 5 related solely to the Board's action on 3 and 4, action on it, too, was implicitly deferred until July.

50. Stern to Bechtel, June 26, 1950.

51. *Ibid.*

52. Personal letter, Bechtel to Stern, June 28, 1950.

53. Personal letter, Walter Fisher (secretary of Group for Academic Freedom [formed July 6, 1950, by northern non-signers]) to Professor Louis Wirth of University of Chicago, July 25, 1950: "Various reasons have been given by these individuals [non-signers]

for their actions [decision to sign], the Korean crisis being that most frequently mentioned."

54. Statement read by Tolman at a meeting of non-signers, June 29, 1950. Files of the Group for Academic Freedom, University Archives, University of California, Berkeley.

55. *Ibid.*

56. Minutes of the Group for Academic Freedom, July 6, 1950. Files of the Group, University Archives, University of California, Berkeley. The group took in only non-signers from the northern section of the Senate. There was no comparable group organized among the few remaining non-signers in the south. The non-Senate academic employees dismissed on June 23, and others of their sympathetic colleagues, organized the Academic Assembly at Berkeley in early June as a successor to the Non-Senate Academic Employees organization which throughtout the controversy had represented the views of those academic employees not of Senate rank. The Academic Assembly enjoyed a membership of some 190 during the summer of 1950. (Personal letter, John Brittain, chairman, Academic Assembly, to Professor Louis Wirth, University of Chicago, July 24, 1950.) The Academic Assembly did not figure influentially with the Regents or, for that matter, with the Group for Academic Freedom.

57. Statement of policy of Group for Academic Freedom, July 6, 1950.

58. Kent was not a member of the group as he had recently signed. He had been among the more active non-signers during the controversy, however, and had been responsible in part for the organization and work of the Group for Academic Freedom.

59. Minutes of an Executive Session of the Group for Academic Freedom, July 13, 1950. Files of the Group, University Archives, University of California, Berkeley.

60. Ehrman to Neylan, July 5, 1950. Neylan Papers on the Loyalty Oath, Bancroft Library, University of California, Berkeley.

61. Personal letter, Woods to Sproul, July 12, 1950. At least one meeting of the committee was held with a member of the Board, when on July 16, members of the committee met personally with Admiral Nimitz. Woods reported to the President that the session was considered by the Committee to be "successful." (Personal letter, Woods to Sproul, July 17, 1950.)

62. Either through personal letters sent directly to members of the Board (e.g., Harold Taylor, president of Sarah Lawrence College, to Regent Dickson, July 13, 1950), or public statements (e.g., Robert Hutchins, president of University of Chicago, June 24, 1950), steps were taken to convince key Regents to support the recommendations of the Senate committees. These measures proved ineffectual.

63. Personal letter, Tolman to Sproul, July 17, 1950. Files of the Group for Academic Freedom, University Archives, University of California, Berkeley.

64. Notes of meeting taken by Tolman. Files of the Group for

Academic Freedom, University Archives, University of California, Berkeley.

65. Of the seventy-three persons stricken from the list of 157, twenty had filed resignations prior to June 30, 1950, twenty-seven had signed, twenty either had been reported late to the President by the hearing committees or had been reexamined by the President and/or the hearing committees and found to be wholly recommendable, two had not received appointment letters and, therefore, had had no opportunity to sign, and four had been erroneously reported as not signing when in fact they had. (Report of the President to the Regents, July 21, 1950. Office of the Secretary of the Regents, Berkeley.)

66. Minutes of the Regents of the University of California, Regular Session, verbatim transcript, July 21, 1950. Office of the Secretary of the Regents, Berkeley.

67. The vote was:

Aye	No	Absent
Fenston	Ahlport	Sprague[b]
Haggerty	Canaday[a]	Griffiths[c]
Hansen	Collins	McFadden[d]
Heller	Ehrman	Dickson[d]
Merchant	Harrison	Giannini[e]
Nimitz	Jordan	
Simpson	Knight	
Sproul	Neylan	
Steinhart	Pauley	
Warren		

[a]Regent Canaday, a vice-president of Lockheed Aircraft Corporation in Los Angeles, had taken his place on the Board July 1, 1950, as an ex officio voting member succeeding Regent Hale. Canaday was president of the Alumni Association of the Los Angeles campus. The president of that association, in alternate years with the president of the California Alumni Association (Berkeley), served on the Board in a voting capacity.

[b]Regent Sprague, a physician, who had been flown from his home in southern California in Regent Pauley's airplane, was very ill and found it necessary to leave the meeting before the vote was called. He would probably have voted to dismiss (no). His vote would have evened the roll call ten to ten and the motion would have failed.

[c]Regent Griffiths had collapsed from exhaustion following the June 23 meeting of the Board and remained too ill to attend in July. His vote would likely have been to accept the President's recommendations (aye).

[d]Regent McFadden, president of the State Board of Agriculture, and Dickson, both traveling out of the state, on the basis of their previous attitude, would most likely have voted to dismiss (no).

ᵉRegent Giannini had announced his resignation as Regent on April 21, 1950. The resignation, however, had not yet been accepted by the Governor. Had he decided to be present, Giannini would probably have voted to dismiss (no). Had all the Regents been in attendance, the vote would most likely have been to dismiss by a majority of two.

68. Moffitt had been a Regent of the University for thirty-seven years (1911–1948) and for many years Board chairman. He had served in 1920 as chairman of a Regents' committee to negotiate with the Senate the agreements upon which the University's system of faculty participation in the affairs of the University was based. Monseigneur Charles A. Ramm, who had been a Regent of the University for thirty-two years (1912–1944), had also served on the same subcommittee.

69. Minutes of the Coordinating Committee, July 21, 1950.

70. Minutes of the Group for Academic Freedom, July 22, 1950. Files of the Group, University Archives, University of California, Berkeley.

71. Personal letter, Weigel to Moffitt, Stevens, Deutsch, and Davisson, August 2, 1950.

72. Minutes of the Group for Academic Freedom, August 3, 1950. Files of the Group, University Archives, University of California, Berkeley.

73. *Ibid.*

74. The statement was the work mostly of Regents Neylan and Harrison. Neylan Papers on the Loyalty Oath, Bancroft Library, University of California, Berkeley.

75. Authored by Professor Joel Hildebrand.

76. Personal letter, Tolman to Hicks, August 11, 1950. Files of of the Group for Academic Freedom, University Archives, University of California, Berkeley.

77. Personal letter, Tolman to Hicks, August 17, 1950. Files of the Group for Academic Freedom, University Archives, University of California, Berkeley.

78. Unidentified non-signers' letter to Hicks, August 10, 1950. Files of the Group for Academic Freedom, University Archives, University of California, Berkeley.

79. Hicks to Bechtel, August 3, 1950.

80. Personal letter, Bechtel to Hicks, August 9, 1950.

81. Personal letter, Esberg to McCaffrey (executive manager of the Alumni Association), August 18, 1950.

82. Personal letter, Fletcher to McCaffrey, August 22, 1950.

83. Personal letter, McLaughlin to Hicks, August 10, 1950.

84. Copies of letters in loyalty oath files, California Alumni Association, Alumni House, University of California, Berkeley.

85. See n. 67.

86. Personal letter, Toll to Bechtel, August 10, 1950. "I think my vote [July 21, 1950] would have been with the majority [to retain]

rather than the minority [to dismiss]. . . . It seems to be most important to terminate the controversy by refusing to reconsider. . . ." Toll's reasoning was that to dismiss would be to "conclude a program designed to rid the University of Communists by discharging only a group of forty faculty members who have been investigated and pretty clearly determined not to be Communists — leaving on the faculty without investigation a tremendous number of people which may include any number of Communists."

87. The more public of the pressures brought to bear was a pamphlet titled *To Bring You the Facts*, published by the Stevens, Deutsch, Moffitt *et al.*, alumni group and distributed in mid-August, 1950, to thirty college presidents and to all officers and council members of the alumni associations of the Los Angeles, Berkeley, Santa Barbara, and Davis campuses. The pamphlet quoted in full letters from Moffitt, Deutsch, and Stevens to the Governor written August 16, 1950, a letter from Hicks to Bechtel written August 3, 1950, and a letter from Deutsch to Regent Fenston written July 17, 1950. The letters argued the faculty view that the President's recommendations be accepted. The opinion expressed in the letters was supported by eighteen alumni of the University whose names appeared in the pamphlet under a joint letter of endorsement. Among those whose names appeared were several of the University's most prominent and influential alumni. The pamphlet was released to the press on August 23 and was widely noticed throughout California.

88. The major metropolitan newspapers, as was earlier noted, most consistently friendly to the faculty position had been the *San Francisco Chronicle*, whose support in its editorials and news coverage had proved unswervingly sympathetic. In July and August of 1950, however, its position was less aggressively pursued, possibly in consideration of reader reaction, which, according to Harley Stevens, had resulted in the cancellation of four hundred subscriptions and two thousand letters of protest against ten letters of commendation. (Personal letter, Stevens to James Conant, August 4, 1950.) The Hearst press, on the other hand, in July and August of 1950, continued its unqualified support of the Neylan faction on the Board and its sharp attack on the non-signers. Regent Neylan had written at least two of the editorials for the Hearst chain himself (appeared in the *San Francisco Examiner* and *San Francisco Call-Bulletin*, August 21, 1950.) (Personal letter, H. S. MacKay, Jr. to editors and publishers of Hearst papers in California, August 14, 1950; personal letter, MacKay to Neylan, August 18, 1950; personal letter, Neylan to MacKay, August 21, 1950. Neylan Papers on the Loyalty Oath, Bancroft Library, University of California, Berkeley.)

89. Woods to Sproul, August 21, 1950.

90. Minutes of the Meeting of the Group for Academic Freedom, August 21, 1950. Files of the Group, University Archives, University of California, Berkeley.

91. *Ibid.*

92. Personal letter, Tolman to Hicks, August 22, 1950. Files of the group for Academic Freedom, University Archives, University of California, Berkeley.

93. *Los Angeles Examiner*, August 24, 1950.

94. Minutes of the Regents of the University of California, Regular Session, verbatim transcript, August 25, 1950. Office of the Secretary of the Regents, Berkeley.

95. *Ibid.*

96. One may wonder, then, as to the purpose of the oath and the contract, both of which presumably were considered by the Regents to be the effective means of implementing the anti-Communist policy. In fact, Canaday thought not only the hearings to be inadequate to their purpose, but the oath as well: "You cannot by requirement of an oath, exclude Communists." (Minutes of the Regents, Regular Session, verbatim transcript, August 25, 1950.)

97. The votes cast were:

Aye (to confirm)		Nay (to dismiss)	
Fenston	Merchant	Ahlport	Jordan
Griffiths	Simpson	Canaday	Knight
Haggerty	Sproul	Collins	McFadden
Hansen	Steinhart	Dickson	Neylan
Heller	Warren	Ehrman	Pauley
		Harrison	Sprague

Regent Nimitz had wired that had he been able to attend he would vote aye — to support the President's recommendations. The message from Nimitz had been read by Warren earlier in the meeting. Had Regent Giannini (whose resignation had not yet been accepted by the Governor) been present, he would in all probability have voted no — to dismiss.

Chapter Seven
The Final Irony

1.   The Group for Academic Freedom
By the authority of all liberty loving people given to us
in sacred trust during our fight at the University of California
in recognition of his meritorious achievements has conferred
The degree of Doctor of Academic Freedom upon
Edward C. Tolman
Chairman of the group — great leader — genius in human relationships — lover of the good and the true — defender of human rights —
Kindest of men — he has been a tower of strength and never failing

inspiration. By witness whereof this diploma is inscribed by the sig-natures of all. Given at Berkeley this Twenty-fifth day of August in The year of our Lord one Thousand nine hundred and fifty, and of this group the first.

(25 signatures)

(Text taken from the original of the diploma by Tolman's daugh-ter, Mrs. T. J. Kent. Personal letter, Mrs. Kent to the author, March 14, 1966.)

2. Minutes of the Executive Committee, Group for Academic Freedom, August 28, 1950. Files of the Group for Academic Free-dom, University Archives, University of California, Berkeley.

3. The southern non-signers did not participate in the legal action, nor did the remaining non-signers in the north.

4. General circular letter to UCLA faculty from Executive Com-mittee, Committee for Responsible University Government, Septem-ber 7, 1950.

5. Personal letter, Neil Jacoby, chairman of Committee for Re-sponsible University Government to Gene Frumkin, editor of the *Daily Bruin* (UCLA student newspaper), November 20, 1950. Loy-alty Oath Collection, Special Collections, University Library, Uni-versity of California, Los Angeles.

6. General circular letter to UCLA faculty from Executive Com-mittee of Committee for Responsible University Government.

7. Personal letter, Franklin P. Rolfe (treasurer of CRUG) to Brewster Rogerson (secretary of Group for Academic Freedom). Files of the Group, University Archives, University of California, Berkeley.

8. Minutes of the Group for Academic Freedom and Sympathetic Signers, September 15, 1950. Files of the Group for Academic Free-dom, University Archives, University of California, Berkeley.

9. Letter from Baldwin Woods to department chairmen, northern section, September 8, 1950.

10. A nearly complete record of these communications may be found in the "Interim Report of the Committee on Academic Free-dom to the Academic Senate, northern section, of the University of California," February 1, 1951, pp. 21–35 and 45–55. Copies of the report may be found in the University Archives, University Library, Berkeley, and in the Office of the Academic Senate, University of California, Berkeley.

11. Minutes of the Group for Academic Freedom and Sympa-thetic Signers, *loc. cit.* Professor O'Brien considered the special call to be a declaration of war on the Senate leadership. (Personal letter, O'Brien to Woods, handwritten and undated [probably between Sep-tember 2 and 6, 1950].)

12. A circumstance already known to the eight.

13. Minutes of the Coordinating Committee of the northern section of the Senate, September 11, 1950. A further consideration

was the reluctance of those opposed to the September 19 meeting to have any Senate assembly prior to the next meeting of the Board of Regents, then scheduled for September 22. (Personal letter Tolman to Deutsch, September 6, 1950. Files of the Group for Academic Freedom, University Archives, University of California, Berkeley.)

14. Minutes of the Group for Academic Freedom and Sympathetic Signers, *loc. cit.*

15. Robert Gordon Sproul, personal records, September 13, 1950.

16. *Ibid.*

17. A sampling of the courses dropped includes: Theories of Social Change, Seminar in the History of the Early Middle Ages, Byzantium: The Eastern Empire to about 700, Civilizations of Eastern Asia, Seminar in tenth and eleventh century texts, Metric Differential Geometry, and Advanced General Psychology. (Compiled from personal statements of non-signers. Files of the Group for Academic Freedom, University Archives, University of California, Berkeley.)

18. Personal letter, George Mallory, assistant secretary of the Regents, to Sproul, September 11, 1950.

19. Program for Financial Assistance to Non-Signers, September 15, 1950. The Group for Academic Freedom had secured gifts from sympathizers, both within and without the University, totaling $30,190. Of this amount only $7,747 remained in mid-September, the difference having gone to finance office expenses, legal expenses, and loans to members. (Financial Statement, September 19, 1950. Files of the Group for Academic Freedom, University Archives, University of California, Berkeley.)

20. Resolution of the Berkeley chapter of the AAUP, September 18, 1950. Files of the Group for Academic Freedom, University Archives, University of California, Berkeley.

21. Tolman to Himstead, September 19, 1950. Files of the Group for Academic Freedom, University Archives, University of California, Berkeley.

22. American Association of University Professors, "Academic Freedom and Tenure in Quest for National Security: A Report of a Special Committee of the American Association of University Professors," *Bulletin*, Vol. 42, No. 1 (Spring, 1956), p. 66.

23. *New York Times*, April 8, 1956.

24. Minutes of the Academic Senate, southern section, September 25, 1950, Vol. 9, p. 34. Office of the Academic Senate, University of California, Los Angeles.

25. University of California, *Faculty Bulletin*, Vol. 20, No. 5 (November, 1950), p. 46.

26. *Ibid.*, p. 43.

27. Report of the Committee on Privilege and Tenure to the Academic Senate, northern section, September 26, 1950, p. 9.

28. *Ibid.*

29. University of California, *Faculty Bulletin*, November, 1950, p. 43.

30. The previous week, Professors Charles Morrey and Frank Newman had visited Deutsch at his home in San Francisco. They successfully persuaded Deutsch to present the motion to censure. Morrey reports that Deutsch was outraged by the Regents' decision to dismiss and by the mild report that was to be submitted to the Senate on September 26, by the Committee on Privilege and Tenure. (Personal letter, Morrey to the author, June 16, 1965.)

31. Report of the Committee on Academic Freedom to the Academic Senate, northern section, September 26, 1950. Office of the Academic Senate, Berkeley.

32. University of California, *Faculty Bulletin*, November, 1950, p. 43. Passage of the Deutsch resolution was by voice vote. The author uncovered only one record noting the vote on the Deutsch resolution. The estimate was that it carried by a two to one ratio. (Personal letter from Brewster Rogerson, secretary of the Group for Academic Freedom, to Paul Dodd at UCLA, October 2, 1950. Files of the Group for Academic Freedom, University Archives, University of California, Berkeley.)

33. *Ibid*.

34. *Ibid*.

35. Proposed resolution (October 3, 1950) submitted to members of the faculty by five Senate members on the Davis campus.

36. Rogerson to Bainton, October 7, 1950. Files of the Group for Academic Freedom, University Archives, University of California, Berkeley. Same wording is also found in a letter from Rogerson to Professor Singleton at Harvard, October 6, 1950.

37. University of California, *Faculty Bulletin*, November, 1950, p. 44.

38. Committee on Privilege and Tenure, northern section, to Sproul, October 19, 1950.

39. *Oakland Tribune*, September 22, 1950.

40. Assembly Bill 61, Chapter 7 — An Act to add Chapter 8 to Division 4, Title 1, of the Government Code, September 26, 1950. All public employees were considered to be "Civil Defense Workers" (Sections 3100, 3101 of Government Code).

41. *Ibid*.

42. *Los Angeles Examiner*, September 27, 1950.

43. *Berkeley Daily Gazette*, October 13, 1950. The news item reported a letter from Kuchel to Olaf Lundberg, University controller, October 13, 1950, in which Kuchel wrote: "I conclude that the legislative intent of the Statute is to include all persons employed by the University of California in the definition of 'all public employees' . . . and that they are, therefore, required to take and subscribe to the oath or affirmation provided for to qualify for payment of compensation or reimbursement for expenses."

44. Minutes of the Board of Regents, University of California,

Regular Session, October 20, 1950. Office of the Secretary of the Regents, Berkeley.

45. *Ibid.*

46. *Ibid.*

47. Memorandum (printed), Lundberg to chairmen of academic and administrative departments, October 23, 1950.

48. Minutes of the Regents of the University of California, Regular Session, October 27, 1950. Office of the Secretary of the Regents, Berkeley.

49. Minutes of the Regents of the University of California, Executive Session, November 17, 1950. Office of the Secretary of the Regents, Berkeley.

50. *Ibid.*

51. Minutes of the Regents of the University of California, Regular Session, December 15, 1950. Office of the Secretary of the Regents, Berkeley.

52. Voting no were Regents Ahlport, Ehrman, Jordan, Knight, McFadden, Neylan, Nimitz, Simpson, Sprague, and Steinhart. Voting aye were Regents Canaday, Dickson, Fenston, Griffiths, Merchant, Pauley, and Sproul.

53. Letter, O. Lundberg, University controller, to Board of Regents, January 12, 1951. The non-signers were struck from the payroll on January 1, 1951.

54. Petition for Writ of Mandate in *Tolman* v. *Underhill*, the District Court of Appeal State of California, Third Appellate District, August 30, 1950; and, Petitioners Reply Brief in *Tolman* v. *Underhill*, the District Court of Appeal State of California, Third Appellate District, November 10, 1950.

55. Brief for Respondents in *Tolman* v. *Underhill* in the District Court of Appeal State of California, Third Appellate District, October 11, 1950; and, Reply Memorandum for Respondents in *Tolman* v. *Underhill* in the District Court of Appeal State of California, Third Appellate District, December 14, 1950.

56. *San Francisco Examiner*, December 23, 1950.

57. *San Francisco Chronicle*, December 23, 1950.

58. Letter (undated but probably early October) to fourteen alumni from Moffitt, Deutsch, Sibley, and Stevens. The fourteen were those whose names appeared in the booklet "To Bring You the Facts" (August of 1950). Also invited to work with the committee was Ivy Lee, Jr., of the San Francisco public relations firm of the same name, who, since late summer, had been engaged by the Group for Academic Freedom to assist in press relations.

59. A Recommendation to the Alumni Council of the California Alumni Association, January 12, 1951, p. 1. Printed privately.

60. *Ibid.*, p. 4.

61. Minutes of the Alumni Council, California Alumni Association, January 12, 1951. Confidential Bulletin No. 265, p. 5. Alumni House, University of California, Berkeley. Committee members ap-

pointed included Tom Carlson, chairman, Stephen D. Bechtel, Paul Davies, Milton Esberg, Jr., Kathryn Fletcher, Henry Schacht, and Francis Steckmest. Bechtel, Davies, Esberg, and Fletcher had served in 1950 as members of the Bechtel committee.

62. Personal letter, Stanley McCaffrey (executive manager of the California Alumni Association) to Toll, January 25, 1951.

63. Personal letter, Toll to Stevens, February 14, 1951.

64. Interim Report of the Committee on Academic Freedom to the Academic Senate, northern section, "The Consequences of the Abrogation of Tenure," February 1, 1951. Copies may be found in the Bancroft Library, in the University Archives, and in the Senate offices — all at Berkeley. The report was the work principally of Professor James Caldwell of English — a non-signer during much of the controversy and closely allied with those members of the faculty most opposing the oath and the policy it implemented. He had also worked with the Hicks committee and served as a member of the Senate's Committee on Academic Freedom.

65. The southern section did not have a Committee on Academic Freedom at this time.

66. Interim Report of the Committee on Academic Freedom, p. 13.

67. Of the 157 recommended in June, 1950, for the dismissal by the President, the following particulars are known: 4 had actually signed but were erroneously reported as non-signers; 26 resigned before June 30, of whom 21 were later stricken from the original Regents' list; and 44 subsequently signed the oath, of whom 31 were reemployed, 10 were not reemployed, and 3 either resigned or declined reemployment.

Of the remaining 83 who did not sign; 8 were nonacademic employees; 12 were nonsalaried academic employees (clinical appointees and lecturers), one of whom would not have been reappointed regardless of the oath; and 63 were salaried academic employees (teaching and research assistants, lecturers, associates, assistants, visiting professors, etc.), of whom 42 would not have been recommended by their departments for reappointment regardless of the oath, and 21 might or might not have been appointed had they signed. (Letter from Robert Johnson, assistant to President Sproul, to Sproul, March 15, 1951.)

68. Interim Report of the Committee on Academic Freedom, p. 14.

69. *Ibid.*, pp. 57, 58.

70. Advance California Reports (A.C.A.) April 13, 1951), on Civ. No. 7946. Third District April 6, 1951, *Tolman* v. *Underhill.*

71. *Oakland Tribune*, April 8, 1951.

72. On April 16, 1951, the California State Senate enacted by a vote of 28 to 0 Senate Concurrent Resolution 41, which urged the Regents to appeal the decision of the District Court of Appeal.

73. Voting aye — to withdraw — were Regents Fenston, Griffiths, Haggerty, Hansen, Heller, McLaughlin (appointed on January 10, 1951), to succeed Giannini, whose resignation had been accepted

by the Governor on October 27, 1950), Merchant, Simpson, Sproul, Steinhart, and Warren. Voting no — not to withdraw — were Regents Ahlport, Canaday, Collins, Dickson, Jordan, Knight, McFadden, Neylan, Nimitz, and Pauley. (Minutes of the Regents of the University of California, Executive Session, April 20, 1951. Office of the Secretary of the Regents, Berkeley.)

74. Same distribution of "ayes" and "noes" as listed in n. 73 above.

75. Regents Pauley, Dickson, Ahlport, Collins, and Knight so indicated. Neylan later joined the five.

76. Prince to the Board of Regents, April 26, 1951.

77. University of California, *Faculty Bulletin*, Vol. 21, No. 1 (Berkeley, July, 1951), p. 3.

78. Regents Harrison, Giannini, and Canaday had voted consistently with the Neylan faction, and Regent Griffiths with the Warren group. All four new Regents were counted among the Warren men.

79. Voting to reject (aye) were Regents Ahlport, Collins, Dickson, Neylan, Nimitz, and Pauley. Voting not to reject (no) were Regents Fenston, Hagar, Hansen, Heller, McLaughlin, Merchant, Olson, Sproul, Steinhart, and Toll. (Minutes of the Regents of the University of California, Regular Session, August 24, 1951. Office of the Secretary of the Regents, University of California, Berkeley.)

80. The forty-eight non-signers seemingly had as their objective "to precipitate action on the part of the Board" to rescind its oath requirement; and as a tactical rather than a principled protest, they chose not to comply. (Letter, Professor James Caldwell to Professor Aaragon, November 28, 1951. Caldwell was one who had chosen not to sign in the fall of 1951 and also had been active with the non-signers in 1949 and 1950. Aaragon was one of the AAUP investigators of the University of California.)

81. Minutes of the Regents of the University of California, Regular Session, October 19, 1951. Office of the Secretary of the Regents, Berkeley.

82. Voting aye were Regents Fenston, Hagar, Haggerty, Hansen, Heller, McLaughlin, Olsen, Simpson, Sproul, Steinhart, Toll, and Warren. Voting no were Regents Ahlport, Dickson, Ehrman, Knight, McFadden, Neylan, Nimitz, and Pauley. Knight and Nimitz each indicated that had the Supreme Court decision on *Tolman* v. *Underhill* been rendered he would probably have voted aye on the McLaughlin resolution. Absent were Regents Collins, Jordan, Merchant, and Sprague — all of whom, except Merchant, could have been expected to vote no. Had all Regents been present the vote would probably have been thirteen to eleven affirmative.

83. Minutes of the Board of Regents of the University of California, Regular Session, verbatim transcript, October 19, 1951. Office of the Secretary of the Regents, Berkeley.

84. Letter, Tolman to Fine, November 5, 1951. Files of the Group for Academic Freedom, University Archives, University of California, Berkeley.

85. The non-signers were in agreement with the terms of the McLaughlin resolution even though it made no provision for their reinstatement. (Letter from Tolman to Professor E. R. Stabler of Hofstra College, Long Island, N.Y., March 11, 1952. Files of the Group for Academic Freedom, University Archives, University of California, Berkeley.)

86. A "Dear Colleague" letter from the Group for Academic Freedom, signed in behalf of the group by Tolman, December 28, 1951.

87. *San Francisco Chronicle*, June 22, 1951.

88. Questions are quoted from Respondents' Answers to the Questions of the Court, Pillsbury, Madison and Sutro, Eugene M. Prince, Francis M. Kirkham, attorneys for the Regents of the University of California, filed in the Supreme Court of the State of California, January 14, 1952; and from Petitioners' Concurrent Brief, Stanley A. Weigel, attorney for petitioners, filed in the Supreme Court of the State of California, January 15, 1952. Answers are derived from each of the briefs noted above.

89. *Advance California Reports*, Official Advance Sheets of the Supreme Court, October 28, 1952, San Francisco, California, p. 722, in the Case of Tolman vs. Underhill. The Recorder Printing and Publishing Company, San Francisco and Los Angeles.

90. *Ibid.*, p. 725.

91. See chap. 9 for a report of those non-signers who chose to sign the Levering oath and accept reinstatement, and of those who refused, of the suit for back pay and privileges filed against the Regents by several of the non-signers, and of the activities of the faculty committees who provided the non-signers with financial assistance.

Chapter Eight
Epilogue

1. The constitutionality of California's state oath may be questioned in the light of more recent court decisions, including among others, *Wieman* v. *Updegraff*, in which an Oklahoma oath was struck down as unconstitutional for punishing unknowing membership by indiscriminate classification of innocent with knowing activity (see United States Reports, Vol. 344, U.S. Government Printing Office, Washington, D.C., 1953); *Baggett* v. *Bullitt*, in which two Washington State statutes requiring the execution of two different oaths by state employees were held unconstitutional for requiring applicants to promise at the risk of perjury and loss of employment to assert their loyalty in phrases considered unduly vague, uncertain, and

broad (see United States Reports, Vol. 377, U.S. Government Printing Office, 1964); *Elfbrandt* v. *Russell,* in which an Arizona oath was struck down for failing to distinguish in its proscription of affiants between knowing membership in an organization having unlawful objectives and the specific intent of an individual member to further those objectives (see United States Reports, Vol. 384, U.S. Government Printing Office, 1966); and *Keyishian* v. *Board of Regents,* in which the United States Supreme Court on January 23, 1967, held constitutionally defective that part of New York state's Feinberg Law which censured mere knowing membership in an organization having unlawful ends without any showing of specific intent to further the illegal objectives. The Berkeley division of the Academic Senate on May 17, 1966, authorized its Committee on Academic Freedom to file an amicus curiae brief in court cases then pending in California challenging the constitutionality of the state oath.

2. Allan M. Cartter, *An Assessment of Quality in Graduate Education: A Comparative Study of Graduate Departments in 29 Academic Disciplines* (Washington, D.C.: American Council on Education, 1966), p. 107.

Chapter Nine
Postscript

1. Compiled from the *San Francisco Chronicle,* October 18, 1952, and from the Group for Academic Freedom Files, University Archives, University of California, Berkeley.

2. Ludwig Edelstein, professor of Greek; Edwin S. Fussell, instructor in English; Ernst H. Kantorowicz, professor of history; Charles L. Mowat, associate professor of history; Stefan Peters, associate professor of insurance; Brewster Rogerson, assistant professor of English; Gian C. Wick, professor of physics.

3. Arthur H. Brayfield, assistant professor of education; Harold W. Lewis, assistant professor of physics.

4. Jacob Loewenberg, professor of philosophy; Pauline Sperry, associate professor of mathematics.

5. Margaret T. Hodgen, associate professor of sociology; John L. Kelley, associate professor of mathematics; Hans Lewy, professor of mathematics; Charles S. Muscatine, assistant professor of English; John M. O'Gorman, assistant professor of chemistry; Leonard Olschki, lecturer in Oriental languages; R. Nevitt Sanford, professor of psychology.

6. John W. Caughey, professor of history; Hubert S. Coffey, assistant professor of psychology; Leonard Doyle, associate professor

of accounting; David Saxon, assistant professor of physics; Edward Tolman, professor of psychology; Harold Winkler, assistant professor of political science.

7. Committee members included Regents Neylan, Ahlport, Dickson, Fenston, Nimitz, and Pauley.

8. Five of the non-signers who had resigned upon being offered appointments sued separately and secured from the Regents in an out-of-court settlement in late 1954 full pay plus 7 percent interest on that amount and nearly $4,000 in court costs.

9. Not to be confused with the fund established in the spring of 1950 by the Committee of Seven.

10. In the north, the Faculty Fund organized the Committee for the Non-Senate Faculty Fund. This subcommittee was concerned only with northern section, non-Senate academic non-signers. Because of the one-year contracts under which non-Senate academic employees were engaged, eligibility was far more difficult to determine than was true for Senate members. Eligible for help was any non-signer serving in 1949–50 as a lecturer, associate, teaching assistant, research assistant, section assistant, or as a laboratory, field, clinical, statistical, or other assistant whose duties were of an academic nature who would have been continued in his appointment during the 1950–51 academic year except for his refusal to sign. Sixteen persons were found eligible for assistance, of whom three declined the help and one set his need at one-half of the amount to which he was entitled. (Summary of Operations on Non-Senate Faculty Fund, November 1, 1950 to January 8, 1951.) The financial obligation was met both from gifts to the Fund by individuals and later from funds of the northern and southern committees as well. The Fund concluded its responsibilities at the end of September 1951 because of the steady scattering of the recipients to other employment and because of a sharp reduction in contributions. During its tenure, the Fund received slightly in excess of $12,000 and disbursed a total of $11,842, which approximated 80 percent of the salaries of the non-signers would have earned had their employment been continuous. Some 375 persons contributed to the fund; and of the thirty-two departments represented among the contributors, seven departments accounted for 50 percent of the total dollars received. (Final Report of the Non-Senate Faculty Fund.)

11. The cost of litigation in the case of *Tolman* v. *Underhill* was borne by the Group for Academic Freedom, which had solicited funds of its own. Legal fees required to recover back pay and privileges were borne by the Faculty Fund as were other non-recoverable expenses to the litigants, i.e., travel, printing, records, clerical help, etc. Funds remaining in the Group for Academic Freedom account ($4,751) were turned over to the Faculty Fund to help defray court costs and attorneys fees.

12. A complete record of the Committee for Responsible Univer-

sity Government may be found in Dean Neil Jacoby's files, School of Business Administration, University of California, Los Angeles.

13. Twenty-three from the Davis camp, forty from the San Francisco Medical Center, and the remainder from Berkeley.

14. A complete record of the Faculty Fund may be found in Dean Milton Chernin's files, School of Social Welfare, University of California, Berkeley.

INDEX

INDEX

Aaragon, R. F., 209

AAUP. *See* American Association of University Professors

Academic Senate, 5–7, 273n. 4; first considers oath, 33; requests Regents to delete or revise oath, 36–37; southern and northern sections urged not to sign, 53–54; asks Regents to rescind oath, 58–59; initial resistance to University policy on communism, 59–61; adopts Adams Resolution, 80–81; enacts ten Broek Resolution, 81–82; unity broken, 82–84; refuses to notice Fox case, 93; southern section's poll, 96; approves University policy on communism while opposing oath, 132–138; moves off-campus, 134; supports Sproul, 164; divides over alumni compromise, 164–165, 169–170; northern section refuses to instruct Committee on Privilege and Tenure, 167–168; leadership of, pressures non-signers, 190, 193–194; reacts to dismissals, 210–214; memorializes Regents to rescind oath, 233; program of financial assistance, 254–255

Acheson, Dean, 128

Activating Committee, 129

Adams, Annette, 225, 226

Adams, George P., 80

Adams Resolution, 80–81, 117

Advisory Committee of Academic Senate, 6, 37–38; reports faculty disagreement with University policy on communism, 28; negotiates with Sproul, 38–40; criticized by faculty, 48–49; narrows its support for oath, 55; urges Sproul to rescind oath, 55; criticized by Regents, 63; confers with Regents, 64–71; seeks Senate acceptance of University policy on communism, 74; withdraws admission of involvement in earlier oath negotiations, 77–78

Ahlport, Brodie (Regent), 25, 201, 236, 237

Alexander Meiklejohn Award, 209

Allen, Raymond B. (President of University of Washington), 12, 17

Alumni Association. *See* California Alumni Association; UCLA Alumni Association

Alumni Committee. *See* Bechtel Committee

Alumni compromise, 181, 182, 201; adopted, 154–157; Senate leadership supports, 160; Neylan's interpretation of, 165, 173; non-signers' understanding of, 173; Neylan faction's assessment of, 191–193

185, 196, 215, 233; organized,
172; assesses damage, 205; reacts to dismissals, 210–214 *passim*; reports to Senate on consequences of oath, 228–230; reacts
to rescinding of oath, 238
Committee on Committees, 171,
172
Committee on Finance and Business Management. *See* Regents,
Board of, of the University of
California
Committee on Privilege and Tenure, 48, 57, 107, 113–114, 159–
166 *passim*, 201, 215; northern
section resigns, 170–172; procedures governing hearings, 172–
173; confers with Bechtel Committee, 174; reports hearings of
non-signers to Sproul, 174–177;
recommendations on non-signers
heard by Regents, 178–182; Regents act on recommendations
of, 185–190, 198–202; reports to
Senate on hearings and Regents'
action, 210–214 *passim*; threatens to resign, 214; reverses earlier unfavorable recommendations, 217
Communist disclaimer. *See* Oath
Communist Party, members of,
fired from University of Washington, 12–13. *See also* University of California: policy on
Conant, James (President of Harvard University), 64
Coordinating Committee, 206
Coplon, Judith, 11, 128
Corley, James (Vice-President of
University of California), 24,
126, 278n. 2
Council of the American Association of University Professors.
See American Association of
University Professors
Crouch, Winston W., 171
CRUG. *See* Committee for Re-
sponsible University Govern-
ment

Daggett, Stuart, 172, 187, 210
Dartmouth College, 229
Davies, Paul, 151, 174, 195

Davis, A. R., 133
Davis–Hicks–Stanley Resolution,
134–136, 139, 141, 152; Senate
vote on, 138
Davisson–Grant Committee, 96,
129, 215; appointed, 87; proposals to Regents, 94–97; negotiations with Neylan committee,
97–104; offers compromise, 111;
confers with Sproul, 112–113;
untenable position, 118–119; re-
sponds to tenure threat, 121–122;
disbands, 132–133
Davisson, Malcolm, 87, 94, 101–
102, 123, 125, 131, 132, 191;
confers with Neylan, 88–90; unwilling to compromise, 110
Deamer, William, 151
Deans and Department Chairmen,
119, 123, 124–125, 147
Dennes, Will R., 57, 110, 172
Dennis v. U.S., 239, 240
Deutsch, Monroe E. (Vice-President and Provost Emeritus of
University of California), 5,
126, 154, 191, 208, 212, 226;
would sign oath, 164; introduces
resolution of censure, 212–213,
214, 220
Dickson, Edward A. (Regent), 42,
43, 88, 125, 142, 149, 222, 231;
appointed Regent, 16; in found-
ing of UCLA, 16; urges withdrawal of Laski invitation, 24
District Court of Appeal, 203, 204,
220, 223, 231, 232; decision in
Tolman v. Underhill, 230
Dodd, Paul, 125, 142, 146
Durant Hotel, Berkeley, 146, 149,
162
Durr, Clifford J., 92
Durrell, Cordell, 125
Dykstra, Clarence (UCLA Provost), appointed, 5; grants permission to Phillips, 14; refuses to
cancel Phillips–Benson debate,
15–16; criticized by Regents, 17;
Laski incident, 18–21 *passim*

Edelstein, Ludwig, 208, 252
Ehrman, Sidney M. (Regent), 88,
144, 148, 180, 188, 199, 232;
urges Neylan to abandon oath,

WITHDRAWN